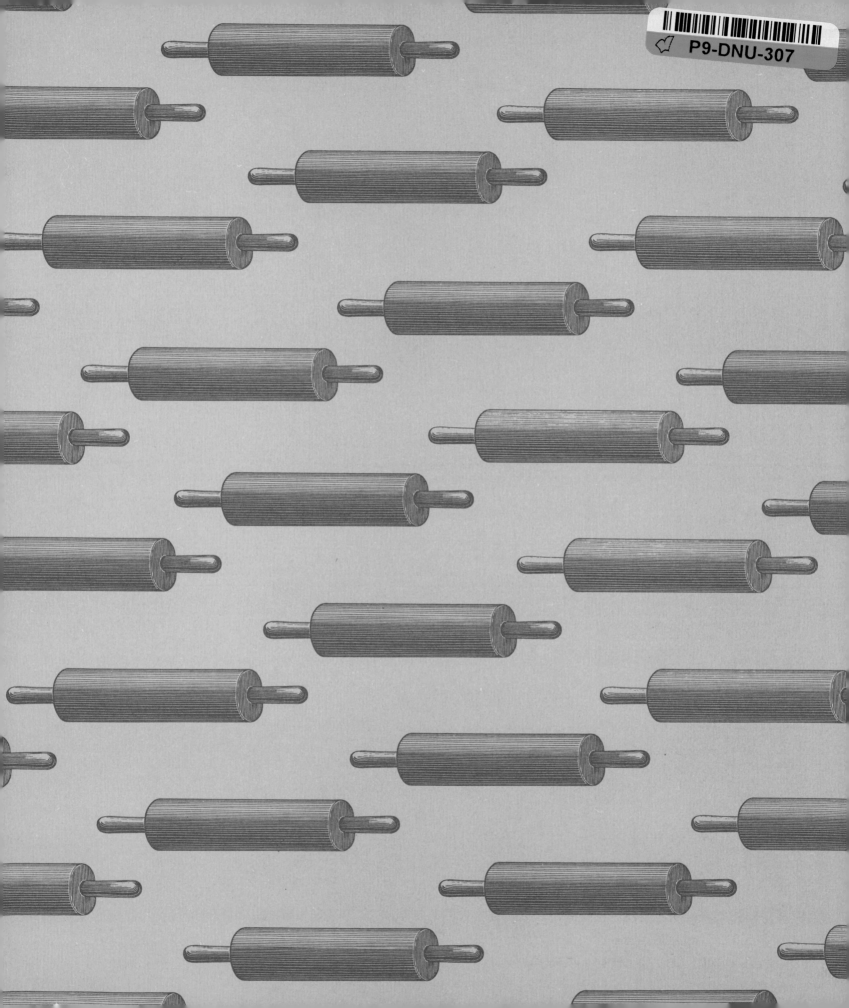

This volume is one of a series that explains and demonstrates how to prepare various types of food, and that offers in each book an international anthology of great recipes.

Pies & Pastries

BY
THE EDITORS OF TIME-LIFE BOOKS

TIME-LIFE BOOKS/ALEXANDRIA, VIRGINIA

Cover: A lattice top for a tart offers a tantalizing preview of the cherry filling within. To create the lattice, short-crust dough was cut into strips with a serrated pastry wheel, and the strips were interwoven on a baking sheet lined with parchment paper *(pages 26-27)*. Chilling then made it possible to transfer the lattice intact to the top of the filled tart prior to baking.

Time-Life Books Inc.
is a wholly owned subsidiary of
TIME INCORPORATED

Founder: Henry R. Luce 1898-1967

Editor-in-Chief: Henry Anatole Grunwald
President: J. Richard Munro
Chairman of the Board: Ralph P. Davidson
Executive Vice President: Clifford J. Grum
Chairman, Executive Committee: James R. Shepley
Editorial Director: Ralph Graves
Vice Chairman: Arthur Temple

TIME-LIFE BOOKS INC.

Editor: George Constable. *Executive Editor:* George Daniels. *Board of Editors:* Dale M. Brown, Thomas H. Flaherty Jr., William Frankel, Thomas A. Lewis, Martin Mann, Philip W. Payne, John Paul Porter, Gerry Schremp, Gerald Simons, Nakanori Tashiro, Kit van Tulleken. *Art Director:* Tom Suzuki; *Assistant:* Arnold C. Holeywell. *Director of Administration:* David L. Harrison. *Director of Operations:* Gennaro C. Esposito. *Director of Research:* Carolyn L. Sackett; *Assistant:* Phyllis K. Wise. *Director of Photography:* Dolores Allen Littles. *Production Director:* Feliciano Madrid; *Assistants:* Peter A. Inchauteguiz, Karen A. Meyerson. *Copy Processing:* Gordon E. Buck. *Quality Control Director:* Robert L. Young; *Assistant:* James J. Cox; *Associates:* Daniel J. McSweeney, Michael G. Wight. *Art Coordinator:* Anne B. Landry. *Copy Room Director:* Susan Galloway Goldberg; *Assistants:* Celia Beattie, Ricki Tarlow

President: Carl G. Jaeger. *Executive Vice Presidents:* John Steven Maxwell, David J. Walsh. *Vice Presidents:* George Artandi, Stephen L. Bair, Peter G. Barnes, Nicholas Benton, John L. Canova, Beatrice T. Dobie, Carol Flaumenhaft, James L. Mercer, Herbert Sorkin, Paul R. Stewart

THE GOOD COOK

The original version of this book was created in London for Time-Life Books B.V.
European Editor: Kit van Tulleken; *Design Director:* Louis Klein; *Photography Director:* Pamela Marke; *Planning Director:* Alan Lothian; *Chief of Research:* Vanessa Kramer; *Chief Sub-Editor:* Ilse Gray; *Production Editor:* Ellen Brush; *Quality Control:* Douglas Whitworth

Staff for *Pies & Pastries:* *Series Coordinator:* Liz Timothy; *Head Designer:* Rick Bowring; *Text Editor:* Ann Tweedy; *Anthology Editor:* Markie Benet; *Staff Writers:* Alexandra Carlier, Jay Ferguson, Mary Harron, Thom Henvey; *Designer:* Zaki Elia; *Researchers:* Ursula Beary, Nora Carey, Margaret Hall, Eleanor Lines, Deborah Litton; *Sub-Editors:* Katie Lloyd, Sally Rowland; *Design Assistant:* Cherry Doyle; *Editorial Department:* Pat Boag, Deborah Dick, Beverly Doe, Philip Garner, Brian Sambrook, Molly Sutherland, Julia West, Helen Whitehorn

U.S. Staff for *Pies & Pastries:* *Series Editor:* Gerry Schremp; *Assistant Editor:* Ellen Phillips; *Designer:* Ellen Robling; *Chief Researcher:* Barbara Fleming; *Picture Editor:* Christine Schuyler; *Staff Writers:* Carol Dana, David M. Schwartz; *Researchers:* Mariana Tait (techniques), Ann Ready (anthology), Karin Kinney; *Assistant Designer:* Peg Schreiber; *Art Assistant:* Robert K. Herndon; *Editorial Assistants:* Brenda Harwell, Rosalie Yates

CHIEF SERIES CONSULTANT

Richard Olney, an American, has lived and worked for some three decades in France, where he is highly regarded as an authority on food and wine. A regular contributor to such influential journals as *La Revue du Vin de France* and *Cuisine et Vins de France,* he also has written numerous articles for other gastronomic magazines in the United States and France. He is, too, the author of *The French Menu Cookbook* and of the award-winning *Simple French Food,* has directed cooking courses in France and in the United States, and is a member of several distinguished gastronomic societies, including La Confrérie des Chevaliers du Tastevin, Les Amitiés Gastronomiques Internationales, and La Commanderie du Bontemps de Médoc et des Graves. Working in London with the series editorial staff, he has been basically responsible for the planning of this volume, and has supervised the final selection of recipes submitted by other consultants. The United States edition of *The Good Cook* has been revised by the Editors of Time-Life Books to bring it into complete accord with American customs and usage.

CHIEF AMERICAN CONSULTANT
Carol Cutler, who lives in Washington, D.C., is the author of three cookbooks, including the award-winning *The Six-Minute Soufflé and Other Culinary Delights.* During the 12 years she lived in France, she studied at the Cordon Bleu and the École des Trois Gourmandes, and with private chefs. She is a member of the Cercle des Gourmettes, a long-established French food society that is limited to just 50 members.

SPECIAL CONSULTANT
Jolene Worthington received degrees in pastry making and candymaking from the Culinary Institute of America in Hyde Park, New York, and worked as a restaurant pastry chef for many years. Formerly the Test Kitchen Chef in recipe development at *Cuisine* magazine, she conducts classes in cooking and pastry making at Cook's Mart in Chicago. She has been largely responsible for the step-by-step photographic sequences in this volume.

PHOTOGRAPHER
Aldo Tutino, a native of Italy, has worked in Milan, New York City and Washington, D.C. He has won a number of awards for his photographs from the New York Advertising Club.

INTERNATIONAL CONSULTANTS
GREAT BRITAIN: *Jane Grigson* has written a number of books about food and has been a cookery correspondent for the London *Observer* since 1968.

Alan Davidson is the author of four cookbooks and the founder of Prospect Books, which specializes in scholarly publications about food and cookery. *Pat Alburey,* special consultant for this volume, is a member of the Association of Home Economists of Great Britain. She has been responsible for some of the step-by-step photographic sequences in this volume. *Alice Wooledge Salmon,* special consultant for this volume, is a chef who has worked at *Ma Cuisine* restaurant and at the Connaught Hotel in London. She is a contributor to many publications, including the *Journal of the International Wine and Food Society.* FRANCE: *Michel Lemonnier,* cofounder and vice president of Les Amitiés Gastronomiques Internationales, is a frequent lecturer on wine and vineyards. GERMANY: *Jochen Kuchenbecker* trained as a chef, but has worked for 10 years as a food photographer in several European countries. *Anne Brakemeier* is the co-author of three cookbooks. ITALY: *Massimo Alberini* is a well-known food writer and journalist, with a particular interest in culinary history. His many books include *Storia del Pranzo all'Italiana, 4000 Anni a Tavola* and *100 Ricette Storiche.* THE NETHERLANDS: *Hugh Jans* has published two cookbooks and his recipes appear in a number of Dutch magazines. THE UNITED STATES: *Judith Olney* received her culinary training in England and France. She conducts cooking classes from her home in Durham, North Carolina, and has written two cookbooks. *Robert Shoffner,* wine and food editor of *The Washingtonian* magazine for six years, has written many articles on food and wine.

Correspondents: Elisabeth Kraemer (Bonn); Margot Hapgood, Dorothy Bacon, Lesley Coleman (London); Susan Jonas, Lucy T. Voulgaris (New York); Maria Vincenza Aloisi, Josephine du Brusle (Paris); Ann Natanson (Rome).
Valuable assistance was also provided by: Bona Schmid, Maria Teresa Marenco (Milan); Judy Aspinall, Karin B. Pearce (London); Carolyn T. Chubet, Miriam Hsia, Christina Lieberman (New York); Mimi Murphy (Rome).

For information about any Time-Life book, please write:
Reader Information, Time-Life Books
541 North Fairbanks Court, Chicago, Illinois 60611

Library of Congress CIP data, page 176.

CONTENTS

Sweet Artifice

Mrs. John Baines, the redoubtable matriarch of Arnold Bennett's turn-of-the-century novel *The Old Wives' Tale*, had strong views on the subject of pastry. She believed that "in pastry making, everything can be taught except the 'hand,' light and firm, which wields the roller. One is born with this hand or without it. And if one is born without it, the highest flights of pastry are impossible." Having infinite faith in her own hand and none in those of her servants or daughters, she made the family's pies and tarts herself, every Friday.

For all her general good sense, Mrs. Baines was overstating the case considerably. Fragrant, golden apple pies, éclairs bulging with pastry cream and gleaming with chocolate icing, and even many-layered strudels are created not by lucky cooks endowed with inborn manual gifts, but by thoughtful cooks who understand the materials and principles of their art—and spend a little time practicing.

This book teaches everything needed for an understanding of the art of pastry making. On the following pages are step-by-step demonstrations explaining the preparation of elements that appear in all types of pastry—the sugar syrups, glazes and fondants used for decoration, the satiny creams that enrich so many pastry assemblies, and the meringues that serve as toppings for pies or as tart shells in their own right. Each of the next three chapters is a comprehensive guide to a particular type of pastry dough: specifically, short crust, puff and chou. The chapters begin by showing methods of making the basic doughs, and continue with lessons in the many ways of shaping, filling and cooking those doughs. The final chapter in the first half of the book concerns some of the exotica of pastry—the making of such delicacies as Austrian and Hungarian strudel, Middle Eastern phyllo, deep-fried pastries and meringue shells.

The second half of the volume is an anthology of more than 200 recipes, gathered from cookbooks representing the world's cookery literature. The anthology complements the techniques demonstrations: By using the recipes to develop the skills learned from the demonstrations, any cook can indeed reach the "highest flights of pastry."

An evolving genre

Pies and other pastries appear in hundreds of guises, but almost all are composed in essentially the same way: Containers made of dough are shaped to hold sweet fillings such as fruits, egg-rich custards or delicate creams. The pastry doughs all are based on the same ingredients—flour, fat and water. Like bread and pasta doughs, pastry doughs are descendants of the primitive grain-and-water pastes that served as food staples in Neolithic times, 10,000 years ago.

The evolution of these crude pastes into the delicate confections now called pastry began at the margins of recorded history. Among the earliest pastry makers are those shown on a bas-relief in the tomb of Pharaoh Ramses II at Thebes; the sculpture proves that 30 centuries ago, Egyptian bakeries sold a variety of sweets—coarse ones, by today's standards—made from grain meal and enlivened by fruits, honey and spices. In ancient Greece, pastry making was more masterful: The Fifth Century B.C. playwright Aristophanes refers to all sorts of pastry creations, including a tart filled with grapes and almonds that was served daintily wrapped in fig leaves. Similar ingredients were used later in Roman pastries, and by the Fourth Century A.D., the business of pastry making had flourished to such a degree that its practitioners had their own guild, the *pastillarium*. Recipes surviving from the period include some for tarts filled with cheese and some for tarts filled with custard.

Despite the colonizing efforts of imperial Rome, Western Europe in the early Christian era appears to have languished in a kind of culinary dark ages; when it came to cooking, the simple imperative of nourishment overshadowed creativity and refinement. In the rich kingdoms of the Middle East, however, the situation was quite different. The Seventh Century banquets of Persia's Sassanid kings, for instance, were noted for their opulence, and descriptions of these feasts—of which there were many—offer enticing catalogues of pastries, many of them flavored with almonds.

At that time, the peoples of the Middle East used foods unknown in Europe. Sugar cane had been cultivated in the area since the armies of Alexander the Great brought it from India in the Fourth Century B.C. (Europeans made do with honey.) From the Orient came the spices and nuts—cinnamon, ginger, nutmeg, cloves, almonds and walnuts—that gave such distinction to Arabic cuisine.

These delicious flavorings appeared in Spain after the Muslim invasion in the Seventh Century, and they spread more widely as a result of the Crusades of the 11th Century and the development of trade routes between East and West. At first, European cooks used them with wild abandon. Sugar was sprinkled on everything, sweet or savory, and the employment of spices was startling, to say the least. Consider, for instance, the apple pie of Taillevent, the famous 14th Century chef to the Valois kings of France. His pie was filled with figs and raisins, as well as apples that had been pounded to a pulp and soaked in wine—and the flavorings were saffron, cinnamon, ginger, anise, sautéed onion and chopped raw purslane, a sharp-tasting herb much favored at the time.

Because Venice was the great Medieval trade center, importing thousands of tons of spices each year from Alexandria and Beirut, Italian cooks were the first to absorb the advanced lessons of Arabic cuisine. The earliest known European cookbook, *De Honesta Voluptate et Valetudine (Of Honest Indulgence and Good Health),* published in 1474, contained hundreds of recipes by a man named Martino, described as cook for "the Most Reverend Monsignor, the Chamberlain and Patriarch of Aquileia" (Aquileia was a town near Venice). Martino used sug-

ar as the Arabs did, to make dishes that were specifically sweet, and his pastries were also full of spices of the Middle East.

The year 1570 saw the publication of the first Western book that clearly explored the Arabic art of pastry making, as gleaned from Arabic treatises on food translated in Venice. This thorough and copiously illustrated volume was the work of Bartolomeo Scappi, chef to Pius IV, a pope well known for his love of pies. Scappi offered more than 200 recipes, including one for a kind of puff pastry made with lard.

By then, the Italians' techniques for producing delectable pastries had begun to spread into France—partly through the agency of the notoriously gluttonous Catherine de' Medici, who brought her own pastry chefs with her when she married the Duke of Orléans in 1533. A century later came the first French publication devoted exclusively to pastry making. Appearing in 1655 and attributed to the chef La Varenne, the book was distinguished by careful instructions for measurements and for temperature control during baking, and it described the same techniques for making short-crust and puff pastry that we use today.

With this book, pastry making was marked in the West as a recognized art—one that could be taught. From that day to this, cookbooks and cooking instructors have devoted a large part of their attention to the techniques of handling dough and fillings. In 18th Century London, for instance, a cook named Edward Kidder published *Receipts of Pastry and Cookery,* in which he carefully listed dates and times for the pastry-making lessons he offered to fashionable ladies. (Kidder also claimed to have invented a new kind of puff pastry; the method described in his

book is quite similar to that for the flaky-pastry dough demonstrated on pages 50-51.) The first cookbook by an American was Amelia Simmons' *American Cookery,* published in Hartford, Connecticut, in 1796. This writer, who pathetically described herself as "an American orphan," advertised the "best modes for making Pastes, puffs, pies [and] tarts."

Fancies and furbelows

Pies and pastries are meant for delight rather than for sustenance; in most cases, they serve as dessert, a pleasurable treat at the end of a meal. It is not surprising, therefore, that pastry cooks devote so much effort to presentation, for food like this must tempt the eye as well as the tongue. Dough, being malleable, is particularly suited to decorative and inventive arrangements, a fact exploited by pastry chefs since the early days of the art of pastry making.

The "four and twenty blackbirds baked in a pie" of the old nursery rhyme, for instance, are not at all apocryphal: Pastries of this dramatic type were much favored for Renaissance banquets. Martino himself provides explicit instructions for "the making of pies that Birds may be alive in them and fly out when it is cut up." And there are reliable records of pies that were large enough to enclose live rabbits, dwarves and even a 28-piece orchestra. (The pastry was cooked before the occupants entered it, obviously.)

The apogee of this form of culinary entertainment was reached by Robert May, the 17th Century English author of *The Accomplisht Cook or The Art and Mystery of Cookery.* In his book, May proudly described a banquet that included, among other dubious creations, a huge pastry stag and two giant pies, one filled with live frogs and one with blackbirds. When the first pie was cut open, "out skip some frogs, which make the ladies to skip and shreek," as might well be expected. Then the birds were released from their pastry prison, and the beating of their wings extinguished the candle flames, leaving the party in darkness. May's conclusion was that "flying birds and skipping frogs, the one above, the other beneath, will cause much delight and pleasure to the whole company."

May's interest in pastry presentation was not confined to creating pandemonium, however. He also offered abundant illustrations of happier means of decorating pastries, many of which are used today.

Short crust, for instance, is so flexible that—as May suggested—it can be woven into a lacy lattice top for pies *(pages 26-27);* it can also be cut into decorative shapes to embellish a turnover *(page 35).* Puff-pastry dough can be molded into tiny cornucopias *(pages 58-59),* and chou paste can be piped from a pastry bag to make miniature swans, or formed into puffs that are piled up as spectacular, towering pyramids *(page 70).* In open-faced tarts, the filling provides handsome effects: Fruit slices handled like fans will fall into the shell in perfectly overlapped, concentric rings *(pages 36-37);* whole fruits can be arrayed in neat rows of alternating color. In many cases, a garnish is the means of pleasing, and a pastry bag, when deftly used, will transform whipped cream or meringue into flower-like puffs or ribbon-like scrolls *(page 45).*

The basic materials

The success of a finished pastry, plain or fancy, depends in part on the quality of the basic materials, especially flour and fat, for these determine the texture of the dough. All pastry requires wheat flour as a base. Only this flour contains the gluten proteins that, activated by liquid, unite the flour particles into a cohesive dough. The type of wheat flour to choose depends on the dough you wish to make. Most pastry doughs, such as short crust and chou paste, are made with all-purpose flour, which contains a mixture of hard and soft wheats that affords a gluten content high enough to make the doughs resilient without loss of tenderness. Puff-pastry dough, which produces the lightest and most delicate of pastries, is made from a mixture of all-purpose flour and low-gluten cake flour. On the other hand, doughs that must be strong enough to stretch into huge, transparent sheets, such as strudel and phyllo, should be made of strong, high-gluten bread flour.

Fat serves to tenderize the flour, and also adds flavor to a dough. Among the various fats used in pastry making, unsalted butter contributes the most luxurious flavor, and it is recommended throughout this book. Another possibility is lard—rendered pork fat. Used either on its own or in combination with butter, lard has a bland taste and produces a more tender and crumbly result than butter does; if you wish to use it, reduce the fat proportions by about 15 per cent to account for lard's higher fat content—about 99 per cent compared to 80 to 85 per cent for butter. Do the same if you wish to substitute vegetable shortening or margarine for all or part of the butter. In Mediterranean countries, olive oil is sometimes used to make pastry; it yields a very soft and distinctively flavored dough and is substituted for butter in a proportion of 4 to 5.

Knowing your oven

Of all the equipment you will use to prepare pastries, your oven is the most important. Be aware, first of all, that thermostats are not always accurate. It is wise to monitor the temperature of your oven with an oven thermometer: Preheat the oven to the desired temperature and move the thermometer from place to place inside it to find out whether or not it heats evenly.

You may well discover that the oven has hotter and cooler areas. Usually, the top and back areas of the oven are hotter

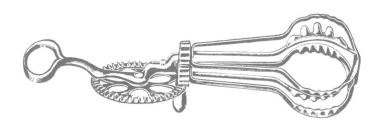

than the bottom, and it is best to bake pastries on the middle shelves, turning them around during baking to ensure that they cook evenly. In any case, do not bake more than two or three large articles at a time. No oven can generate enough heat to compensate for overloading.

For crisp pastry, dry heat is essential. Avoid baking pastry with a steam-producing dish such as a stew, which might contaminate the pastry's flavor in addition to spoiling its texture.

An accompaniment of wine

In many countries, pastries are served as snacks to accompany strong black coffee—as in the famous coffee houses of Vienna—or hot chocolate, as in Spain. But when pastries are served as dessert, wine is a natural accompaniment.

The best wines for the purpose are the white, naturally sweet dessert wines—the French Sauternes and Barsac, the

German *Beerenauslese* and more rarely found *Trockenbeerenauslese,* and the sweet Hungarian Tokay. All these wines are made from grapes that are harvested late. Their juices are concentrated into a fragrant essence, which gives the wines a wonderful depth and richness. To prevent them from being heavy, the wines should be served well chilled; two hours in the refrigerator or an ice bucket will bring them to the proper temperature—45° to 50° F. [7° to 10° C.]—without making them so cold as to mute their taste.

Pastries served with wine should always be less sweet than the wine that accompanies them; otherwise, the wine's subtle flavors will be masked. Some ingredients are best enjoyed without wine. Chocolate, for example, overwhelms a wine, and very creamy fillings may interfere with the enjoyment of a wine's flavor. Acid fruits such as strawberries or lemon may undercut the richness of a sweet wine, but apples, pears and peaches make excellent companions, as does any filling prepared with almonds. The *Pithiviers* shown on page 46, for instance, would be magnificent with a Sauternes; the apple tart shown on pages 36-37 would also balance the qualities of a fine, sweet wine. There are many other such marriages, and the search for new partnerships provides much scope for pleasurable excitement—the same absorbing adventure as is found in exploring the varied art of pastry making itself.

Transforming Sugar into Syrups and Glazes

Syrup made of sugar and water—and perhaps flavored with fruit—provides varied embellishments for pastry. Depending on its original sugar-water ratio and the density to which it is cooked, syrup can be transformed into everything from lustrous glazes to crackly caramel.

For most purposes, the syrup should have a high sugar-to-water ratio—four parts of sugar to one part of water is used here—so that the mixture will cook quickly to the desired density. For fruit-flavored glazes, the proportion of sugar should be reduced to allow for the sweetness of the fruit; one and one half parts of sugar to one part of water is typical.

The top demonstration shows the four densities of syrup most common in pastry making: simple syrup and three candy syrups—small thread, soft ball and caramel. Simple syrup is used to poach fruit and produce glaze. At the small-thread stage, the syrup can serve as a bath for crisp pastries *(pages 78-79)*. When further heated to the soft-ball stage, syrup cools to a pliable mass suitable for making fondant *(pages 10-11)*. Syrup heated to caramel can be poured over pastry to form a hard, smooth coating *(page 68)* or spun into an amber veil *(page 70)*.

Although boiling sugar and water is simple, it must be done with care to prevent the syrup from crystallizing into a hard, lumpy mass. After the sugar has been put over low heat, stir gently until it dissolves, then brush down sugar grains from the sides of the pan *(Step 1, top)*. Test the syrup frequently, and—if you like—confirm the tests with a candy thermometer set in the pan after the sugar dissolves.

Syrup suitable for drenching flaky pastries such as phyllo *(pages 78-79)* can be flavored simply by adding a lemon slice, some fresh lemon juice and—if desired—a few whole cloves to a sugar-and-water mixture before cooking it; because the lemon reacts chemically with the sugar, the syrup requires approximately 20 minutes of cooking to reach the small-thread stage.

Fruit glaze is made by poaching fruit in simple syrup, then straining and reducing the syrup. Jelly or jam can replace fruit glaze: Jelly need only be melted; jam requires straining *(box, opposite)*.

Four Stages of Syrup Making

1 **Simple syrup.** Mix sugar and warm water in a heavy pan, and let the sugar soak for 10 minutes. Stir gently over low heat to dissolve the sugar. With a pastry brush dipped in hot water, dissolve any sugar grains on the sides of the pan. Bring the syrup to a boil.

2 **Small-thread syrup.** After about 20 seconds of boiling, start testing for the small-thread stage. Let some of the syrup dribble from the spoon. If it falls in a fine, short, elastic thread *(above)*, it is ready. This stage gives a thermometer reading of about 215° F. [102° C.].

Flavoring with Fruit

1 **Poaching fruit.** Prepare simple syrup *(Step 1, top)*. Over low heat, add fruit—here, pear halves—in one layer. Cover the fruit with parchment paper, cover the pan and simmer until the fruit is barely tender. Lift out the fruit and reserve for tarts or pies.

2 **Straining syrup.** Ladle the desired amount of poaching syrup—in this case, about 1 cup [¼ liter]—into a fine-meshed strainer set over a small, heavy saucepan. Straining eliminates bits of fruit that might cloud the glaze; do not press down on the mesh of the strainer.

3 **Soft-ball syrup.** Boil simple syrup for about five minutes. Drop a little into ice water and lift out the solidified lump. If you can roll the syrup into a ball that flattens rapidly, it is at the soft-ball stage — a thermometer reading of 234° to 240° F. [112° to 115° C.]. To arrest cooking, stand the pan in cold water.

4 **Caramel.** Boil simple syrup for eight to nine minutes, until it begins to turn a pale amber color and reaches the caramel stage — a thermometer reading of 335° F. [169° C.]. Caramel darkens rapidly and soon burns. While the caramel is still slightly lighter than the color you want, place the pan in cold water to arrest the cooking *(above)*. Use the caramel immediately, before it cools and sets. To keep caramel liquid for a short period of time, put the pan in hot water.

3 **Testing the glaze.** Boil the syrup over high heat for 10 minutes, or until it thickens enough so that it will fall from the spoon in a large, sticky drop *(above)* — the glaze will register about 220° F. [105° C.] on a candy thermometer. Remove the glaze from the heat and allow it to cool briefly before using it.

An Expeditious Glaze

Straining jam. In a small, heavy pan, dilute jam — here, apricot — with a little water to keep the jam from scorching. Then, stirring constantly, melt the jam over low heat. To eliminate bits of fruit pulp, press the melted jam through a fine-meshed strainer into a clean pan. Reheat the jam until it forms a sticky drop *(Step 3, left)*. Cool the glaze briefly before using it.

Icings Based on Fondant

Although they are more commonly associated with cakes than pastries, icings provide a fine finish for such desserts as napoleons *(pages 56-57)* and éclairs *(pages 66-67)*. The pastry chef's favorite icing is based on fondant, a paste that can be kept for months in an airtight container. Whenever icing is required, all or part of the fondant can be quickly melted, diluted with simple sugar syrup and flavored as desired.

Fondant—from the French *fondre*, to melt—takes time to produce, so it should be made in a quantity large enough to yield several batches of icing *(demonstration, below; recipes, page 167)*. The procedure is simple enough: A sugar syrup is cooked to the soft-ball stage *(pages 8-9)*, cooled slightly, and then manipulated to transform the liquid into a thick, white amalgam of syrup and minute suspended crystals that are imperceptible to the tongue. Success depends on certain tricks and cautions, however.

To achieve the requisite velvety texture, a special syrup is needed: The usual sugar-and-water mixture is supplemented with corn syrup—a sweet that does not crystallize. Even a spoonful or so of corn syrup helps keep large sugar crystals from forming as the fondant cooks.

Crystals can form if the solution is "seeded" by stray sugar grains or rough surfaces. The surface onto which the syrup is poured must be perfectly smooth—and any sugar syrup that clings to the pan must be left there. Even the thermometer should be handled gingerly; do not roll it around in the syrup or it may induce crystallization.

The kneaded fondant will become more pliant when it is allowed to ripen: Wrap it in foil or plastic, and let it rest at room temperature for at least an hour—up to 12 hours is better. It is then ready for use or for storage in a cool place.

To turn it into icing, fondant is melted over hot water, then thinned *(Step 4)*. At no time should it be allowed to warm to more than 96° F. [36° C.], lest its creamy shine disappear.

For chocolate-flavored fondant icing *(box, right)*, melted chocolate may be added to the fondant before it is thinned. Alternatively, fondant icing may be flavored with black coffee, freshly brewed and boiled down until it is reduced to an essence, or with strained fresh lemon or orange juice.

Whether flavored or not, fondant icing should be used as soon as it is prepared. It will begin to harden the moment it is removed from the heat. If necessary, however, the icing can be stored in a tightly covered jar for up to four months and remelted briefly before use.

1 **Pouring the syrup.** Prepare a cool, smooth work surface — a large baking sheet or, as here, a marble slab — by sprinkling it with a little cold water. Add corn syrup to a sugar-syrup mixture and cook to the soft-ball stage *(pages 8-9)*. Quickly pour the syrup onto the work surface; the water will prevent the syrup from sticking.

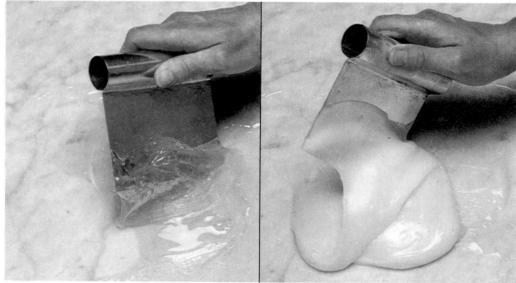

2 **Working the syrup.** Let the syrup cool slightly — three minutes should be adequate. With a flat instrument such as a narrow spatula, a pastry scraper or, as shown in this demonstration, a sugar scraper, work the syrup by repeatedly scooping it up from the edges and folding it into the center *(above, left)*. Continue folding the syrup in this manner for about 15 minutes, until it becomes thick and opaque *(above, right)*.

A Chocolate Variation

1 **Heating chocolate.** Break semisweet baking chocolate into a heatproof bowl. Partially fill a small pan with water and bring it almost to a boil. Remove the pan from the heat and set the bowl of chocolate over it.

2 **Melting the chocolate.** Stirring continuously, break up the chocolate with a spoon. Work gently to avoid tipping the bowl. Stop stirring only when all of the chocolate has melted.

3 **Flavoring the fondant.** When the chocolate is completely smooth, pour it into the bowl with the melted fondant. Stir briefly, then add the simple syrup and stir all of the ingredients together. Use the icing at once.

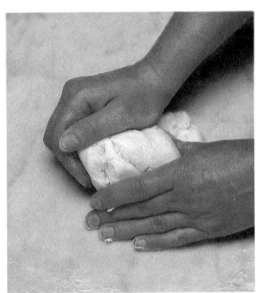

3 **Kneading the fondant.** Knead the cooled syrup with your hands for about 10 minutes, repeatedly folding it and pressing it until it is smooth, white and firm. For a smoother texture, enclose it in plastic wrap or foil, and let it ripen for at least one hour before use.

4 **Preparing fondant icing.** Fill a small saucepan halfway with hot water. Put as much fondant as you need into a small, heatproof bowl and set the bowl over the water *(above, left)*. Place the pan over low heat. When the fondant begins to melt, gradually stir in a little simple syrup made with two parts of sugar to one part of water. Continue stirring the fondant and adding syrup without letting the temperature of the mixture exceed 96° F. [36° C.]. As soon as the consistency becomes that of thick cream *(above, right)*, use the icing.

Pastry Cream: A Classic, Satin-textured Filling

A gently cooked mixture of egg yolks and sugar, thickened with flour and blended with milk, becomes pastry cream: the custard filling for myriad desserts.

Pastry cream may underlie fruit in a tart *(pages 42-43)* or it may be layered with fruit as a filling for meringue shells *(page 86)*. In napoleons *(pages 56-57)*, pastry cream and whipped cream are interleaved with layers of puff pastry, whereas in éclairs *(pages 66-67)*, pastry cream alone fills the interiors. The cream may also be lightened with beaten egg white and stiffened with gelatin for use in a *gâteau Saint-Honoré (pages 68-69)*.

For all these uses, pastry cream must be satin-smooth, a consistency ensured by painstaking preparation *(recipe, page 166)*. The egg yolks and sugar must be whipped to the ribbon stage; the flour must be sifted. After the milk is added, the mixture needs straining to remove any lumps. Keeping the cooking heat low prevents the yolks from scrambling.

The ways pastry cream may be flavored are as diverse as its uses. Coffee beans or a vanilla bean—the choice here—are two possibilities: Both are cooked in the milk and removed before it is added to the eggs. Alternatively, vanilla extract, melted chocolate, praline, coffee essence, liqueurs or brandy may be stirred into the pastry cream as a final step.

1 **Beating yolks.** Separate eggs, dropping the yolks into a bowl; reserve the whites for other uses. Whisk the yolks until they are smooth. Gradually add sugar, and beat until the mixture is light-colored and falls from the whisk in a thick ribbon *(above)*. Sift in flour, add a pinch of salt and beat well.

2 **Adding the milk.** Pour milk into a small, heavy saucepan, add a 2-inch [5-cm.] piece of vanilla bean and bring to a boil over medium heat. Remove the vanilla bean. Pour the milk into the bowl by letting it run out of the pan in a thin stream, simultaneously whisking it into the egg-yolk mixture.

3 **Straining.** Wash and dry the saucepan if it contains any residue from the boiled milk. Holding a fine-meshed sieve over the pan, strain the pastry-cream mixture into the pan.

4 **Cooking the pastry cream.** Return the pan to the burner. Stirring constantly but gently with the whisk, bring the mixture to a boil over low-to-medium heat *(above, left)*. Still stirring, boil the mixture for two to three minutes, or until the pastry cream becomes thick enough to coat the wires of the whisk *(above, right)*.

5 **Chilling.** Transfer the pastry cream to a small bowl and let it cool for five minutes, stirring occasionally. Gently press plastic wrap against the surface of the cream to prevent a skin from forming. Chill the cream for at least an hour before using it.

Meringue: A Multipurpose Amalgam of Egg Whites and Sugar

Another egg-and-sugar compound is meringue: an uncooked foam of egg whites and sugar that—when baked—creates a fluffy or crisp topping to garnish tarts or pies *(pages 44-45)*, or forms a strong shell that will support a filling *(page 86)*. By varying the ratio of egg white to sugar and the method of mixing the two, it is possible to produce meringues that range from soft, spreadable mixtures to firm ones for molding or piping.

For any meringue, the egg whites must be allowed to reach room temperature before they are beaten; whites will rise, or mount, to only about 60 per cent of the maximum potential volume when they are cold. If possible, beat the egg whites in a copper bowl; a chemical reaction that occurs between copper and egg-white albumen will stabilize the foam. Most important, the bowl and whisk or beater must be scrupulously clean; any trace of fat will interfere with the foaming of the egg whites.

The firmness of a meringue is determined primarily by its content of sugar, which strengthens the whites. A spreading meringue is achieved by using a relatively low proportion of sugar—about 2 tablespoons [30 ml.] to each egg white. After the whites have mounted to the soft-peak stage, the sugar is gradually incorporated, with the whisking continuing until the foam reaches the firm-peak stage *(top demonstration)*.

Firmer meringues are produced by using 4 tablespoons [60 ml.] of sugar to each white. The sugar may be incorporated in the same way as for the spreading meringue. However, an especially sturdy form can be created by adding the sugar in two stages—first beating in some of it, then folding in the rest *(bottom demonstration)*. The sugar grains that are folded in remain undissolved, imparting a crunchy texture to the baked meringue.

Once any meringue is assembled, it must be used immediately. If allowed to stand, the egg whites will give off moisture and lose their volume, and the dissolved sugar will "weep" beads of liquid sugar that will become hard bits of caramel when the meringue is baked.

Whisking in Sugar for a Smooth Finish

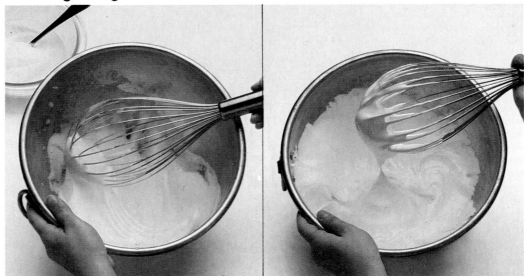

Beating in sugar. Separate eggs, dropping the whites into a large bowl—preferably copper. Reserve the yolks for another use. Let the whites warm to room temperature, then place a folded, dampened towel under the bowl to steady it. Using a rotary or electric beater or—as shown—a large balloon whisk, beat the whites until the foam forms soft, rounded peaks *(above, left)*. Continuing to beat, sprinkle in all of the sugar you plan to use—adding it about 2 tablespoonfuls [30 ml.] at a time. Stop beating as soon as the foam rises in firm peaks *(above, right)*.

Folding in Sugar for a Crunchy Effect

Adding sugar in stages. Beat egg whites to the soft-peak stage *(top demonstration, left)*. Whisk in half of the sugar you plan to use—sprinkling it in about 2 tablespoons [30 ml.] at a time *(above, left)*. Continue whisking until the foam forms firm peaks *(above, center)*. Then, using a rubber spatula, gradually fold in the remaining sugar by lifting the whites from the bottom of the bowl over the top of the mixture. To avoid deflating the foam, stop folding as soon as the meringue is properly mixed.

1
Short Crust
A Versatile Dough Family

Short-crust dough—the foundation of legions of pastries, from homey apple pie to the elaborate tarts that glitter in the windows of Parisian *pâtisseries*—is an uncomplicated blend whose traits derive from an invisible reaction. When flour is moistened, its gluten proteins develop into a microscopic webbing that unites the flour particles into a cohesive dough. Unchecked, the gluten development produces a hard dough and a tough pastry. For this reason, fat—usually unsalted butter because of its pleasing taste—is included in all short-crust doughs: The butter coats some of the flour particles and prevents moisture from activating their gluten. Such dough, when baked, becomes flaky and crisp—its precise texture depending in large part on the amount of butter it contains.

A basic short crust *(pages 16-17),* for example, includes the minimum of fat and a small amount of water; it yields sturdy yet tender pastry. Rich short crust *(pages 18-19)* contains more butter and little or no water, liquid being provided principally by eggs instead; it has less gluten development than basic short crust and produces more fragile and crumbly pastry. Crumbliest of all is refrigerator dough *(pages 20-21),* composed almost entirely of low-gluten cake flour, butter and sugar.

Each of these doughs has multiple uses, although not all can be used for every kind of pastry. Basic short crust is the most versatile: It can yield two-crust and lattice-top pies, deep-dish pies, open-faced pies or tarts, and turnovers. Rich short-crust and refrigerator doughs are too fragile for turnovers and most top crusts, but both can be used in open-faced pies or tarts and refrigerator dough can even form a simple lattice.

All short-crust doughs are absorbent, and care must be taken to prevent moisture in the fillings from making the crusts soggy. Protective stratagems depend on the shape of the pastry. Turnovers and two-crust, lattice-top and deep-dish pies all must be completely baked with the filling inside. Because the doughs would absorb liquid, fillings for these pies are limited to relatively dry ingredients such as fruit, and even fruit must be prepared to minimize juiciness *(page 27).* For open-faced pies or tarts, the choice of fillings is broader: These shells can be partly baked to set the dough and reduce its absorbency before a filling is added and baking is completed *(pages 38-39).* Or they can be fully baked, then filled with cooked ingredients. Both procedures are called baking blind.

A tart reveals an unusual Provençal filling—a sweet spinach custard enlivened by pine nuts. To prevent the custard from penetrating the rich short-crust shell, the shell was partially baked blind, or empty, before the filling was added and baking completed.

Making Basic Short-Crust Dough

The forming of a basic short-crust dough is a straightforward operation: Butter is combined with all-purpose flour, and water is added to make the ingredients cohere *(recipe, page 162)*. For a perfectly light and tender pastry, however, two rules should be scrupulously followed: The ingredients must be kept cold and the dough itself must be handled as little and as rapidly as possible.

Your first object in mixing the dough is to distribute pieces of butter evenly throughout the flour, thereby preventing some—but not all—of the gluten development that the water will cause later. If the butter softens, however, it will coat too many flour particles and the dough will not cohere well.

For proper distribution, use your finger tips—not your warmer palms—to rub the chilled butter lightly together with the flour, as demonstrated in Step 2 at right. Some cooks minimize handling by cutting the butter into the flour with a pastry blender or two knives *(box, opposite, bottom)*, a technique that produces a less uniform mixture that bakes to a flakier pastry. Or you can place the flour in a food processor, drop in chilled butter

pieces and operate the processor in brief spurts; mixing will be completed in a matter of seconds. Whichever technique you use, be sure to hold the mixing time to a minimum; otherwise the butter will soften, yielding oily pastry.

Finish making the dough by adding just enough ice water to make it cohere *(Step 3, right, top)*. Too little water produces an unmanageably mealy dough and a crumbly pastry; too much water produces a sticky, glutenous dough and a tough pastry. Start with less water than you think you need; add more, a drop or two at a time, if it is required. Take care not to overwork the dough: Excessive handling—like excessive water—causes too much gluten development.

Short crust should be refrigerated for at least one hour after it is formed. Chilling firms the butter and relaxes the gluten, making the dough less elastic and thus easier to roll out. Before refrigerating it, enclose the dough in plastic wrap or foil so that air will not dry it. Short-crust dough can be stored this way for two days. It can also be frozen for up to a month; defrost it overnight in the refrigerator before rolling it out.

1 **Preparing ingredients.** Measure chilled, unsalted butter and cut it into pieces. Measure all-purpose flour and ice water. Add a pinch of salt to the flour to flavor it and sift them together through a strainer or sifter into a large mixing bowl *(above)*.

4 **Finishing the dough.** Quickly stir in the water with a knife to distribute the water evenly without overworking the dough *(above, left)*. Gather the mixture together with one hand; if it feels crumbly and dry, add more water gradually, until the dough begins to cohere *(center)*. Press the dough into a ball *(right)*. To make the dough easier to roll out, enclose it in plastic wrap or foil and chill it in the refrigerator for at least an hour before using it.

2 **Rubbing the butter into the flour.** Add all of the butter to the flour and salt. Using the tips of your fingers and thumbs, pick up a small amount of butter and flour, lightly rub them together and let the mixture fall back into the bowl *(above, left)*. Continue for about two to three minutes, until all of the butter is incorporated and the mixture resembles very coarse bread crumbs *(right)*.

3 **Adding the water.** Use a spoon to make a shallow well in the flour-butter mixture; spoon in a little ice water *(above)*. Because some types of flour absorb more water than others, the quantity of water you need will vary; always start with a minimum amount.

An Alternative Approach: Working with Knives

1 **Cutting in the butter.** Sift flour and salt into a bowl. Add chilled butter that has been cut into pieces. Using two table knives in a rapid crisscross motion, cut the butter into the flour until the mixture looks like coarse crumbs.

2 **Adding the water.** Sprinkle a little ice water over the mixture and blend it in with a knife. Then use your hands to gather the dough lightly together. Add a little more water if necessary; the mixture should cling together but it should not feel damp *(above)*.

3 **Finishing the dough.** Lightly press the dough together and form it into a ball. Enclose the dough in plastic wrap or foil to prevent drying, and chill the dough for an hour before use.

An Enrichment of Butter and Eggs

Rich short-crust dough *(recipe, page 162)* is made by techniques akin to those used for basic short crust, but its ingredients are calculated to produce a sweeter, more fragile result. For rich short crust, all-purpose flour is sweetened with super-fine or confectioners' sugar, which blends in evenly, contributes tenderness and helps the dough to brown during baking. More butter is used for this dough than for basic short crust, and the liquid is provided by eggs rather than water.

Because of the viscosity of eggs and the consequent danger of overhandling the dough when they are incorporated, special mixing tactics are needed. A good way to ensure even distribution is to mix the eggs with the butter before blending in flour. Use butter that is cool but malleable: Cold butter cannot easily be combined with the eggs, and warm butter would spread too much in the flour, producing an oily pastry.

Many cooks mix the butter and eggs together in a well—a bowl-like cavity—made in a mound of sifted flour and sugar. This permits the dry ingredients to be gathered in a little at a time, so that the flour mixture is evenly and thoroughly coated with the butter-and-egg paste. In this demonstration, the ingredients are mixed on a cool, marble work surface—a particularly useful way of handling a large volume of ingredients. Small quantities of dough, however, can be prepared just as easily in a mixing bowl.

Making rich short crust by hand takes about five minutes, but a food processor produces it in seconds. If you use softened butter, add all of the ingredients to the processor container and blend them by operating the processor in short spurts. If the butter is hard, cut it up by hand and blend it with the dry ingredients first; then add the eggs and blend again.

However you produce the dough, the addition of the sugar will make it stickier and more difficult to handle than basic short crust. The dough will therefore require longer chilling in the refrigerator—at least two hours.

1 **Assembling ingredients.** Soften unsalted butter by leaving it at room temperature for 15 minutes. Measure the flour and sugar—in this demonstration, confectioners' sugar. Combine the flour, sugar and a pinch of salt in a strainer or sifter. Sift the dry ingredients into a mound.

2 **Adding butter and eggs.** With your hand, make a deep well in the center of the mound of dry ingredients. Place the softened butter in the center of the well; break the eggs over the butter.

5 **Blending the ingredients.** Continue to chop in the flour, flipping the bottom of the mixture to the top. After about two minutes, the dough will be coarse and mealy *(above, left)*. If the dough is too dry to absorb all of the flour-sugar mixture, add a little ice water—a drop or two at a time—until the dough begins to cling together. Work it until it is rough and crumbly *(right)*.

3 **Mixing moist ingredients.** Using the fingers of one hand, pinch the butter and eggs together repeatedly until they are lightly blended *(above, left)*. Work quickly, so that the butter does not become oily; after about a minute, the mixture will have the consistency of a slippery paste *(right)*.

4 **Adding dry ingredients.** Use a narrow metal spatula or table knife to gather in the dry ingredients. Flip the flour mixture, little by little, over the butter-and-egg mixture *(above),* and then chop the ingredients with the spatula or knife, using quick, light movements.

6 **Finishing the dough.** Use your hands to push the crumbly dough mixture together, pressing gently so that the crumbs cohere and form a loose mass *(inset)*. Form the dough into a ball *(right),* enclose it in plastic wrap or foil, and chill it in the refrigerator for at least two hours before rolling it out.

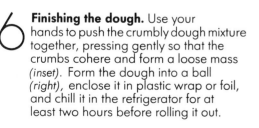

Cookie-like Refrigerator Doughs

Refrigerator doughs *(recipes, pages 162-163)* are based on the same ingredients as rich short crust: flour, butter, sugar and eggs. The ingredients, however, are chosen and combined so that gluten development is minimal: The flour is low-gluten cake flour, and the proportions of butter and sugar are high. The result is a soft dough, quite crumbly when cooked.

The baked pastry, in fact, resembles a large cookie, and the mixing of the dough is more like cookie making than pastry making. To give a light, even texture, the butter is creamed, then combined with the other ingredients. Once mixed, the dough is far too soft and sticky to roll. It must be refrigerated—hence the name of the dough—for four hours to firm up.

Like cookie dough, refrigerator doughs are subject to infinite variation. They may be sweetened with either granulated sugar or confectioners' sugar; the latter should be sifted *(box, below)* to eliminate lumps. The doughs can also be enhanced with all sorts of flavorings and texture-altering ingredients. The gamut of flavorings includes vanilla extract, rum, lemon juice, cocoa, grated lemon peel and spices. Various textural effects may be achieved by adding dry bread or cake crumbs, or by lightening the dough with baking powder. The most popular additions, however, are ground nuts—prominent among the elements used in this demonstration *(recipe, page 163)*.

For the best flavor, the nuts—whether almonds, hazelnuts, pistachios, pecans or walnuts—should be freshly shelled. Once shelled, almonds, pistachios and hazelnuts can be stripped of their inner skins so that the dough will have a uniform color. Parboil almonds or pistachios for a minute or two to loosen the skins; hazelnuts should be toasted in a preheated 350° F. [180° C.] oven for 15 minutes. After these treatments, almond skins will slip off easily; pistachios and hazelnuts should be rolled back and forth inside a towel.

Any of the nuts can be ground in a food mill or food processor. When using a processor, first cool the nuts completely. Then, grind the nuts by operating the machine in short spurts, stopping when they are crumbly but still dry. Overgrinding would make them oily.

1 **Flavoring flour.** Using a strainer or sifter, sift cake flour into a large bowl. Add ground cinnamon, baking powder and salt, and stir the ingredients with a spoon to blend them together.

A Simplified Version

Sweetening the mixture. Stir salt into sifted cake flour and sift the two together *(Step 2)*. Cream butter *(Step 3)* and sift confectioners' sugar onto it *(above)*. Beat in the sugar, then stir in an egg, grated lemon peel and cinnamon. Fold in the flour and chill the dough *(Step 6)* for rolling.

4 **Enriching the dough.** Stir the ground nuts into the butter mixture. When they are completely incorporated, stir in the ground bread crumbs *(above)*.

5 **Completing the dough.** Add the flavored flour mixture to the butter-sugar mixture. With the spoon, fold and stir the ingredients until the flour mixture is evenly incorporated. The resulting dough will be soft and sticky.

2 **Sifting.** To aerate the ingredients and blend them thoroughly, sift the flour mixture onto a sheet of wax paper. Remove the crusts from stale white bread and grind the bread in a food processor to make crumbs. Grind shelled and peeled nuts — in this case, almonds and hazelnuts. Reserve the crumbs and nuts in separate bowls.

3 **Creaming butter.** With a wooden spoon, beat cold butter, mashing it against the sides of a mixing bowl until it is soft and fluffy *(above, left)*. Beat in sugar by spoonfuls, then beat in an egg and an egg yolk *(right)*. Stir in grated lemon peel and vanilla extract.

6 **Chilling the dough.** Put the dough on a sheet of aluminum foil or wax paper, and pat it into a large flat cake to facilitate later rolling. Wrap the dough cake in foil and refrigerate it for at least four hours, or until it is hard. When it is stored this way, the dough will keep for up to four days.

The Shaping and Baking of Two-Crust Pies

Whether you make an old-fashioned two-crust pie like the one demonstrated here or any of the array of pies, tarts and turnovers shown on the following pages, the rule for rolling short-crust dough is the same: For tender crusts, the dough must be handled quickly and lightly to keep it cool and to avoid overworking it.

Start with chilled dough, and roll out the pastry elements—top and bottom crusts, for instance—one at a time, keeping the rest of the dough in the refrigerator. A cool marble slab is a particularly good surface for rolling. For the best control of pressure, use a pastry pin *(right)* or a heavy-duty ball-bearing rolling pin. To prevent sticking, dust the work surface with flour—but very lightly: Too much flour could make the pastry tough. To ensure an even thickness, roll the dough sheet from the center to the edge, turning the sheet as you work so you can roll in all directions. Use light strokes; heavy pressure will overwork the dough.

The two-crust pie at right is made from basic short-crust dough *(pages 16-17)*; rich short-crust and refrigerator doughs are too crumbly to form top crusts. Like other pastries, the pie is best baked in a light-colored, satiny-surfaced metal pan that reflects some oven heat; dark metal or glass pans absorb heat so readily that the pastries could easily overbrown.

Fillings for two-crust pies are based on all sorts of ingredients, including vegetables, meats, cheese and—most popular of all—fresh fruits such as cherries, berries or the apples used here *(recipes, pages 88-106)*. Thickening agents must be added to fresh fruits to give the filling body and keep it from turning the pastry soggy.

Usually, the thickening agent is flour, but starches such as cornstarch, arrowroot or tapioca may be used instead. (Tapioca is the obligatory choice for plum or cranberry fillings; these fruits are so acidic that they inhibit the thickening action of the other starches.) If you use flour, simply stir it into the prepared fruit. Tapioca, too, can be stirred into the fruit, but the filling should be allowed to rest for 15 minutes so that the tapioca's grains can swell and soften. Cornstarch and arrowroot should be dissolved in a little cold water or juice before they are added to the fruit.

1 **Preparing the filling.** In a bowl, mix together a little flour, salt, sugar and spices — in this case, freshly grated nutmeg and ground cinnamon. Peel, core and slice apples. Add them to the bowl and, using your hands, mix the apples with the dry ingredients until the fruit is evenly coated.

2 **Rolling.** Halve chilled basic short-crust dough; return one piece to the refrigerator. Place the other piece on a floured work surface and flatten it with a rolling pin. Working from its center, roll the dough away from yourself, using quick, light strokes. Give the dough quarter turns to form an even surface.

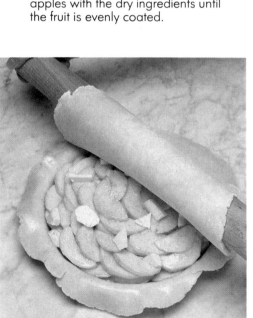

5 **Filling.** Put in the apple mixture; sprinkle on grated lemon peel, lemon juice and pieces of butter. To make a lid, roll the rest of the dough into a round about ⅛ inch [3 mm.] thick and about 2 inches [5 cm.] larger than the pan. Moisten the edges of the shell with cold water and unroll the lid over it.

6 **Trimming the excess.** With scissors or a sharp knife, trim excess dough from around the edges of the pie, leaving a ½-inch [1-cm.] margin of dough all around it.

3 **Lining the pan.** Continue turning and rolling the dough until it forms a round about ⅛ inch [3 mm.] thick. To ensure that the round is big enough to fill the pan and overlap the sides, hold the pan over the dough as a guide; the pastry should be about 2 inches [5 cm.] wider than the pan all around *(inset)*. Roll the dough slightly thinner and wider, if necessary. Then roll the dough loosely around the rolling pin and unroll it over the piepan *(above)*.

4 **Forming the shell.** Use your fingers or a small, wadded-up piece of dough to press the dough firmly into the pan. Try not to stretch or tear the dough; if you do, patch damaged areas with extra bits of rolled dough.

7 **Decorating the edge.** Hold the pie in one hand and, with the thumb and forefinger of the other hand, pinch and twist the edge of the dough to form a decorative seal. With a knife tip, slit the lid in several places to allow steam to escape as the pie bakes.

8 **Serving.** Bake the pie in a preheated 375° F. [190° C.] oven for 50 to 60 minutes, or until the pastry is firm and golden brown, and the fruit is tender when tested with a skewer inserted through the slits in the lid. Let the pie cool before serving; hot pastry is fragile.

Fashioning the Lid of a Deep-dish Pie

Deep-dish pie, a simplification of a basic two-crust pie *(pages 22-23)*, consists merely of a filling piled into a baking dish, covered with dough and baked. Any filling suitable for a two-crust pie is appropriate for a deep-dish pie. Moreover, fresh-fruit fillings such as the blueberries used in this demonstration are thickened for the deep-dish version just as for a two-crust pie, although the only purpose is to avoid soupiness (there is no danger of the lid becoming soggy). Deep-dish pie does call for some special handling of the dough because the pie has no bottom shell to anchor its lid.

To provide anchorage for the dough, use a baking dish with a broad, flat rim on which to lay the dough. The dish should be made of ceramic or other nonreactive material; aluminum pans might interact with the acid in many pie fillings, giving them an off taste.

For strength, the dough that forms the lid should be a basic short crust. To prevent shrinkage—which could make the lid collapse into the filling—the dough should be very well chilled and very lightly handled.

To reinforce its edges, the dough lid should be at least two layers thick all around its circumference. A simple way to achieve this is to roll the dough slightly larger than the rim of the baking dish, then fold under a border all around the edge. A neater border is achieved by the technique shown here: A collar of dough is fitted onto the rim of the dish and the dough lid is then sealed to the collar.

As with two-crust pies, the deep-dish lids are pierced to allow the escape of steam. Either slit the pie lid with a knife tip once you have it in place or, for a more decorative effect, fashion prettily shaped vents in advance (the task demands the support of a hard, flat surface). Make these vents with aspic cutters—small tools like cookie cutters, available at kitchen-equipment shops—or cut elaborate shapes with a small, sharp knife.

To promote browning, the pie lid can be brushed with milk before baking. For a glossy finish, brush the lid with egg and water. Or, after baking, coat the lid with confectioners' sugar moistened with water or milk; the sugar will harden to an icing-like glaze.

1 Preparing the filling. Rinse blueberries in cold water and sort them, removing stems and discarding wizened or soft, overripe berries. Place the blueberries in a bowl, add sugar to taste, and sift a little flour over the berries. Stir the mixture well; sprinkle on fresh lemon juice and stir again.

2 Rolling out the dough. On a lightly floured surface, roll chilled basic short-crust dough into a sheet large enough to cover the top of your baking dish, allowing a margin of 3 inches [8 cm.] all around. The sheet should be about ⅛ inch [3 mm.] thick.

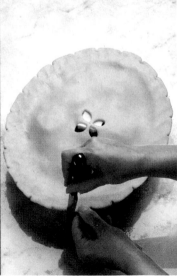

6 Covering the pie. Gently fold the dough lid in half and position it precisely over half of the pie, so that the edges of the lid align with those of the dough collar. Unfold the lid *(above, left)*, aligning the second half over the other side of the collar. Press the lid onto the collar to seal it, keeping the edges aligned by pressing the flat of a knife blade against them *(center)*. Press the dull edge of the knife blade into the dough at regular intervals around the lid to crimp it decoratively *(right)*.

3 **Shaping a lid.** Invert the baking dish onto the dough, but do not press it onto the sheet; this would mark the lid. Shape the lid by cutting the dough all around the dish, ¼ to ½ inch [6 mm. to 1 cm.] beyond the rim. Make a collar by cutting a concentric circle outside the first *(above)*; the dough ring should be ¼ to ½ inch wider than the rim of the dish. Remove the dish and set it upright.

4 **Fitting the collar.** Remove excess dough from outside the collar. Cut through the collar on opposite sides to divide it for easy lifting. Brush water onto the rim of the pie dish. Press half of the dough collar onto the rim of the dish, letting it overhang on the outside by ¼ to ½ inch. Press the second half of the collar into place; the cut ends of the halves will overlap by about ½ inch.

5 **Filling the pie.** Using aspic cutters or a knife, cut decorative steam vents in the center of the dough lid. Butter the baking dish and pour the blueberry mixture into it. Scatter slices of butter over the fruit, then brush the dough collar lightly with water.

7 **Baking.** Brush the pie lid with an egg that has been beaten with 1 tablespoon [15 ml.] of cold water. Then bake the pie in a preheated 400° F. [200° C.] oven for 10 minutes. Reduce the heat to 325° F. [160° C.] and bake for another 15 to 20 minutes, until the crust is golden brown and the fruit tender. Let the pie cool and firm for 15 minutes.

8 **Serving.** Cut a neat wedge of crust from the pie lid and set it aside. Spoon a portion of filling onto a plate, then cover it with the reserved wedge of crust. Garnish, if you like, with whipped cream, sour cream or, as here, tart cream *(recipe, page 166)*.

A Woven Lattice to Invite the Eye

If strips of basic short crust are arranged on top of a pie filling, a two-crust pie is transformed into a lattice pie—a splendid showcase for brightly colored contents, and one that lends itself to a variety of ornamental effects. The strips may, for instance, be given scalloped edges by cutting them with a serrated pastry wheel *(right)* instead of a knife. They can also be endowed with a ribbon-like appearance by twisting them several times before laying them on the pie, instead of simply laying them flat.

The overall pattern of the lattice offers further scope for variation. To make the simplest of lattice tops, dough strips are laid in evenly spaced rows across a filled pie shell, then topped with more strips set at right angles to form squares or set obliquely to form diamonds. In this demonstration, a more elaborate lattice is created by weaving two sets of strips together. The weaving is done on a baking sheet, and the entire lattice is transferred intact to the top of the pie; weaving

done directly on the filled pie may produce a messy, filling-spattered lattice.

Fresh fruits, because of their pretty colors, are the usual choices for lattice-pie fillings. They are thickened just as for two-crust and deep-dish pies, not only to prevent soupiness or a soggy crust, but also to keep the fillings from bubbling up through the lattice and possibly charring on top when the pie is baked.

The pie shown here contains an old-fashioned filling—red strawberries and green-tinged field rhubarb *(recipe, page 103)*. Rhubarb, which renders much of its liquid, requires some preliminary treatment. It is cut into pieces, mixed with sugar, then left to stand for an hour or so: The sugar will draw out the fruit's liquid, a process known as sweating.

To capture its tart flavor, the liquid can be drained from the rhubarb, thickened with cornstarch, then mixed into the filling *(Step 3)*. Because of the time required, you should begin preparing the rhubarb before shaping the dough.

1 **Cutting strips.** Using the inverted piepan as a template and a table knife as a tool, incise a circle on wax paper to serve as a guide. Set the paper on a baking sheet. Roll basic short-crust dough into a round 2 inches [5 cm.] larger than the circle. Guiding a knife or pastry wheel *(above)* with a ruler, cut the dough into ½-inch [1-cm.] strips.

4 **Glazing.** Fit rolled-out, basic short crust into the piepan, trimming the dough to within ½ inch [1 cm.] of the rim. Pour the filling into this shell. Remove the lattice from the refrigerator, then slip a spatula underneath it to free it from the wax paper. Brush it with a glaze of lightly beaten egg whites.

5 **Covering the pie.** Brush the rim of the shell with water. Place the baking sheet on the shell so that the lattice is aligned with the edges of the pie. Holding the wax paper and baking sheet together, gently slide them out from under the lattice and, at the same time, adjust the lattice so that it settles onto the rim of the shell.

6 **Trimming and crimping.** With scissors, trim the lattice strips to meet the edges of the shell *(above, left)*. Press each strip end onto the rim of the shell, then flute the rim by pinching the dough around your forefinger at ½-inch [1-cm.] intervals *(above, right)*.

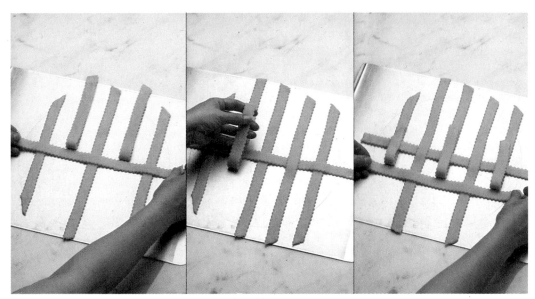

2 **Forming the lattice.** Leaving a 1-inch [2½-cm.] margin at each side, lay parallel dough strips across the wax-paper circle at 1-inch intervals. Fold alternate strips back and lay a strip across the unfolded strips *(left)*. Lower the folded strips over it *(center)*. Fold back the strips that now lie under the crosswise piece, and lay a second crosswise strip parallel to the first, 1 inch away *(right)*. Unfold the folded strips over it. Repeat to form a lattice about 1 inch larger than the circle. Chill for 15 minutes.

3 **Making a filling.** Cut rhubarb into 1-inch [2½-cm.] pieces. Add sugar and let the rhubarb sweat for about an hour. Drain the liquid into a pan, stir in cornstarch and simmer for about five minutes, until thick. Pour it over the rhubarb. Stir in grated lemon peel and hulled strawberries.

7 **Baking.** Bake the pie in a preheated 450° F. [230° C.] oven for 15 minutes; reduce the heat to 350° F. [180° C.] and bake for 35 minutes more, or until the crust is crisp and brown *(above)* and the fruit is tender.

Stratagems for Handling Refrigerator Dough

Rich, sweet refrigerator doughs *(pages 20-21)* are far too crumbly to form the tops of two-crust or deep-dish pies, but if properly molded and baked, they yield delectable, cookie-like shells for lattice-top or open-faced tarts, large or small. High proportions of butter and sugar can make the doughs difficult to work with; the techniques for shaping, filling and baking them are therefore different from those used for other short crusts.

Both plain and nut refrigerator doughs are soft and sticky until well chilled—and neither should be rolled until it is very hard indeed. Do not warm the dough to make it more malleable; smack it with a rolling pin to flatten it, then—working quickly and using as much pressure as needed—roll it out. If the dough softens as you work, chill it until it is hard again; otherwise, it will become unmanageable.

Unlike rolled short-crust, refrigerator-dough sheets are fragile and inflexible. If you try to roll them around the rolling pin or lift them with your hands to fit them into their molds, they will break

up: Move the dough from place to place on a rimless baking sheet.

To mold a large, freestanding pastry such as the Austrian *Linzertorte* shown at right and below, use a bottomless rectangular or round flan form—available at kitchen-equipment shops—set on a baking sheet. The molded dough will shrink slightly during baking, allowing you to lift the flan form from the cooked pastry. The dough can also be molded in piepans or cake pans, or in tartlet pans such as the barquettes used on the opposite page, at bottom.

Refrigerator doughs are baked at lower temperatures—their high sugar content makes them susceptible to burning—and therefore set more slowly than basic or rich short crust. For this reason, refrigerator doughs are not suitable for fresh fruit fillings: Even when thickened, these fillings exude enough liquid to penetrate the doughs and make them soggy. Drier fillings such as jam or almond cream *(page 31)* are best; raspberry jam fills both pastries demonstrated here.

Molding with a Flan Form

1 **Rolling.** On a lightly floured surface, beat chilled refrigerator dough with a rolling pin to flatten it. With firm, quick strokes, roll the dough into a sheet ¼ inch [6 mm.] thick and several inches larger all around than your flan form. (A pound [½ kg.] of nut dough is used in this demonstration to line a 4-by-12-inch [10-by-30-cm.] form.)

4 **Making a lattice.** From a second sheet of dough, cut equal-length strips ½ inch [1 cm.] wide. Lay strips diagonally across the filled pastry, about 1 inch [2½ cm.] apart, pressing them onto the pastry rim. Over them lay strips diagonally in the opposite direction. Press a blanched hazelnut, if you like, into each intersection of the strips.

5 **Unmolding.** Bake the tart for 35 to 40 minutes in a preheated 350° F. [180° C.] oven until the top is crisp and brown. Let it cool and firm for a few moments, then lift the flan form straight up off the top of the tart. Tilt the baking sheet slightly to slide the tart gently onto a serving dish, holding the parchment paper against the sheet so that it is left behind.

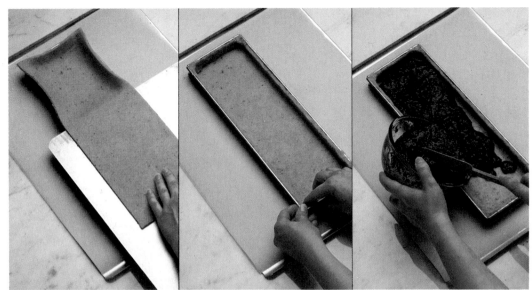

2 **Trimming.** Set the flan form on the dough sheet as a template and, with a knife, trim the dough into a rectangle about 1 inch [2½ cm.] larger than the flan form all around. Transfer the flan form to a parchment-lined baking sheet. Starting at one narrow end of the rectangle, slide a second, rimless baking sheet under the trimmed dough.

3 **Molding.** Place the dough on its baking sheet over the flan form so that the far end of the dough is positioned about an inch [2½ cm.] beyond the far end of the form's rim. Hold the near end of the dough in place with one hand and pull the baking sheet back out from under it *(above, left)*; the dough will drop into the flan form. Pinch the dough against the sides of the form all around *(center)*, making sure no dough projects above the rim, which could hamper unmolding later. Fill the molded pastry almost to the rim *(right)* — in this case, with 2 cups [½ liter] of raspberry jam.

Baking in Barquettes

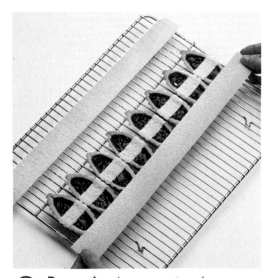

1 **Lining molds.** Roll out chilled refrigerator dough and cut it into rectangles 1 inch [2½ cm.] larger than the tartlet molds. A pound [½ kg.] of plain dough is used here to line eight barquettes. Dipping your fingers in flour, press each rectangle into an unbuttered mold, forcing excess dough against the rim to cut it off.

2 **Baking the tartlets.** Set the tartlets on a baking sheet and fill each one; in this demonstration, raspberry jam is used. Bake the tartlets for 20 minutes in a preheated 375° F. [190° C.] oven, until crisp and brown. Let the tartlets cool until lukewarm, then gently lift them from their molds and set them side by side in a straight row on a wire rack.

3 **Decorating.** Lay two strips of parchment paper across the row of tartlets, covering the ends and leaving a ½-inch [1-cm.] space exposed in the centers. Sift a heavy layer of confectioners' sugar over the exposed centers, then carefully lift away the strips of parchment paper, leaving a neat white belt on each tartlet.

An Efficient Method for Producing Tartlets

Tartlets made from crumbly refrigerator dough must be molded one by one *(page 29)*, but those formed from the more flexible basic or rich short-crust doughs can be shaped assembly-line fashion, as demonstrated here. The key to mass production is the same dough-handling technique used to line an individual piepan. A sheet of dough is rolled loosely around its rolling pin, then unrolled over the tartlet pans and gently pressed down into them. Next, the pin is rolled across the tops of the dough-covered pans to trim away excess dough in one smooth swoop.

For this procedure to work successfully, you need equal-sized sharp-rimmed tartlet pans: Pans with flat lips will not cut through the dough. Arrange the pans close together on a dampened towel so that they will not slide about. To press the dough sheet into the pans, use a small ball of lightly floured excess dough; your fingers might pierce the dough sheet.

Tartlets this small may contain any of the fillings used for larger pies, but if the small pastries are to be eaten with the fingers, as is frequently the case, the filling should be a firm mixture that will not spill out messily when the pastries are bitten into. Jams are a good choice, as are pecan or chess fillings *(recipes, pages 131 and 108-110)*. Or you can use the classic, rum-scented almond-cream filling demonstrated in the box opposite. Known as frangipane, it supposedly is named in honor of Cesar Frangipani, an Italian Renaissance nobleman, and was one of the delicacies introduced to France by Catherine de' Medici in the 16th Century.

Frangipane, mild and fragrant, lends itself to a variety of garnishes. In this case the finished tartlets are given a coating of amber-colored apricot glaze and a decoration of almonds and pistachios. A thin coat of melted chocolate or fondant icing *(pages 10-11)* would also complement the almond flavoring, or you could use small whole fruits, such as cherries, that have been marinated in the liqueur used to flavor the frangipane.

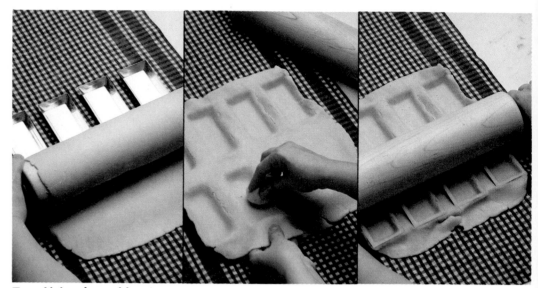

1 **Lining the molds.** Align tartlet pans on a damp towel, spacing them about ¾ inch [2 cm.] apart. Roll a sheet of short-crust dough ⅛ inch [3 mm.] thick around the rolling pin *(page 23)*, then unroll it over the pans *(above, left)*. With a small ball of dough scraps, gently press the sheet down into each pan *(center)*. Then roll the pin firmly across the tops of the pans to cut out the shells *(right)*. Pull away excess dough.

4 **Garnishing the tartlets.** Arrange two almond slices in the depression in the center of the filling, separating the slices with a pistachio. If you like, you can instead use chocolate-covered almonds, cherry halves or pieces of candied fruit.

2 **Filling the tartlets.** Prepare a fruit glaze *(pages 8-9)* with apricots and glaze the bottom of each tartlet. To keep it fluid, set the pan of glaze in a pot of hot water. Spoon the frangipane *(box, below)* into the tartlets to within ¼ inch [6 mm.] of the top and smooth the filling. Place the tartlets on a baking sheet and bake them in a preheated 425° F. [220° C.] oven for 10 to 15 minutes, or until they are lightly browned.

3 **Glazing the tartlets.** Blanch and peel pistachios. Toast sliced, unblanched almonds in a 350° F. [180° C.] oven until golden — about five minutes. When the tartlets are cool enough to handle, invert each one over your hand and lift off the pan; use a knife, if necessary, to loosen the tartlet. Set the unmolded tartlets on a rack. When cool, brush the tops with the warm glaze.

Frangipane: A Rich Almond Filling

The classic almond-cream filling, called frangipane, begins with almonds that have been shelled, blanched and peeled, then finely ground in a nut grinder or in a food processor. The almonds are stirred into a batter-like mixture of butter, sugar, eggs, flour and flavorings—traditionally, almond extract and rum *(recipe, page 166)*. Both the taste and texture of the mixture may be altered.

You can, for instance, replace the almonds with finely ground hazelnuts, and the almond extract and rum with vanilla extract, lemon juice, kirsch or orange-flower water.

To alter the texture of the filling, simply eliminate the flour in the recipe, as described on page 54. The flour in the filling acts as a thickener: When the filling is baked in the tart shell, the mixture becomes cakelike in consistency. Without the flour, the mixture will remain more custard-like and closer in texture to pastry cream.

1 **Stirring in the nuts.** Grind blanched and peeled almonds in a nut grinder or food processor until they are like fine, dry meal. Cream together butter and sugar, beating the ingredients to incorporate air and make them fluffy. Beat in eggs, one at a time. Stir in the almonds and mix thoroughly.

2 **Adding the flavoring.** Stir in flavorings: Dark rum and almond extract are used in this demonstration. Sift in flour and stir until all of it is absorbed.

An Upside-down Tart of Wine-drenched Fruit

One way of ensuring that a tart shell does not absorb liquid from a fruit filling is to bake the assemblage upside down, with the shell on top and the filling underneath, then reverse the tart onto its serving plate. A short-crust shell of this nature requires basic short-crust dough for strength and a filling of firm fruits that will hold their shapes when unmolded: Apples, apricots or pears are all suitable.

The fruits can simply be sliced, mixed with flavorings such as sugar, and then cooked under a pastry lid. If you wish to leave the fruits in large pieces, first sauté the pieces in butter or poach them in a sweet liquid such as sugar syrup *(page 8)*, softening them so that they will cook through in the same time as the pastry.

In this demonstration, pear halves are poached in sweetened red wine for about one hour. The wine adds flavor and gives the pale fruit a reddish-purple color. In addition, its acidity slows the breakdown of the fruit's cell structure and helps keep the pears intact during cooking. Even so, you should use underripe pears of a firm-fleshed variety such as Anjou or Bosc: Fully ripe or soft-fleshed fruit might well break despite the wine's effect. Choose a good wine, one that is deeply colored, young and full-bodied: Cooking concentrates the flavor, and the quality of the wine will be reflected in the finished tart.

To prevent the filling from being too moist, pour the poaching liquid into a saucepan after the pears have been softened and reduce it over high heat to a thick syrup *(Step 5)*. Return the thickened syrup to the pears, cover them with rolled-out dough and bake the tart. If possible, use the same pan for poaching and baking: By transferring the pears to a baking dish, you risk breaking them.

To prevent juices from seeping into the pastry and making it soggy after the tart is baked, unmold the tart at the last possible moment. Serve it warm or cold, accompanied, if you like, by thick cream.

1 Preparing the pears. Assemble firm, slightly underripe pears, red wine, sugar and ground cinnamon. Peel, halve and core the pears. Arrange the halves, cored surfaces up, in a shallow, heavy, nonreactive pan — stainless steel, enameled iron or tin-lined copper — fitting the wide ends of the pears against the edge of the pan.

2 Adding the wine. Fill the center of the pan with more pear halves, their narrow ends pointing outward so that the fruit will form an attractively symmetrical design when the tart is unmolded. Sprinkle sugar and cinnamon over the pears. Pour enough wine into the pan to almost cover the fruit.

6 Preparing the lid. Roll basic short-crust dough into a round slightly larger than the pan and about ¼ inch [6 mm.] thick. Pierce the dough repeatedly with a fork to form steam vents. Make a border about ½ inch [1 cm.] wide by folding in the edge of the dough round; press the edge flat, crimping it with a fork *(above)*.

7 Covering the pears. Carefully lift the dough and place it over the pears with the folded border downward. Bake the tart in a preheated 375° F. [190° C.] oven for about 40 minutes, until the pastry is golden brown and crisp.

3 **Poaching the pears.** Place the pan of pears and wine over high heat. Bring the wine to a boil, cover the pan, reduce the heat and simmer the pears for one hour, or until tender. Test the fruit by gently inserting the tip of a knife into a pear half *(above)*; the knife should penetrate the fruit easily.

4 **Draining the pears.** Holding the lid of the poaching pan against the pears to keep them in place, pour the liquid into a small, nonreactive saucepan *(above)*. Put the saucepan over high heat and bring the poaching liquid to a boil, stirring it with a wooden spoon. Adjust the heat so that the liquid bubbles, but does not boil over.

5 **Making the syrup.** Boil the liquid for 10 minutes, or until it has been reduced to about one third its original volume and has become a thick syrup. Pour the syrup evenly over the pears.

8 **Serving the tart.** Remove the tart from the oven and let it cool for at least a few minutes to firm the filling. When you are ready to serve the tart, invert a serving plate over the pan *(inset)* and turn the plate and pan over together. If the pan's handle keeps you from unmolding the tart into the center of the plate, slide it into place with your hand.

Turnovers: Packages for Full-bodied Fillings

Among the free-form pastries that can be shaped without the aid of piepans or tart pans, turnovers are the easiest to make: Sheets of flexible short-crust dough are simply folded over a filling and sealed around it, then baked, as shown at right, or—sometimes—fried *(box, below)*.

Baked turnovers—always made with basic short-crust dough because of its strength—are folded into rectangular or semicircular packages as large as pies or as small as cookies. Whatever their size or shape, they require thick, firm fillings; very juicy mixtures might seep through the sealed edges. In the demonstration at right, a large rectangular turnover is filled with a precooked mixture of dried fruits and nuts *(recipe, page 102)*, but many other ingredients, cooked beforehand or not, may be baked in the pastry packages. An English Banbury tart, for instance, is stuffed with a lemon-scented filling of cracker crumbs, eggs and raisins *(recipe, page 106)*.

Turnovers that will be deep fried also are always made with basic short-crust

dough. The turnovers should be small, so that they will cook through quickly: Because of the high heat used for deep frying, the dough will become crisp in a matter of moments—not long enough to do much more than warm a filling. For this reason, the turnovers should be filled with precooked mixtures such as mincemeat, jam or—as used in this demonstration—dried fruits.

For successful deep frying, careful regulation of the oil temperature is essential. If the oil is too hot, the pastries may char; if it is too cool, they will take longer to cook, causing them to absorb oil and become greasy. The frying oil should therefore be heated ahead of time until its temperature reaches 375° F. [190° C.] on a deep-frying thermometer. If you do not have a deep-frying thermometer, you may test the oil's temperature by dropping into it a small piece of dough; the oil should sizzle instantly. To avoid lowering the temperature of the oil during the frying process, cook the little turnovers a few at a time.

1 **Preparing the filling.** Simmer chopped, dried prunes and apricots in a little water until soft—about 10 minutes. Stir in sugar, salt, fresh lemon juice, and cornstarch that has been dissolved in cold water. If you like, add nuts; chopped, toasted walnuts are used here. Pour in a dash of brandy or kirsch and stir over medium heat until the mixture thickens. Set aside to cool.

Pastry Half-moons Quickly Deep Fried

1 **Filling the pies.** Prepare a filling; an apricot-prune-nut mixture *(Step 1, above, right)* is used here. Cut rolled-out short-crust dough into 3- or 4-inch [8- or 10-cm.] rounds, using a cookie cutter or a glass. Spoon about 1½ tablespoons [22 ml.] of filling onto half of each circle. Moisten the edges of the dough and fold over the tops.

2 **Sealing the pieces.** Crimp the cut edges of each turnover together by pressing them all around with the tines of a fork that has been dipped in a little flour. Invert each turnover and lightly crimp the edges on the reverse side to ensure a tight seal.

3 **Frying.** Pour 3 inches [8 cm.] of oil into a heavy pan. Heat the oil to 375° F. [190° C.]. Drop in a few turnovers at a time and fry for five to six minutes, turning once. When the turnovers have risen to the surface and their edges have browned, remove them from the oil with a skimmer. Drain on paper towels, then cool on a rack.

2 **Shaping.** Roll basic short-crust dough ¼ inch [6 mm.] thick and cut out a 14-inch [35-cm.] square. To move the square without tearing, fold it in half, then in quarters, placing wax paper between the layers. Using a large spatula, transfer the dough to a parchment-covered baking sheet. Unfold the square and spoon filling over half of it.

3 **Sealing.** Brush the edges of the square with water. Fold the top half over the filling to make a neat package. To seal, press the cut edges with the tines of a fork, or run a floured ravioli cutter lightly over the dough margins *(above)*. Remove and discard the thin dough strip cut off by the ravioli cutter.

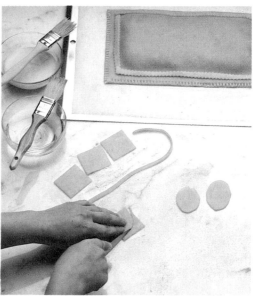

4 **Decorating.** Beat an egg with water to make a glaze. Cut four narrow strips of dough, using a serrated pastry wheel. Brush the strips with water and lay them around the edges of the turnover. With a knife, cut the remaining dough into a long strip and several small squares. Roll this strip under your fingers to shape it into a stem. Cut the squares into fruit and leaf shapes.

5 **Glazing.** Moisten the dough cutouts with water and apply them to the top of the turnover to simulate a leafy branch with fruit on it. Pierce the top of the pastry with a knife tip — near the decorations, to disguise the holes. Brush the surface with the egg glaze *(above)*. Bake the turnover in a preheated 425° F. [220° C.] oven for 20 minutes, or until the pastry is golden. Slide the turnover onto a wire rack to cool, then transfer it to a platter and cut it into squares for serving *(right)*.

Splendid Arrays on a Free-form Base

Few varieties of short-crust pastry lend themselves to such spectacular presentations as a free-form tart. Made of either basic or rich short crust, it can be shaped into a circle, oval, rectangle or any other form the cook devises, and it may be as large as the oven will hold. Because the sides of the tart are not supported by a pan, the dough sheet should be thicker than usual—¼ inch [6 mm.] is about right. Otherwise, forming the tart shell is simple: The dough is rolled into the desired shape and the edges are pinched up to make a low rim. The effort in making a tart of this type should be expended in preparing the filling ingredients and displaying them to best advantage.

Most often, fillings for sizable, free-form tart shells are fruits, left in large pieces that lend themselves to handsome arrangements and retain their shapes during cooking. Crescent-shaped apple slices are used here (recipe, page 88), but slices or halves of peaches, apricots, plums and pears, or whole berries or pitted cherries, also make appealing fillings, either alone or in combination.

Many fruits require no more preparation than peeling, pitting or coring, and cutting. Apples, peaches, pears and apricots, however, have a low ascorbic-acid content, and their pale flesh turns brown when it is exposed to the air. To avoid discoloration, drop the peeled fruits into acidulated water—water combined with fresh lemon or lime juice in the proportion of 5 or 6 tablespoons [75 or 90 ml.] of juice to each quart [1 liter] of water.

Fruit will exude a certain amount of juice during baking, and this could make the pastry shell soggy. The best preventive tactic is to choose firm, slightly underripe fruit, which will develop flavor as it bakes but render less juice than when very ripe—and also will hold its shape better. If you do use soft, ripe fruit, sugar it after, not before, baking: Sugar helps draw out juice. To further protect the shell—and add a bonus of flavor—you can coat it with fruit jam before filling and baking it. If the fruit is exceedingly juicy, sprinkle the shell with absorbent bread or cake crumbs instead of jam.

For a glittering finish, coat the baked tart with a jelly or jam glaze (pages 8-9), red currant for dark-colored fruits, apricot for light ones. For a rich, golden brown finish, you can run the glazed tart under the broiler, covering the shell rim (Step 6) to prevent scorching.

4 **Arranging the apple slices.** Pick up a sliced apple half in both hands. Set the half just inside the rim of the tart shell, pressing down slightly to fan out the slices. Continue arranging slices this way to fill the shell with overlapping concentric rings (left). Sprinkle the apples with a little sugar (inset) and bake in a preheated 350° F. [180° C.] oven for about 50 minutes, or until the apples are soft and the crust is golden.

1 **Shaping the shell.** Roll dough — here, rich short crust — into a round ¼ inch [6 mm.] thick. Using the pin, transfer the dough round to a buttered baking sheet. Moisten the edge of the round, then fold over about 1 inch [2½ cm.] of the edge, pleating it to form a rim. Chill the shell if it feels soft.

2 **Preparing apples.** Halve each apple and seed it with a melon baller. Trim out the cores, peel the halves, and place them in acidulated water. Then cut the halves into thin slices. Holding the slices together, dip the half again into the water, then set it on paper towels to drain.

3 **Coating with jam glaze.** Gently heat apricot jam to melt it, then force it through a fine-meshed strainer to remove lumps. With a pastry brush, apply a thin layer of the jam glaze to the tart shell. To keep the glaze fluid, set the pan of jam in a larger pan partly filled with hot water.

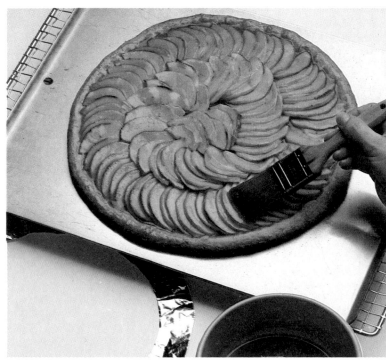

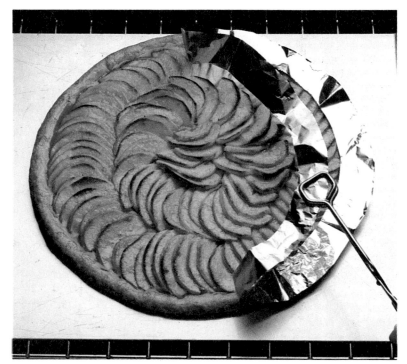

5 **Glazing the tart.** Brush the apricot-jam glaze generously over the sliced apples. Cut a ring of aluminum foil wide enough to cover the rim of the pastry shell and place this collar over the rim, leaving the glazed fruit exposed.

6 **Coloring the apples.** Slide the glazed tart under a preheated broiler and cook for two to four minutes, or just until the edges of the fruit are nicely browned. Lift off the foil collar with tongs. Loosen the tart from the baking sheet with a spatula and gently slide the tart onto a cutting board or serving platter.

Blind Baking a Shell to Ensure Its Crispness

Unless a tart is being baked upside down *(pages 32-33)*, uncooked dough cannot be used to contain moist fillings; it would quickly absorb liquid and become soggy. But inversion of the assembly is not the only solution to this difficulty: A more common stratagem is blind baking—prebaking the shells when empty.

The duration of blind baking depends on the nature and handling of the filling. If you wish to cook the filling in the shell, the empty shell is baked until it is set but not fully done; if the filling is to be cooked separately *(page 43, Step 4; page 44, Step 1)* or needs no cooking, the empty shell is cooked completely. Either way, the same procedure is followed, whether with basic short-crust, rich short-crust or refrigerator dough *(pages 16-21)*.

Any of these doughs may be blind-baked in a piepan, but to produce a handsome, freestanding tart, you will need either a flan form set on a baking sheet—the choice for this demonstration—or a false-bottomed tart pan similar to the one shown on pages 42-43.

The dough cannot be simply molded in the pan and baked: Without the pressure of a filling, the shell would blister and buckle and its sides would collapse. To provide the necessary support, the shell must be lined with wax or parchment paper or with aluminum foil, then filled with weights—dried peas or beans or small metal weights sold especially for this purpose. Once the pastry has set during baking, the paper and weights are removed and the shell is returned briefly to the oven to dry and crisp.

Although suitable for any moist or dry filling, including the fruits and jams used with unbaked shells, partly baked shells are most often prepared for custards and creams. These fillings can be flavored in an astonishing variety of ways—with chocolate, with liqueurs, with fruits and even with vegetables. In this demonstration, a sweet pastry cream is flavored with puréed spinach *(recipe, page 137)* to produce a filling popular in the South of France. Other vegetable flavorings for fillings are pumpkin, sweet potato, squash, carrot, green tomato, sorrel and chard *(recipes, pages 133-138)*.

1 Cutting a liner. Fold a square of parchment paper into quarters and center the folded corner in the flan form. Cut off the outer edge 2 inches [5 cm.] beyond the rim of the form. To make the quarter circle flexible, press the folded edges together, forming successively smaller wedges.

2 Molding. Place a round flan form on a buttered baking sheet. Fit rolled-out dough—basic short crust, here—into the form and trim it so that it is about 1¾ inches [4 cm.] wider than the form all around. Fold this excess dough into the form, pressing it against the sides to make a double thickness.

6 Making the filling. Prepare pastry cream *(page 12)*. Trim the stems from spinach and parboil the leaves for one minute. Drain the leaves, chop them fine and squeeze out excess liquid. Stir the spinach into the pastry cream, then stir in vanilla extract, a little salt and grated lemon peel. Pour the filling mixture into the tart shell.

7 Baking. Set the tart in a preheated 375° F. [190° C.] oven and bake for 25 minutes, until the filling is firm. Cool the tart, then slide a spatula under it to loosen it. Slide the tart to the edge of the sheet and rest that edge on a plate or board. Steady the flan form with one hand and pull out the sheet so that the tart slides onto the plate.

3 **Decorating the rim.** Press the dull edge of a knife blade into the pastry rim all around to crimp it. Unfold the paper and fit it into the molded shell; the edges of the paper should project an inch [2½ cm.] or so above the rim.

4 **Buttressing the shell.** Pour dried beans or peas — chick-peas are used here — into the lined shell up to the rim. (The beans will not be edible after baking, but can be used repeatedly for this purpose.) Press the beans against the flan form to make sure the sides of the pastry are well supported.

5 **Prebaking.** Bake the shell in a preheated 400° F. [200° C.] oven for 15 minutes. Lift out the paper and beans, and prick the bottom of the shell with a fork to let steam escape and prevent buckling. Bake the empty shell for three to five minutes, until dry, then let it cool while you make the filling.

8 **Garnishing.** Sauté pine nuts in a little oil for one or two minutes until they are golden. Drain them on paper towels. Gently lift the flan form off the spinach tart (above). Sprinkle the pine nuts on the tart (right) and serve hot or cooled.

A Two-Step Case for a Smooth Cheese Mixture

Cheesecake—a crisp shell containing a creamy, cheese-based filling—is sometimes made with a crumb crust and may be shaped as a shallow, open-faced pie or tart *(recipes, pages 120-125)*. But the classic American version of the dessert has the deep, freestanding short-crust shell that is shown here—a casing that presents special challenges of construction and baking.

To produce such a deep pastry, the cheesecake must be baked in a spring-form pan, which has ring sides that can be unclamped and lifted off the bottom after baking. Because the filling is moist, partial prebaking of the shell is in order. However, the depth of the shell—about 3 inches [8 cm.]—would require an impractically large amount of supportive dried beans or peas if blind baking were done in the usual manner. Furthermore, the high sides of the shell might collapse when the beans or peas were removed.

The solution is to prebake only the base of the shell—its most vulnerable part—on the removable bottom of the pan. Then the ring can be clamped in place and lined with strips of raw dough to complete the shell. Filled with the cheese mixture and baked briefly at high heat, then for a long time at low heat, the sides and bottom of the shell will merge and crisp evenly.

Fillings can be made with almost any soft, white cheese. Cream cheese is used here, but farmer or pot cheese, ricotta, drained and sieved cottage cheese, or a combination of these would be equally delicious. In this demonstration, the filling is enriched with eggs and heavy cream, sweetened with sugar, flavored with vanilla extract and grated lemon and orange peels, and thickened with a little flour *(recipe, page 121)*. For a slightly sharper taste, tart cream *(recipe, page 166)*, sour cream, yogurt or buttermilk might replace the heavy cream. Other flavors can be introduced by adding raisins or candied fruits, spices, nuts or chocolate *(recipes, pages 120-125)*.

Cheesecakes should be cooled, then refrigerated after baking to make their fillings firm enough to slice. They may be served on their own, or topped with a fruit glaze *(pages 8-9)* or fresh fruits such as strawberries or pineapple.

1 **Prebaking the base.** Prepare basic short-crust dough, then divide it in half. Put one piece on the buttered bottom of a spring-form pan. Roll the dough to cover the bottom; the dough will be about 1/8 inch [3 mm.] thick. Using a fork, pierce the dough all over. Bake in a preheated 400° F. [200° C.] oven for 15 minutes, prick any bubbles that may have developed, and continue baking for five more minutes, or until pale gold. Cool.

4 **Beating in the eggs.** To ensure that the eggs and extra yolks are thoroughly incorporated in the mixture, beat them in one at a time, using the mixer or wooden spoon *(above)*. When all of the eggs have been added, stir in heavy cream. Keep stirring until the filling is smooth and satiny.

5 **Filling the shell.** Pour the filling into the prepared shell. Bake the cheesecake in a preheated 450° F. [230° C.] oven for about 15 minutes to give the top of the filling a light golden color. Reduce the heat to 200° F. [100° C.] and bake for one hour, or until the pastry is brown and the filling is firm to the touch.

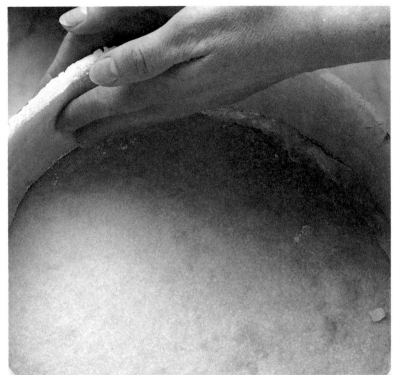

2 **Completing the shell.** Butter the spring-form ring so that it will be easy to remove after the pastry is baked; set the ring on the bottom of the spring-form and lock the clasp. Because a single strip breaks easily, roll the remaining dough into two strips a little wider than the depth of the ring. Fit the strips inside the ring and press their bottom edges onto the baked pastry. Trim the top edges to the level of the ring.

3 **Preparing the filling.** For the filling, assemble whole eggs, egg yolks, heavy cream and vanilla extract. In a large bowl, combine sugar, flour and the grated peels of a lemon and an orange. Place softened cream cheese in another bowl and, using an electric mixer or — as here — a wooden spoon, beat the cream cheese until it is smooth. Add the sugar-and-flour mixture to the cheese and mix well.

6 **Removing the ring.** To set the cheesecake, leave it in the pan at room temperature for two hours. Unlock the clamp and gently lift off the ring *(above)*. Slide a wide spatula under the pastry to loosen it from the pan bottom, and ease the cake onto a serving plate. Chill the cheesecake thoroughly before serving it in wedges *(right)*.

Last-minute Mergings of Shell, Filling and Garnish

Fully baked, freestanding short-crust shells are blind-baked in the same way as partially prebaked shells *(pages 38-39)*, with some minor changes.

Large shells can be shaped in flan forms or in the false-bottomed tart pan chosen here. Miniature shells are shaped in tartlet pans such as those shown on the opposite page. These small shells, like large ones, need bracing during the first part of baking. Bake the dough-lined pans in stacks of up to four pans each; each pan will brace the dough underneath, and just the topmost pan is lined with paper and filled with weights. This technique works only with sloping-sided pans: Straight-sided ones will not fit together properly.

Baking times and temperatures depend on the type of dough. Shells made with basic short-crust dough, lined and weighted, are baked for 10 minutes at 400° F. [200° C.] to set the dough. Then the paper and weights are removed and the shells are baked a further 10 to 12 minutes, until dry and crisp. Rich short-crust shells begin baking at the same temperature; however, for the final 10 to 12 minutes of baking the oven temperature must be reduced to 375° F. [190° C.] because the sugary dough burns easily. Refrigerator-dough shells contain more sugar, and are baked at 375° F. throughout — 10 minutes with the lining and weights, and 10 to 15 minutes without.

The shells may be baked as much as a day in advance and stored in a cool place other than the refrigerator, where they would become soggy. Fill the shells just before serving. Fillings include creams, custards and fruit, used alone or in alliances like those shown here: These tarts hold a filling of pastry cream *(recipe, page 166)* underneath a splendid layer of fresh fruit. If you use firm pears, apricots or peaches for such a treatment, poach them first in sugar syrup *(page 8)* to soften them. Poaching also enhances flavor and, as with the orange-topped tart below, provides the bonus of a glaze.

A Pinwheel of Oranges

1 **Lining the pan.** Roll dough ⅛ inch [3 mm.] thick and fit it into a buttered false-bottomed tart pan. Here, ½ pound [¼ kg.] of short crust lines a 9-inch [23-cm.] pan. Roll the pin over the pan to trim the dough *(left)*. Press the dough against the pan ring *(right)*. Line and weight the pan *(page 39)*, and set it on a baking sheet.

5 **Arranging the fruit.** Starting at the rim of the shell, lay the drained oranges on the pastry cream in two circles, overlapping the slices in one direction for the outer circle and in the opposite direction for the inner one.

6 **Glazing.** Boil down about a cup [¼ liter] of the reserved poaching liquid for 10 to 15 minutes, until it is thick enough to form a glaze. Brush the glaze onto the oranges. Then transfer the tart to a serving plate and garnish it, if you like, with whole mint leaves.

2 **Baking.** Bake the shell for 10 minutes in a preheated 400° F. [200° C.] oven. Remove the paper and beans, prick the bottom of the shell, and bake for 10 to 12 minutes more, until golden. To unmold, balance the pan on a large can or crock; the ring will slide down *(above, left)*. Let the tart cool a moment, then, using a spatula, slide the shell off the pan bottom onto a rack *(right)*.

3 **Poaching oranges.** Peel oranges, removing the bitter white pith. Slice the oranges thin, pick out any seeds, and poach the slices for one minute in a simple sugar syrup *(page 8)* flavored with orange liqueur. To drain the oranges, put them on a parchment-covered baking sheet that has been propped at an angle so liquid can run off. Reserve the liquid.

4 **Filling the tart.** Make a pastry cream, flavoring it, if you like, with orange liqueur. For this tart, 1 cup [¼ liter] of pastry cream is used. Using a narrow-bladed metal spatula, spread the cream in the bottom of the cooled tart shell to a depth of about ½ inch [1 cm.].

Stripes of Grapes

1 **Stacking pans.** Line tartlet pans with rolled-out dough *(page 30)* — ½ pound [¼ kg.] of basic short crust for eight tartlets, in this case. Set a pan on a baking sheet, butter the bottom of another pan and fit it into the first. Repeat, making stacks of four pans each. Line and weight the top shells.

2 **Baking.** Bake the shells in a preheated 400° F. [200° C.] oven for 10 minutes. Cool them until you can handle them. Lift out the paper and beans, separate the stacks, and set the pans on the baking sheet. Prick the shell bottoms with a fork and return the shells to the oven for 10 to 12 minutes.

3 **Filling.** When the pans are cool enough to handle, lift out the baked shells and set them on a wire rack to cool thoroughly. Fill the tartlets with a shallow layer of pastry cream such as this vanilla-flavored cream. Add the topping — alternate rows of seeded red and green grapes are shown.

Pristine Toppings of Meringue

Among the many toppings for pies and tarts, a fluffy mountain of meringue, cooked briefly so that it browns on the outside but remains soft within, is one of the most appealing. Meringue toppings may be made with either spreading or molding meringue *(page 13)*; the latter produces a slightly firmer texture. In either case, whisk the egg whites and sugar together at the last possible moment; otherwise, the egg whites will become watery. Ideally, the meringue should be put on a filling that is at room temperature: A hot filling may cause the meringue to "weep," producing amber beads on its surface as it bakes. A chilled filling may make the meringue drip moisture that will prevent the topping from clinging to its base.

You can apply spreading meringue to a filling simply by distributing it with a large spoon, broad-bladed knife or narrow spatula—the approach used for the lemon meringue tart demonstrated at right and below *(recipe, page 111)*. Or you can create more elaborate toppings by forcing molding meringue from a pastry bag *(box, opposite)*. These nylon or plastic-lined muslin bags—available at kitchen-equipment shops—can be fitted with interchangeable metal tubes that mold the piping material into strips of various widths or shapes.

Both plain and decorative pastry tubes range in size from No. 0, which has a tip 1/32 inch [3/4 mm.] wide and produces fine lines, to No. 9, which has an 1 1/16-inch [2-cm.] tip and is used for piping wide strips of heavy mixtures such as chou. Any such tube is simply dropped, tip down, into the pastry bag; the opening at the narrow end of the pastry bag is small enough to hold the tube in place, letting its tip protrude.

Once the meringue is spread, it should be baked at once, until it sets and turns golden brown. Do not let it overcook, lest the egg whites toughen. For a dark surface, sprinkle the meringue with a little sugar before baking.

1 **Cooking lemon filling.** Combine fresh lemon juice, grated lemon peel, sugar, eggs and butter in a small pan. To keep the ingredients from overheating and curdling, place the pan on a trivet set in a larger pan filled with enough hot water to cover the trivet by 1 inch [2½ cm.]. Stirring constantly, cook the mixture for 30 minutes, until thick and creamy.

4 **Decorating and baking.** Using a broad-bladed knife or narrow spatula, spread the meringue over the filling, slightly overlapping the rim of the tart shell: The meringue will shrink a little as it cooks in the oven. Roughen the surface of the meringue by dipping in the blade and lifting it quickly *(left)*; the resulting peaks will brown attractively in the oven. Sprinkle the meringue with sugar *(right)* and set the tart in a preheated 375° F. [190° C.] oven for five minutes, or until the topping begins to color.

5 **Serving.** Serve the tart hot or at room temperature. To cut the tart, first slice through the meringue layer with swift strokes of a dampened knife to form the number of wedges desired; wipe and remoisten the knife as necessary. Then, with a clean dampened knife, cut through the filling and crust.

2 **Setting the filling.** Remove the saucepan from the heat and pour the filling into a large shallow bowl to cool to room temperature. The filling will thicken slightly as it cools.

3 **Assembling the tart.** Make a fully baked tart shell (pages 42-43) and unmold it onto a large ovenproof plate. With a spoon, fill the shell evenly with the lemon mixture. Leave the rim of the shell exposed — and clean — to provide a smooth surface to which the meringue topping can adhere. Make spreading meringue and pile it thickly over the filling (inset).

Deft Use of a Pastry Bag

1 **Filling the pastry bag.** Make molding meringue. Fit a No. 6 star tube into a pastry bag. Hold the bag in one hand, fold back the top and, with a spatula, fill the bag half-full of meringue. Unfold the bag and shake it up and down — over the bowl, to catch any drips — to eliminate air bubbles.

2 **Securing the bag.** Hold the bag horizontally in one hand over the bowl. With the other hand, twist the top of the bag together just above the filling. With a steady, gentle pressure, use the hand holding the twisted top to force a little meringue into the bowl to start the meringue flowing evenly.

3 **Piping a border.** To make a border, hold the tip of the tube at a 45-degree angle inside the rim of the lemon tart. Using a curving motion, pipe overlapping crescents of meringue around the filling, just inside the rim. Bake as described in Step 4, opposite.

2
Puff Pastry
A Layered Miracle of Lightness

Adding butter in a sheet or dabs
Tricks of construction
Baking in stages
Gleaming glazes and icings
Adapting to fillings soft or firm
How to use scraps

A wedge of *Pithiviers* (pages 54-55) reveals a soft filling of almond-flavored cream sandwiched between pieces of crisp, airy puff pastry. For decoration, the edges of the dough were scalloped and the surface was inscribed with a spiral pattern before the pastry was baked.

Puff-pastry dough takes longer to make than any other type, but the results more than justify the time invested: It produces some of the most delectable desserts in the entire pastry repertoire. A simple dough formulation of flour, salt, water and butter is the starting point. This dough, rolled out into a sheet, is repeatedly folded and rolled together with a sheet of butter; each rolling-and-folding operation is followed by thorough chilling, which firms the butter and relaxes the gluten developed by the manipulation. In all, the process may take as long as eight hours.

The end product is a composite sheet consisting of more than 700 paper-thin dough layers separated by layers of butter—and also by air that has been trapped during rolling. During baking, moisture in the dough turns to steam and puffs the pastry while the folded-in butter keeps the layers discrete, producing a finished pastry that is incomparably light, crisp and rich. (More quickly made versions of puff-pastry dough are demonstrated on pages 50-51; these do not rise as dramatically as the classic type.)

Desserts made with puff-pastry dough are formed in ways similar to those used for short-crust creations. For instance, the dough can be shaped into free-form shells, filled with fruit or pastry cream and baked; during cooking, the weight of the filling will keep the shell bottom fairly flat, but the unweighted edges will puff up into high and delicate sides *(pages 52-53)*. In the spirit of two-crust pies, two sheets of puff-pastry dough can be shaped into covered pastries such as the almond-cream-filled *Pithiviers* shown at left, named for the French town where it is said to have been invented. Another French creation, known as a *jalousie* (literally, "shutter"), has a slashed top crust that exposes decorative lines of filling in much the same way as a lattice-top pie does.

Puff-pastry dough, like short crust, can be blind-baked for particularly crisp results, then assembled with prepared filling ingredients. Turnovers are formed this way, as are the small, hollow cones called cream horns (they usually hold sweetened whipped cream, although other fillings such as butter cream may be used). The most famous desserts of this type, however, are napoleons *(pages 56-57)* —baked sheets of puff pastry stacked in layers with pastry cream. In France, where they originated, these pastries are aptly known as *mille-feuilles,* or "thousand leaves."

The Classic Way to Incorporate Butter

The initial step in the making of classic puff-pastry dough is the same as for short crusts: Flour is combined with butter and ice water, and the resulting dough is refrigerated before it is rolled out into a sheet. This preliminary dough differs from most short crusts, however, in that its base is a mixture of all-purpose and cake flours. The low-gluten content of cake flour provides insurance against toughness that might otherwise result from the repeated handling. Also, less butter is used than for short crust because large amounts of butter will be incorporated later.

To form the puff-pastry dough, you will need to shape a sheet of butter somewhat smaller than the sheet of the preliminary dough. Most butter is too watery to produce a successful puff-pastry dough, and it should be kneaded to remove excess liquid (box opposite, bottom) before it is flattened with a rolling pin into a sheet. (Hand-churned butter is an exception.)

The butter sheet first is enfolded in the dough sheet. This parcel is then rolled, folded in thirds and rolled again, an operation that is repeated five times. With each rolling, the layers of butter and dough become thinner—and with each folding, the layers build up in a geometric progression.

The chilling that is required after each rolling-and-folding operation is the main reason why puff-pastry dough takes such a long time to make. As the dough is repeatedly worked, it requires progressively longer periods of refrigeration to keep it manageable and to ensure its tenderness. The first chilling lasts only 30 minutes; the final one requires four hours.

Because these processes are so time-consuming, the production of puff-pastry dough in large quantities is well worthwhile. Enclosed in plastic wrap or aluminum foil, the dough will keep for two or three days in the refrigerator and for up to three months in the freezer.

1 Preparing the dough. Sift all-purpose flour, cake flour and salt into a bowl, add cold butter and rub the ingredients together with your finger tips until the mixture is mealy. Gradually add ice water to bind the dough; then pat it into a ball. Sprinkle flour into a plastic bag to prevent sticking (above); put the ball in the bag and chill it for 30 minutes.

2 Flattening the butter. Let the chilled dough stand for a few minutes at room temperature. Meanwhile, to prevent sticking, put parchment paper on a work surface; place chilled, kneaded butter on top and cover with another sheet of paper. With the rolling pin, flatten the butter into a square about ¾ inch [2 cm.] thick.

6 Rolling folded dough. Pressing evenly but lightly, so as not to squeeze out the butter, roll the dough into a rectangle three times as long as it is wide. Pat the edges of the dough with the sides of your hands to keep the edges neat. Brush off extra flour to keep the pastry from becoming tough and dry.

7 Folding the dough. Fold one end of the rectangle over the center, then fold the other end over the first, aligning them so that they form three layers of dough. Seal air inside the layers by pressing the edges of the dough down lightly with the rolling pin.

3 **Rolling the dough.** Remove the dough from the plastic bag and place it on a lightly floured work surface. Roll the dough into a square about ½ inch [1 cm.] thick and large enough for its corners to fold over and envelop the butter. Use light, quick strokes when you roll the dough, turning it so that it is flattened evenly.

4 **Positioning the butter.** Peel the top sheet of parchment paper from the butter. Invert the butter over the rolled-out dough, placing it diagonally on the dough. Then peel the second sheet of paper from the butter.

5 **Enclosing the butter.** Draw up the four corners of the dough one at a time and fold them over the butter to meet and overlap slightly in the center *(above)*, leaving a ½-inch [1-cm.] margin of dough all around the butter. Press the seams of the envelope gently together with your fingers or with the rolling pin.

Reducing Butter's Moisture

8 **Finishing.** Repeat Steps 6 and 7 — rolling the dough to the same size as in Step 6 and turning it to keep the folded edges at right angles to the rolling pin *(above)*. Indent the dough *(right)* to show the number of rollings. Wrap and chill the dough for an hour. Repeat Steps 6, 7 and 8 twice, doubling the chilling time after each repetition.

Kneading butter. Place chilled butter on a floured surface and flatten it with a rolling pin. Sprinkle on a little flour. Using the heel of your hand, fold and press the butter for about five minutes. The flour will absorb some liquid, and additional liquid will appear as drops on the work surface. Chill the butter before rolling it out.

Flaky Dough: A Timesaving Variant

The cook who does not have the time to form a classic puff-pastry dough *(pages 48-49)* can substitute either of the more quickly made doughs shown here. They will not be as tender—nor rise as high—as classic dough, but both give extra spirit to tarts and are quite effective when used for such pastries as cream horns and turnovers *(pages 58-59)*, which do not depend on the exceptional rising properties of classic puff pastry.

Of the two alternatives, flaky dough *(right; recipe, page 164)* is the lighter and crisper. To make it, a preliminary flour-butter-and-water dough is formed, rolled into a rectangle, dotted with butter and folded into a package. The butter should be malleable but still cold: If it is too hard, the little pieces will tear the dough; if it is too soft, it will melt during rolling and ooze out the sides of the parcel.

The sequence of rolling, buttering and folding is repeated twice more, with chillings between each sequence to relax the gluten and make the dough easier to roll. Because flaky dough is folded and rolled fewer times than the classic puff-pastry dough, it has fewer layers of butter, air and dough, and therefore will not rise as high. The butter is added to the dough in stages—and in pieces rather than as a sheet—to ensure that it is distributed as widely and easily as possible.

A rough puff dough *(box, opposite)* is not as close in composition to classic puff-pastry dough. It consists of nothing more than basic short-crust dough *(pages 16-17)* that is folded and rolled two or three times. Several dough layers are formed during the process of rolling and folding—enough to raise the pastry slightly. But no additional butter is used; therefore, rough puff pastry does not have the clearly defined layers and the richness of the classic version.

1 **Preparing dough.** Sift all-purpose and cake flours, and salt into a bowl. Beat butter to soften it, and divide it into four equal portions. Using your finger tips, lightly rub one portion into the flour until the mixture looks like bread crumbs. Chill the remaining butter. Gradually add ice water to the flour mixture and work the dough until it is smooth and comes cleanly away from the sides of the bowl *(inset)*. Cover with plastic wrap and refrigerate for 30 minutes to relax the dough and firm the butter.

4 **Folding the dough.** Fold the unbuttered third of the rectangle of dough over the center. Fold over the buttered top third *(above, left)*. To keep the layers uniform, press the open sides of the package together with your hands *(above, right)*; to keep the butter from squeezing out, gently press down on the edges of the dough package with a rolling pin.

2 **Rolling out the dough.** Sprinkle a little flour onto a work surface to prevent sticking. Roll the dough into a rectangle about ½ inch [1 cm.] thick and about three times as long as it is wide. Pat the sides of the rectangle into straight lines so that the rolled-out dough can be folded neatly.

3 **Adding butter.** With a brush, remove any surplus flour from the dough. Use a narrow-bladed spatula to dot one third of the chilled butter over two thirds of the dough. Leave a border of about ½ inch [1 cm.] around the edge of the dough to prevent the butter from being squeezed out during rolling.

5 **Resting the dough.** Line a shallow baking dish or small tray with plastic wrap or kitchen foil. Place the dough on the lining and cover the dough with more plastic wrap or foil to prevent it from drying out. Refrigerate the dough for 15 minutes, unwrap it and put it on a lightly floured work surface.

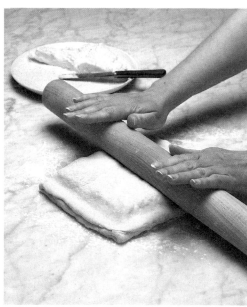

6 **Completing the dough.** Repeat Steps 2 to 5 twice more, incorporating all of the chilled butter. To distribute the butter evenly, always roll the dough at a 90-degree angle to the folds. Roll, fold and then chill it for two or three hours before rolling it out for use.

A Lightened Short Crust

To ensure tender short-crust pastry, make a basic short-crust dough *(pages 16-17)* and chill it for one to two hours before rolling and folding it as described below. You can speed the process of making rough puff dough by eliminating the chilling after the first folding sequence.

1 **Layering.** On a floured work surface, flatten chilled short-crust dough with a rolling pin. Roll the dough into a rectangle *(Step 2, left)*, then fold it in thirds. Give the dough a quarter turn and roll it into a rectangle once again.

2 **Completing the folding.** Fold the ends of the rectangle to meet in the center, then fold the dough in half to make four layers; chill for 30 minutes. Roll, fold into four layers and chill twice more before rolling out the dough for use.

Constructing a Tart with High-rising Sides

The simplest puff pastries are open-faced tarts. Like short-crust tarts, they may be baked with a filling or completely blind-baked and filled later. However, shaping and baking procedures for puff-pastry dough differ somewhat from those used for short crust.

Any puff-pastry dough *(pages 48-51)* may be used for shells, although the classic version gives the most delicate effect. Tart pans or molds are unnecessary for the shaping of these doughs. Instead, the chilled, rolled-out dough can be cut to form a base—a rectangle, circle or triangle—and then placed on a baking sheet. Strips of dough set along the top edges of the base puff vertically during baking to form a rim for the shell.

When cutting the dough, always use a very sharp knife: A dull knife dragged through the dough would stretch it and cause uneven rising. Move the dough with the aid of a large spatula, as shown in Step 4: The rolling-pin method would stretch the sheet.

A puff-pastry shell to be blind-baked need not be weighted, as is short crust, because the rising rim needs no bracing. Prick the bottom to provide holes for the escape of steam, thereby controlling the amount of puffing; then bake the shell. If you bake the shell with a filling, the ingredients will weight the bottom and pricking is not necessary.

Because the shell's rim rises, the top of the filling must be higher than that of the dough before baking begins. For this reason, the filling must be firm enough to hold its shape. Uncooked fruits, such as the cherries used here, are best. For a crisp bottom crust, the fruit should be sweated *(page 26)* to rid it of excess juice; the drained juice can then be thickened and returned to the filling.

Puff-pastry tarts start baking in a hot oven, which encourages production of the steam that causes puffing. Once the layers have puffed, the heat is reduced so that the dough can crisp without the pastry browning too much.

1 **Trimming the dough.** Unwrap chilled puff-pastry dough, cut off the amount required — in this case, 1 pound [½ kg.] — and refrigerate the rest. On a cold, unfloured surface, roll the dough into a rectangle about ¼ inch [6 mm.] thick. Using a ruler and a very sharp knife, trim the edges to form a perfect rectangle; here, the rectangle is cut 14 by 9 inches [35 by 23 cm.].

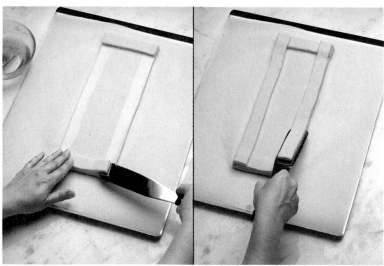

5 **Applying the rim.** Moisten a 1-inch [2½-cm.] border along the edges of the tart base. Slide a narrow spatula under a short dough strip and press the strip onto one end of the tart base, aligning the outer edges of the strip and base. Place the other short strip at the opposite end of the base *(above, left)*. Moisten both ends of the top of each short strip. Again using the spatula and aligning the edges, fold each long strip crosswise and unfold it onto the side of the rectangle with the ends of the strip overlapping the short strips *(above, right)*.

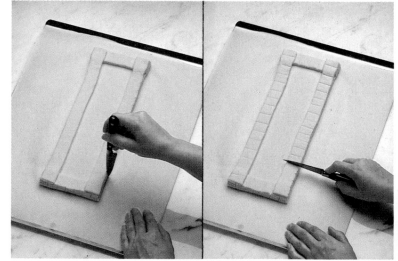

6 **Decorating the shell.** With the dull edge of a knife blade, make indentations at ½-inch [1-cm.] intervals all around the sides of the tart shell *(above, left)*. Decorate the top of the dough-strip rim in the same way *(above, right)*. Instead of parallel cuts, you can make a crosshatch pattern with the knife or crimp the edges with a fork. Refrigerate the pastry shell for at least 30 minutes.

2 **Cutting the base and sides.** Line a rimless baking sheet with parchment paper. Halve the dough rectangle lengthwise. From one of the smaller rectangles thus formed, slice three lengthwise strips, each 1 inch [2½ cm.] wide. The uncut rectangle will form the tart base; the strips will become the rim.

3 **Cutting the ends.** Measure the width of one end of the uncut dough rectangle. Then cut one of the dough strips into two pieces, each as long as the rectangle is wide. Refrigerate all of the trimmings for another use.

4 **Transferring the dough.** Lay a strip of wax paper on top of the tart base and fold the base in half crosswise, enclosing the paper. Slide a long, wide metal spatula under the base and, supporting the base with your other hand, transfer the dough to the lined baking sheet. Gently ease out the spatula and unfold the dough onto the sheet. Remove the wax paper.

7 **Adding the filling.** Toss pitted Bing cherries with sugar — in this case, 4 cups [1 liter] of fruit and 1 cup [¼ liter] of sugar — and let them sweat for 30 minutes. Drain off the juice, stir in dissolved cornstarch and simmer until clear and thick. Stir in the cherries, then pile them in rows in the shell. Sprinkle with a little sugar.

8 **Baking.** Brush the top of the shell with an egg-and-water glaze *(inset)*. Bake in a 425° F. [220° C.] oven for 20 minutes, or until the sides begin to brown. Reduce the heat to 375° F. [190° C.] for 25 minutes. Let the tart cool slightly, then slide it onto a serving board.

Two Inspired French Inventions

Because of the way it rises, puff-pastry dough can be shaped into filled, two-crust pastries and baked without the support of a pan or mold. The structure of the pastry depends on the filling you wish to use.

A soft filling—jam, for instance, or poached fruit used alone or layered with pastry cream—requires a conventional container such as the one shown at right in the top demonstration. The base of this pastry is a free-form shell with built-up sides, constructed as explained on pages 52-53; classic puff-pastry dough is used here, but flaky dough would also do. Once it is filled, the shell is covered with a second sheet of dough—the lid. In this case, the lid for the rectangular shell is slashed to reveal the filling; the French call such a pastry a *jalousie*.

Another, more unusual sort of two-crust puff pastry—exemplified by the French *Pithiviers* at bottom—requires a filling firm enough to hold its shape when molded. In this instance, a stiff almond cream, or frangipane—prepared as shown in the box on page 31, but without the flour that would make it cake-like—is shaped into a hemisphere and placed on a round of dough. The mound of filling serves as a mold for the lid. If you like, you can make the filling with walnuts or hazelnuts instead of almonds, and shape it into an oval, a rectangle or a triangle. The pastry base and lid should be cut to echo the shape of the block.

A Revealing Top for a Rectangular Case

1 **Filling.** Trim dough into two equal-sized rectangles; in this case, 1 pound [½ kg.] of puff-pastry dough is rolled ⅛ inch [3 mm.] thick and cut into 14-by-5-inch [36-by-13-cm.] rectangles. Place a rectangle on a lined baking sheet. With strips 1 inch [2½ cm.] wide, form a rim on this base. Add filling—1½ cups [375 ml.] of strawberry jam are used here.

2 **Making the lid.** Fold the second rectangle in half lengthwise. Lay a ruler along the fold. With the dull edge of a knife, mark off 1½-inch [4-cm.] margins at both ends, leaving a 1½-inch border on the opposite edge. Then score lines between the margins at intervals of about ½ inch [1 cm.]. Slice through the dough along the scored lines.

Scalloped Edges for a Circular Envelope

1 **Cutting rounds.** With a bowl as a guide, cut a base—here, 10 inches [25 cm.] across—from puff-pastry dough rolled ¼ inch [6 mm.] thick. Chill on a lined baking sheet. Roll more dough slightly thinner, cut a lid 1 inch [2½ cm.] larger than the bowl, and chill; 2 pounds [1 kg.] of dough are used here.

2 **Filling.** Make almond-cream filling—in this instance, 2 cups [½ liter]—and mold it into a hemisphere by pressing it into a bowl lined with plastic wrap. Chill for one hour. Invert the bowl onto the center of the puff-pastry base to unmold the filling; peel away the wrap. Moisten the rim of the base.

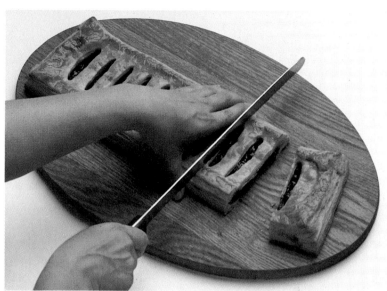

3 **Covering the shell.** Moisten the shell rim. With the aid of a large spatula, set the folded lid on one long side of the shell, aligning the edges. Carefully unfold the dough lid so that it completely covers the shell. Press the edges together all around, and score a crosshatch design on the border with the dull edge of the knife *(page 52, Step 6)*. Refrigerate the shell for half an hour.

4 **Baking and serving.** Glaze the lid with an egg wash *(page 53, Step 8)*. Bake in a preheated 425° F. [220° C.] oven for 30 minutes, until well puffed. Reduce the heat to 350° F. [180° C.] and bake for 30 minutes more, until golden brown. Let the pastry cool slightly, then carefully slide it onto a serving board or platter. Serve warm or cooled, cutting the pastry into cross sections with a long, serrated knife that will slice through the layers without distorting them.

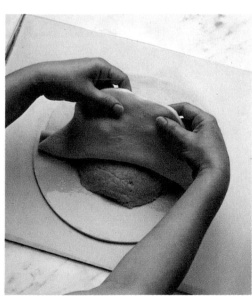

3 **Covering.** Fold the dough lid in half and position it over one side of the filling, aligning the cut edge with the rim of the base. Carefully unfold the lid over the filling. Press the edges of the lid and base together to seal them.

4 **Shaping scallops.** Invert over the covered mound of filling a bowl large enough to leave a 2-inch [5-cm.] border of dough all around. With the dull edge of a knife blade, scallop the border by pressing toward the bowl at regular intervals. Remove the bowl.

5 **Decorating.** Pierce the center of the lid to make a steam vent. Decorate the mound with shallow, curving incisions *(above)*. Chill for half an hour. Glaze with egg wash *(page 53, Step 8)*. Bake at 425° F. [220° C.] for 30 minutes, then at 375° F. [190° C.] for 30 minutes more, until golden brown *(page 46)*.

A Brilliant Marriage of Cream and Pastry

Blind-baked to make it crisp and rigid, classic or flaky puff-pastry dough can be layered with soft, creamy fillings to yield multitiered desserts—round, cake-like confections or the rectangular napoleons shown here. These creations depend for effect on thin, perfectly flat pastry layers of miraculous delicacy—the result of special baking techniques.

The dough, rolled out very thin and pricked all over to minimize puffing, is baked in a sheet large enough so that it overhangs the edges of a jelly-roll pan. The overhang exerts a downward pull that helps keep the dough flat (and also compensates for the dough's tendency to shrink at the edges). Because sheets of this size tend to remain damp on the underside, the baked dough is turned over to finish cooking.

Once baked and cooled—warm pastry is quite absorbent—the pastry can be trimmed into clean-edged pieces of identical shape and size, ready to layer with filling. The filling should be spread only a few hours before serving; even cool puff pastry absorbs liquid in time.

For a pleasing textural contrast to the pastry layers, choose rich, creamy fillings. Flavored pastry creams *(page 12)*, whipped cream or a combination of the two make delicious fillings; you can also spread some pastry layers with jam, or press fresh fruit such as chopped strawberries into the cream filling.

To decorate the assembled pastry, coat the top layer with unflavored fondant icing *(pages 10-11)* and stripe the fondant with thin ribbons of melted chocolate, as demonstrated here. Or you can simply sprinkle the top of the pastry with a thick layer of confectioners' sugar and burn a crosshatch pattern into the sugar by briefly laying on it a skewer that has been heated red-hot, either under the broiler or over a gas flame.

1 Baking. Roll out puff-pastry dough about 1/16 inch [1 1/2 mm.] thick; here, 1 pound [1/2 kg.] of dough is rolled and cut into a 20-by-14-inch [50-by-36-cm.] rectangle. Cover an inverted jelly-roll pan with parchment paper. Lay the dough on the paper, letting the edges drape. Prick the dough all over to provide steam vents. Bake in a 425° F. [220° C.] oven for 12 minutes, until golden.

5 Assembling. Prepare filling—in this case, 2 cups [1/2 liter] of vanilla-flavored pastry cream. Lay a pastry rectangle on a platter or serving board. Spoon on a 1/2-inch [1-cm.] layer of pastry cream; level with a spatula. Cover with another pastry rectangle and spread this one with another layer of pastry cream. Top with the third pastry layer.

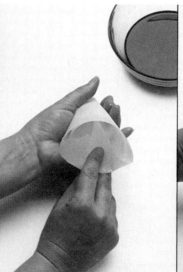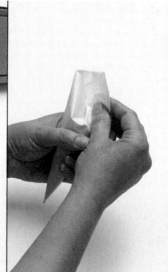

6 Making a piping cone. Cut a 10-inch [25-cm.] square of parchment paper diagonally in half to make two triangles. Holding the right-angled point of one triangle, curl one short side of the triangle until the underside of its oblique-angled point meets the right angle, thus forming a cone. Hold the points together and curl the other half of the paper around the cone *(above, left)* until all three points meet. Fold the points into the open end of the cone to secure it *(center)*. Half-fill the cone with melted chocolate *(box, page 11)* and fold the open end over the chocolate *(right)*.

2 **Puncturing air pockets.** Set the pan on a wire rack to cool the pastry. Reduce the oven temperature to 350° F. [180° C.]. With the tip of a sharp knife, puncture any bubbled areas in the pastry to deflate them.

3 **Completing the baking.** When the pastry is cool enough to handle, lift it up by the corners and carefully invert it onto the jelly-roll pan. Peel away the parchment paper. Return the pastry to the oven for five to 10 minutes to dry and crisp. Lift the pastry off the pan and cool it on the rack.

4 **Cutting out the layers.** When the pastry is cool, slice off the uneven edges to make a perfect rectangle. Using a ruler and a long, sharp knife, cut one lengthwise third from the rectangle. Lay this piece on the remaining pastry, carefully aligning the edges *(above)*, to serve as a guide in slicing the pastry into two more pieces of the same size.

7 **Frosting the pastry.** With a spatula, spread a thin layer of fondant icing—here, ½ cup [125 ml.] of vanilla-flavored icing is used—on the top pastry layer. Hold the chocolate-filled paper cone on its side to prevent leaks and, using scissors, clip off the tip of the cone to make a small opening.

8 **Decorating.** Pipe parallel lines of chocolate across the pastry *(inset)*. Immediately draw the dull edge of a knife down the center of the pastry at right angles to the piped lines. Turn the platter around and draw the knife along each side of the pastry *(above)*. Chill for 30 minutes to set the icing. To serve, cut the pastry into cross sections, using a serrated knife and a light, sawing motion.

Molding or Folding Small Hollow Shapes

To fashion individual pastries of maximum crispness, puff-pastry dough is first blind-baked, then filled. Two pastry containers are demonstrated here. At right, strips of dough are wrapped around conical metal molds, available at kitchen-equipment shops. Below, dough is folded around pillows of foil to make turnovers.

Professional cooks bake such pastries at a constant temperature, but this can be risky: The pastries may emerge fully cooked on the outside but, because of the molds or foil, moist within. A safer course is to cook them in three stages: Puff them in a hot oven; reduce the heat to crisp them; then, after removing the molds or foil, dry them out in a slow oven.

Although any sweet filling used for tarts is appropriate for these pastries, creams give an especially pleasing textural effect. Cones filled with sweetened whipped cream are called cream horns *(recipe, page 141)*. Whipped cream is also chosen for the turnovers here, along with a garnish of fresh peach slices.

Strips Spiraled Around a Metal Cone

1 **Shaping.** Slice puff-pastry dough into strips; here, 1 pound [½ kg.] of flaky dough is rolled ¼ inch [6 mm.] thick, trimmed to 10 by 24 inches [25 by 60 cm.], then cut into ten 1-inch [2½-cm.] strips. Moisten each strip and wrap an end over the tip of a mold. Rotate the mold *(inset)* to wind the strip in overlapping layers. Brush with egg white, dust with sugar and set on a lined baking sheet.

Squares Closed over Pillows of Foil

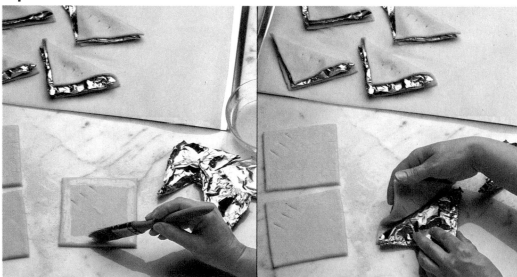

1 **Shaping.** Fold long strips of foil into thick triangles slightly larger than the planned turnovers. Cut squares of dough — flaky dough rolled ¼ inch [6 mm.] thick is cut into 4-inch [10-cm.] squares here. Cut slits near the top of each square to prevent overpuffing, and brush the edges with melted butter *(above, left)* to prevent sticking. Fold each square into a triangle around a foil triangle *(right)*. Place on a parchment-lined baking sheet and bake at 425° F. [220° C.] for about 25 minutes. Reduce the heat to 350° F. [180° C.] and bake for 10 minutes more, until golden.

2 **Extracting the foil.** Set the sheet of turnovers on a wire rack to cool and reduce the oven heat to 180° F. [85° C.]. As soon as the turnovers can be handled, ease out the foil by compressing it with your fingers. Dry the interiors of the pastries by returning them to the oven for about 45 minutes. Cool them on a wire rack.

2 **Filling.** Chill the pastries for 30 minutes. Then bake them in a preheated 425° F. [220° C.] oven for 25 minutes; reduce the heat to 350° F. [180° C.] and bake for 10 minutes. Unmold. Dry the pastries in a 180° F. [85° C.] oven for 45 minutes. Cool on a rack. Brush apricot-jam glaze *(box, page 9)* inside and fill the cones with sweetened whipped cream — a No. 6 star tube is shown.

3 **Serving the cream horns.** Sprinkle blanched, peeled and chopped pistachios over the whipped cream, if you like. When all of the pastries are glazed, filled and garnished, arrange them like the spokes of a wheel on a round platter. Serve them at once.

3 **Preparing the fruit.** Immerse peaches in boiling water for about 10 seconds to loosen their skins; plunge them into cold water for a moment, then peel them and slice them. Drop the slices into acidulated water *(page 37)* to prevent discoloration.

4 **Filling.** Pat the slices dry with paper towels and slide a few slices into each turnover. Using a No. 6 star tube, pipe a band of whipped cream around the edges of the turnover *(above).* Garnish with peach slices and confectioners' sugar *(inset).*

Fanciful Morsels Made with Scraps

Scraps left over from making pastries with classic or flaky puff-pastry dough need not be discarded; given proper treatment, they can be amalgamated to produce pastries themselves.

Storage is the first consideration. The scraps can be refrigerated for two days or kept in the freezer for up to two weeks. If frozen, they must be defrosted for a day in the refrigerator before use.

The scraps are not simply gathered into a ball and rolled out, as are short-crust scraps. If the puff-pastry dough is to rise during baking, the chilled scraps must be fitted together on a flat surface so that their dough and butter layers remain intact and are at least roughly aligned. Once assembled this way *(box, below, right)*, the scraps can be joined by rolling them into a single sheet. This sheet, in turn, should be rolled and folded twice, then chilled before use.

The dough thus formed will not rise as dramatically as newly made dough, but it is airy and crisp nonetheless, and is effective for making small, sugary pastries such as the French *palmiers* demonstrated here. *Palmiers* are formed by cutting sugared and elaborately folded sheets of puff-pastry dough into cross sections, then spreading the ends of the U-shaped pieces and baking them until they are crisp.

The French have a wide range of descriptively named small pastries often made from dough scraps. *Alumettes glacées* —literally, "glazed matchsticks"— are thin, icing-coated pastry strips. *Papillons,* or "butterflies," are formed by twisting stacked strips of dough in the center so that layers of wings form on either side. And *sacristains (recipe, page 140)* —named for the church sacristan's staff they resemble—are strips of pastry twisted like corkscrews and sprinkled with chopped nuts as well as with sugar.

1 Rolling the dough. Sprinkle a work surface evenly with sugar and roll puff-pastry dough into a rectangle ⅛ inch [3 mm.] thick. Sprinkle the rectangle with sugar and run the rolling pin over it lightly to press the sugar grains into the dough. Measure the rectangle to find the middle of one long side, and mark this point lightly with the dull edge of a knife blade.

A Patchwork of Trimmings

1 Assembling the pieces. On a flat surface, arrange chilled classic or flaky puff-pastry dough scraps in a rough rectangle, overlapping the pieces slightly to form a solid sheet. Do not moisten the dough to make the pieces stick; they will do so without being dampened.

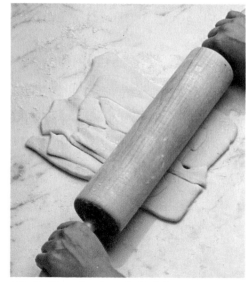

2 Rolling the dough. Roll the scraps into a flat rectangle about ¼ inch [6 mm.] thick. Fold the sheet and roll it as described on pages 48-49, Steps 7 and 8. Fold and roll again. Fold the sheet in half, with wax paper at the center to prevent sticking. Enclose it in plastic wrap and chill it for at least 30 minutes.

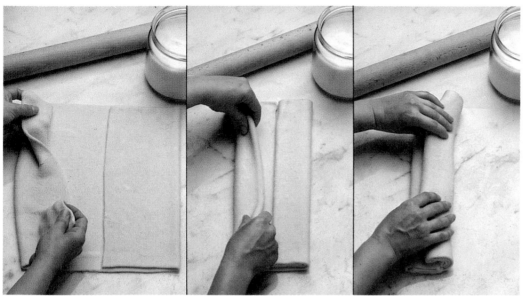

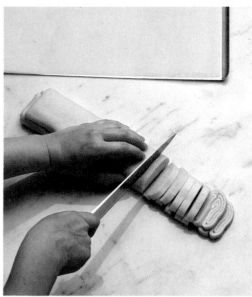

2 **Folding the dough.** Fold the short edges of the rectangle to meet at the middle *(above, left)*. Sprinkle more sugar on the dough and run a rolling pin lightly over it. Bring the folded edges of the rectangle together to meet in the middle *(center)*, and sugar and roll again. Finally, close the dough from the folded edges the way you would close a book, thereby making eight layers *(right)*. Enclose the dough in plastic wrap and refrigerate it.

3 **Cutting the pastry.** Cover a baking sheet with parchment paper. When the dough is thoroughly chilled — after about one hour — slice it into cross sections that are about ⅜ inch [9 mm.] thick.

4 **Baking.** Arrange the pastries on the baking sheet, leaving 2 inches [5 cm.] between them to allow for expansion during cooking. Pinch the ends of the pieces outward *(left)*. Bake in a preheated 425° F. [220° C.] oven for about 15 minutes, until the bottoms are crisp, then turn the pastries over with a spatula and bake for 10 more minutes, until the *palmiers* are brown *(below)*.

3
Chou

A Paste with Special Properties

Serenely afloat on their platter, chou-paste swans are a charming example of the pastry maker's art. The swan bodies and necks were separately piped from a pastry bag and baked. Then the bodies were split horizontally; the bottoms were filled with sweetened whipped cream and the tops were cut into wings. Necks and wings rest in the cream; the eyes are chocolate.

Chou paste, the inspiration for the pastry cook's airiest flights of fancy, contains the same ingredients as many other pastries—butter, water, flour and eggs—but behaves differently because the ingredients are combined in different proportions and are heated during the mixing process. Chou paste contains 16 times as much water and eight times as many eggs as short-crust doughs; mixed with butter and flour, these ingredients form a soft, batter-like mass that can be shaped with spoons or a pastry bag, then fried or, more commonly, baked. During the second cooking, the moisture in the paste expands as steam; the paste itself, made elastic by the proteins in the eggs, puffs up and out around the steam, then dries to create a structure that is crisp, golden—and hollow.

Baked chou pastries lend themselves to myriad presentations: The pastries not only can assume different shapes, but also are variously stuffed and garnished. Basic chou shapes include rings, the cylinders that form éclairs and the little spheres that become cream puffs. (The form of the puffs gave the paste its name: *Chou* means "cabbage" in French.) These shapes can be filled with pastry cream, whipped cream or ice cream—and many other good things. The French food encyclopedia *Larousse Gastronomique* lists nine varieties of cream puffs alone, including cherry-filled *choux Montmorency,* named for the French cherries, and *choux à la normande,* which, like many dishes of orchard-covered Normandy, includes apples and apple brandy. As for toppings, fondant icing is usual, but caramel or confectioners' sugar may be used instead.

The shapes themselves provide yet another opportunity for elaboration. A little deft piping with a pastry bag and cutting with a knife, for instance, transform puffs into the whimsical swans shown opposite *(demonstration, page 71)*. And filled chou rings and spheres, cemented together with caramel, are the building blocks for edifices of amazing complexity. A large ring on a round of dough, for instance, is the foundation of that crownlike dessert, *gâteau Saint-Honoré (page 69),* named after the patron saint of pastry cooks. The ring is topped with small filled puffs, forming a shell that holds yet another filling. Or puffs can be stacked to form a cone, which is covered with a glittering web of caramel *(page 9);* this pastry tower is known as *croquembouche,* because the hardened caramel literally "cracks in the mouth."

A Twice-cooked Foundation

Making chou paste *(recipe, page 163)* is a simple operation: Butter and water are boiled together, all-purpose flour is added and eggs are beaten in. However, the heat must be carefully controlled at each stage of the process to produce a paste that will inflate into a tender puff when it is subsequently baked or fried.

The butter and water must be brought to a boil quickly, and as soon as they boil the flour should be added; excessive boiling would evaporate water that is needed to produce the steam for puffing. When the paste has formed, it is removed from the heat and cooled slightly before the eggs are added; if the paste is too hot, the eggs might curdle before they can be smoothly incorporated.

Once the eggs have been blended in, chou paste can be put into a pastry bag *(Step 6, inset, opposite page)* and shaped as demonstrated on the following pages. Or it can wait, covered tightly to keep a crust from forming, for up to three hours at room temperature.

1 **Preparing the ingredients.** Put water into a heavy saucepan and place it over low heat. Add butter and chop it into small pieces with a wooden spoon to speed melting. Sift all-purpose flour and salt onto parchment or wax paper.

2 **Boiling the liquid.** Heat the liquid gently, while stirring it to encourage the melting of the butter. When the butter melts, increase the temperature to high to bring the liquid to a boil.

5 **Adding eggs.** Cool the paste for a minute or two. To ensure that no eggshell slips into the mixture, break an egg into a bowl, then add it to the pan *(above, left)*; beat hard to force the egg into the paste, then beat in another egg. As each egg is added, the mixture will separate slightly and be wet and slippery *(above, center)*. As soon as it becomes smooth and homogeneous again *(above, right)*, add the next egg.

3 **Adding the flour.** Immediately slide the flour and salt into the hot liquid, adding all the flour mixture at once; the melted butter will help prevent lumps from forming. Reduce the heat to medium to prevent the mixture from scorching.

4 **Stirring in the flour.** Start stirring the mixture as soon as the flour is added *(above, left)*, and continue until all of the ingredients are thoroughly combined. Stir the mixture vigorously, until the paste forms a solid mass that comes away cleanly from the sides of the pan *(above, right)*. Remove the pan from the heat.

6 **Filling a pastry bag.** Beat until the paste is thick and shiny *(left)*. Use a pastry bag fitted with a tube to shape the chou paste. To fill the bag, fold the top third of the open end back over your wrist, then spoon in the chou paste *(inset)* until the pastry bag is about half-full. Unfold the bag and twist the top tightly to secure its contents.

Cream-filled Éclairs Coated with Chocolate

No matter what form you choose for it, the rules for shaping and baking chou paste remain constant. To prepare the paste for the oven, you can shape it into mounds or strips using two spoons; however, a pastry bag fitted with a plain or decorative tube produces more uniform and attractive results. In this demonstration, for instance, neat strips are piped onto a baking sheet to make éclairs that will be filled with pastry cream.

If you like, you can give the pastries a glossy finish by brushing the tops lightly with a mixture of egg yolk and milk before baking them. Make sure that the glaze does not touch the baking sheet, lest it cement the paste to the sheet and prevent it from rising evenly.

In the oven, cavities form inside the chou-paste shells as the moisture in the paste turns to steam and expands. To ensure proper expansion, bake the pastries at high heat—400° F. [200° C.]—until they feel firm to the touch. Some steam will remain inside the pastries after they are done, and it must be eliminated to achieve properly crisp shells.

You can deal with the steam in either of two ways. Remove the pastries from the oven, pierce the shells with the tip of a knife *(Step 2, right),* and immediately return them to the oven to dry out for a few minutes. Alternatively, pierce the shells, turn off the heat, and let the shells dry in the oven for half an hour.

Once baked and cooled, chou pastries are ready for filling and icing. You can use a pastry bag to force a soft filling through the hole that was formed to let steam escape. Or simply slice off the pastry tops to expose their hollow interiors, spoon in the filling, replace the tops and apply the icing—in this case, chocolate-flavored fondant *(pages 10-11).*

Baking is not the only way to cook chou paste. It may be deep fried *(box, opposite);* it will then cook before the expanding steam inflates it completely, resulting in a crisp, closely textured pastry.

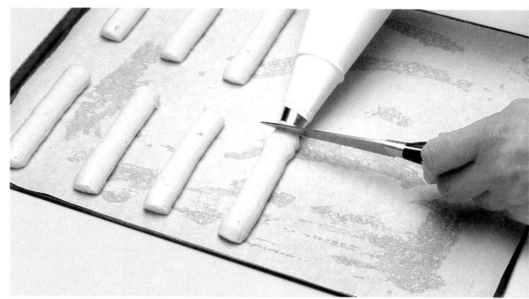

1 Piping. To prevent the paste from sticking, cover a baking sheet with parchment paper; butter the sheet to keep the paper in place. Fit a No. 7 plain tube into a pastry bag, fill the bag with paste *(page 65, Step 6),* and pipe strips 3 to 4 inches [8 to 10 cm.] long, slicing off each length with a knife *(above).* Leave 1½ inches [4 cm.] between the strips to allow for expansion.

2 Baking the shells. Place the éclairs in a preheated 400° F. [200° C.] oven and bake them for 20 minutes, until firm and golden. Remove the éclairs from the oven and pierce both ends of each with a knife *(above);* bake for a few more minutes. Remove the éclairs from the oven and cool on a rack.

3 Filling the bases. While the pastry is baking, prepare the pastry-cream filling and the chocolate fondant icing. Keep the fondant soft in a bowl set over hot water. Slice each cooled éclair lengthwise and spoon the cream into the bottom half. Replace the tops and return the éclairs to the rack for icing.

Deep Frying Ribbons of Paste

Deep frying turns chou paste into deliciously crunchy desserts—as long as you carefully regulate the temperature of the oil. For interesting tastes, flavor the paste with vanilla, rum or lemon juice *(recipe, page 163)*, then drop it directly into hot oil. Here, the paste is piped from a pastry bag to form strips; alternatively, you could push bits of paste from a spoon to form balls.

The paste swells as it comes in contact with the oil; the outside of the pastry crisps to a golden brown. To cook the paste quickly so that it does not absorb oil and become soggy, but not so quickly that it burns, the temperature of the oil should be 375° F. [190° C.]. Check the temperature with a deep-frying thermometer or by dropping a piece of paste into the oil. If the paste sizzles at once, the oil is hot enough. To maintain a consistently high temperature, fry only a few pastries at a time.

1 **Deep frying chou.** Pour 3 inches [8 cm.] of oil into a deep, heavy pan and heat it to 375° F. [190° C.]. Fit a No. 6 plain or star tube into a pastry bag; half-fill the bag with chou paste. Pipe 8- to 12-inch [20- to 30-cm.] lengths into the oil, slicing off each length with a knife.

2 **Serving the pastries.** Turning them once with a slotted spoon, deep fry the pastries for five to seven minutes, or until they are golden. Remove them with the spoon and drain on paper towels. Sprinkle sugar over the pastries and serve them warm or cold.

4 **Icing the éclairs.** Spoon the fondant icing over the top of each of the éclairs *(inset)*. Arrange the éclairs on a dish *(right)* and serve.

Pastries in Partnership

Large chou rings and little chou puffs can be used as the foundations for a range of fanciful desserts *(recipes, pages 147-150)*. For instance, three rings piped concentrically, then baked, split and filled with praline-flavored pastry cream, form a classic dessert named for two French cities: Paris-Brest. A small cream-filled and fondant-iced puff set on top of a larger one and trimmed with piped butter cream becomes a *religieuse (box, opposite)* —so named, it seems, because the shape of the pastry and the color of the coffee- or chocolate-flavored icing *(pages 10-11)* recall a French nun's habit.

Even more elaborate desserts combine both rings and puffs. For example, the *gâteau Saint-Honoré* that is shown at right begins with a ring of chou paste piped onto a round base of rich short crust *(pages 18-19)*. When baked, the assembly becomes a kind of extra-airy tart shell. To make the shell deeper and give it the appearance of a crown, the chou ring is topped with a ring of small puffs filled with pastry cream. The puffs are attached to the ring with caramel *(pages 8-9)*, which hardens as it cools and bonds the puffs firmly in place. The regal case is then filled with pastry cream, in this instance firmed with a little gelatin and aerated with beaten egg whites.

The chou ring and puffs for a *gâteau Saint-Honoré* are formed by forcing the paste through a pastry bag fitted with a plain tube. It would be possible, of course, to shape both ring and puffs with the aid of two large spoons, but the effect would not be nearly so regular and smooth.

Like all chou pastry, the ring and puffs must be cooked at a steady high heat, as described on page 66. Because the puffs take less time to cook than the ring, they are baked separately; if you opened the oven door to retrieve them while the ring was still cooking, the slight drop in temperature could cause the ring to sink.

To fill the baked puffs without cutting them in two, fit a small tube into a pastry bag, load the bag with pastry cream and insert the tube into the pierced base of each puff *(Step 2)*. By squeezing the bag with a firm, even pressure, you can force the cream into the interior of the puff.

1 **Assembling the dough and paste.** Using a No. 7 plain tube, pipe 15 walnut-sized chou-paste balls onto a paper-lined baking sheet. Roll out rich short-crust dough about ¼ inch [6 mm.] thick. Cut it into a 10-inch [25-cm.] round, place it on a buttered baking sheet, pipe a ring of paste around the rim *(above, right)* and prick the top of the short crust. Glaze the balls and ring with beaten egg and milk. Bake the balls for 15 to 20 minutes in an oven preheated to 400° F. [200° C.].

4 **Constructing the case.** In a small, heavy saucepan, make a rich, amber caramel *(pages 8-9)*; remove the pan from the heat to arrest cooking. Dip each puff into the caramel to coat its base, then press it gently onto the chou ring *(above)*. If the caramel hardens before you finish, place the pan briefly over low heat to melt it again. Continue to dip and position the balls until you complete a full circle. Use a spoon to dribble the remaining caramel over the surface of the puffs *(inset)*.

2 **Filling the puffs.** As soon as the chou puffs are done, pierce them and dry them in the hot oven for a few minutes. Cool them on a rack. Then bake the chou ring and short-crust round for 25 to 30 minutes. Make pastry cream *(page 12)*, cool about a third of it in a bowl and pipe it into the puffs.

3 **Preparing the cream.** In a bowl, soften gelatin in a little cold water for two minutes. Set the bowl in a pan of hot water over low heat and stir the gelatin to dissolve it. Then stir the gelatin into the remaining warm pastry cream. Beat egg whites and sugar until stiff *(page 13)*; gradually fold in the cream *(above)*.

Miniature Confections Glossed with Fondant

5 **Finishing the case.** Spoon the cream mixture into the case up to the top of the chou ring. For a simple decoration, make shallow furrows in the cream by running the spoon's edge across the surface. Refrigerate the pastry for half an hour before serving to firm the filling. Cut the pastry in wedges for serving *(above)*.

Making small chou pastries. Pipe rounds of chou onto a prepared baking sheet *(Step 1)* — half of them about 1 inch [2½ cm.] across and half of them about 2 inches [5 cm.] across. Bake the puffs, fill them with pastry cream *(Step 2)*, and dip them in fondant icing — both the filling and icing used here are flavored with coffee. Set the puffs on a rack until the icing hardens. Secure a small ball on top of each large one with a dab of butter cream and decorate each pastry with a collar of butter cream.

A Fantasy of Puffs and Caramel

Of the many chou-paste constructions, *croquembouche,* demonstrated here, is one of the most dramatic—a soaring cone of cream-filled puffs, veiled with amber threads of caramel *(pages 8-9).*

The towering assembly is not so precarious as it might appear at first glance. Bake the chou puffs and fill them with pastry cream *(page 12)*—or with sweetened whipped cream, as here. To build the cone, dip the chou puffs individually into a light, golden caramel *(pages 8-9),* and set the puffs on top of one another, arranging them in circular layers of diminishing size. As the syrup cools, it will harden to hold the puffs firmly in place.

You can build the *croquembouche* on a prebaked base of either short-crust pastry or, as in this demonstration, rich short-crust pastry *(recipe, page 162).* To decorate the assembly, use a fork to spin a fine web of caramel around the cone *(Step 3, inset).*

If you like, you can also pipe stars of whipped cream or butter cream around the *croquembouche* or stud the construction with candied cherries that have been dipped in caramel to help them adhere.

1 **Making the base.** Put a prebaked 8-inch [20-cm.] pastry base on a dish; bake and fill about 150 chou puffs *(pages 68-69).* Make caramel*(pages 8-9)* and, to keep it liquid, place the pan in hot water. Dip one side of each puff into the caramel and set it on the pastry, syrup side down and flat base facing in.

2 **Building the cone.** Complete the first layer by covering the base with more puffs dipped in caramel. Continue building layers—each one slightly smaller than the last—to make a cone. If the caramel begins to harden, renew the hot water or set the pan over low heat to remelt the caramel.

3 **Decorating and serving.** Use a fork to lift threads of caramel and drape them around the assembly until it is covered by a fine web *(inset).* Serve the pastry—starting at the top and gently snapping away one or two chou puffs at a time with a spoon and fork *(far right).*

Sculpting with Chou

Whimsical chou pastries, including the graceful swans shown on this page, are only slightly more difficult to make than chou puffs; they require nothing more than a pastry bag and a little practice.

Shaping and baking procedures are, in fact, essentially the same as for puffs. First, teardrop-shaped puffs are piped onto a baking sheet. Here, a star tube was fitted to the pastry bag to give the bodies a feathery look, but a plain tube also makes satisfactory swans. The swan necks and heads are piped from a bag fitted with a plain tube. Because the narrow necks cook much more quickly than the bodies, the shapes are baked at different temperatures.

Once the puffs are baked and cooled, assembly is simple. The puffs become swan bodies and wings. The bodies, filled with whipped cream or pastry cream, are attached to the wings and necks. Finally the swans are given eyes of chocolate and a dusting of confectioners' sugar to simulate white feathers.

1 Forming bodies. Fill a pastry bag fitted with a No. 6 star tube with chou paste *(page 65, Step 6)*. To make each body, squeeze an oval mound of paste about 3 inches [8 cm.] long onto a prepared baking sheet. Raise the tube to create a ridged center, and ease the pressure on the bag to make a tapered tail. Bake for 30 minutes in a 400° F. [200° C.] oven, as described on page 66.

2 Forming necks. Fit a pastry bag with a No. 0 plain tube and fill the bag with paste. For each neck, pipe an S curve of paste onto a prepared baking sheet. Thicken one end of the line to form a head; thicken the other end to make an anchor for the neck. Make extra necks: The thin shapes are fragile. Bake for 10 minutes in a preheated 375° F. [190° C.] oven.

3 Forming wings. When the puffs and necks are cool and dry, slice off the tops of the puffs parallel to the bases. Then halve each top lengthwise to form the swan wings. Fill the bottoms of the puffs with sweetened whipped cream to form the swan bodies.

4 Assembling the swans. Position the wings — with the cut sides facing outward — lengthwise on top of a swan body, pushing them gently into the cream. Push a neck into the cream at the thicker end of each swan body.

5 Adding eyes. Fill a paper cone *(page 56, Step 6)* with melted chocolate. Clip off the end of the cone, and pipe a tiny dot of chocolate on either side of each swan head to form eyes. Let the chocolate set, then sift confectioners' sugar over the swans.

4
Specialty Pastries

The realm of pastry making encompasses confections that defy categorization. Among them are unusual treatments of familiar dough ingredients, as well as alternatives to the flour-fat-and-water doughs so central to the pastry cook's art. Some of these pastries are simple to prepare; others require enough skill to make them the stuff of legend.

Strudel *(pages 74-75)* is one such hard-to-classify pastry. The pride of Austria and Hungary, strudel dough actually is a descendant of Middle Eastern phyllo dough *(pages 78-79)*—which it closely resembles—brought west in the 16th Century by invading Turks. A rolled strudel's myriad buttery layers are formed from a dough stretched so thin that, as Viennese cooks are fond of saying, you can read a newspaper through it. Some cookbook writers claim that the stretching of this dough is a difficult task best left to professionals. In fact, if you select the proper flour and understand how to handle it, you can readily produce a dough of sufficient strength and elasticity to be manipulated into a giant, filmy sheet. It can then be used to enclose fillings like the lemon-brightened cheese mixture shown opposite, or fragrantly spiced blends of apples, raisins, nuts or even poppy seeds.

Strudels are baked, but similarly strong doughs serve as the bases for delicate deep-fried pastries: These doughs need extra strength so that they can be rolled very thin without losing their coherence. Wrapping such a dough around cylindrical metal molds yields Italian *cannoli (pages 80-81),* crisp tubes that are filled with mixtures of soft ricotta cheese or whipped cream, either of which may be flavored with liqueurs or chocolate, nuts or candied fruits. Another deep-fried pastry is based on a thin dough sheet folded into layers separated by butter and flour; when the dough is cut, shaped and deep fried, its leaves swell apart in a splendid display that has earned this Argentine dessert an extravagant name, *pastelitos de mil hojas,* or "thousand-leaf pastries" *(pages 82-83).*

Unlike strudel and fried pastry, crumb crusts *(pages 84-85)* and meringue shells *(page 86)* require no dough preparation. Crumb crusts are nothing more than bread, cake, cookie or cracker crumbs bound by butter; meringues are egg whites and sugar, stiffly beaten, shaped and slowly baked until dry and firm. These crisp containers are pastries, nonetheless, and belong in every good cook's repertoire.

A crosswise slice reveals the golden paper-thin layers of a perfect strudel. The strudel dough was rolled around a rich filling of cottage cheese, eggs, sugar, butter, sour cream, raisins and lemon peel, then baked *(pages 74-77)*.

Stretching a Strudel Sheet

The unique qualities of strudel dough—the pliability and strength that allow it to be stretched to gossamer thinness—come from a high level of gluten development; this is achieved by turning most of the rules of pastry making upside down.

All-purpose flour is by no means the automatic selection, for example. Some cooks use bread flour, which will yield more gluten. Alternatively, a combination of bread and all-purpose flour, or all-purpose flour alone, produces dough that is slightly easier to knead, if slightly harder to stretch. Whatever the flour, adding a small amount of acid to it will strengthen its gluten. Simply mix a dash of vinegar or lemon juice into the dough.

Besides flour, strudel dough contains eggs (which increase flexibility and richness), water and butter. To ensure an evenly textured dough, all these ingredients should be at room temperature—not chilled as they are for short crust or puff pastry. The butter, in fact, is melted.

The major difference between strudel and other doughs is in the handling. Most doughs are only lightly worked, but strudel calls for vigorous kneading to develop its gluten network. When left to relax after kneading, the dough loses its springiness yet retains its strength.

Rolling and stretching must be done on a large table—the finished sheet may be as large as 6 feet [1¾ m.] square—covered with a floured cloth that facilitates handling the dough.

As the dough is stretched more and more, it will gradually become so thin that it is translucent. If you have long fingernails that might pierce the sheet, stretch the dough with clenched fists. But do not be too concerned if you make a small tear: Once the stretched dough is rolled repeatedly around its filling (page 77), the accumulating layers will prevent any leakage.

1 **Assembling ingredients.** Sift flour and salt into a large mixing bowl, and break eggs into a smaller bowl. Melt butter in a small saucepan and let it cool until tepid. Add lukewarm water and the melted butter to the eggs, and beat them together with a fork until smooth. Add a dash of vinegar to the mixture, if desired.

2 **Combining ingredients.** Make a well in the middle of the flour and fill the hollow with the egg-and-butter mixture. Use your hands to combine the ingredients, gradually drawing the flour into the center: The mixture should be soft and sticky at this point. If it seems dry, add more lukewarm water.

5 **Preparing for rolling.** Cover a large table with a clean cloth. To prevent the dough from sticking, sprinkle the cloth lightly with flour. Place the rested dough in the center of the cloth. To keep the dough moist, brush it with a little melted butter (above).

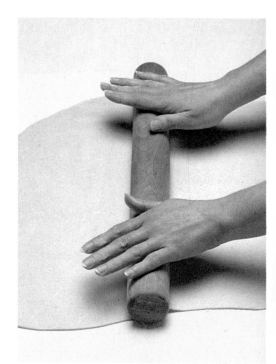

6 **Rolling out the dough.** Roll the dough in a lengthwise direction until it is about ¼ inch [6 mm.] thick. Then move around the table and roll the dough in a crosswise direction until it is about ⅛ inch [3 mm.] thick.

3 **Blending the dough.** Use one hand to scrape up the dough from the sides of the bowl, blending the dough with your fingers. As you work, use your other hand to tilt and rotate the bowl. When the dough is cohesive enough to leave the sides of the bowl clean (above), shape the dough into a ball and place it on a lightly floured surface.

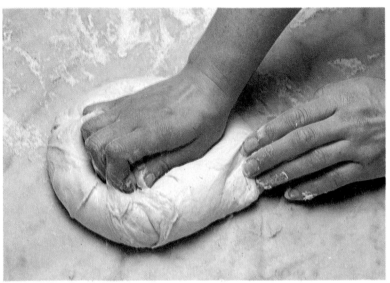

4 **Kneading.** Press the dough with the heel of your hand and push forward (above). Turn the dough slightly and repeat the process. Knead until the dough is not sticky — about 15 minutes. Form a smooth ball with only one seam: Extra seams would make ridges in the sheet. Brush with melted butter, place in a warmed bowl, cover with plastic wrap and let the ball rest for 30 minutes.

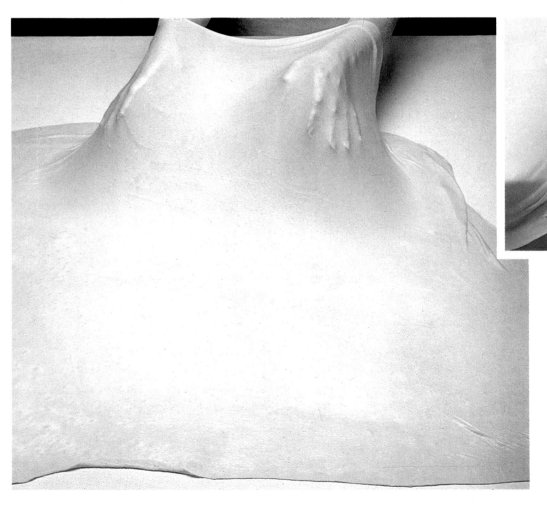

7 **Stretching the dough.** Flour your hands and slip them — palms down — beneath the dough. Working from the center toward the nearest edge, move your hands apart repeatedly until the dough stretches to a translucent sheet across your knuckles. Move around the table, stretching a section at a time. The sheet will drape over the table. Use scissors to trim the border. Let the dough dry for five to 10 minutes — no longer — before using it.

Rolling Rich Mixtures in Strudel

Strudel comes from a German word that means "to roll" and that is how this pastry is traditionally shaped: The stretched dough sheet *(pages 74-75)* is rolled up around a filling. When baked, the core of filling is surrounded by a crisp, golden cylinder of fragile pastry layers. You can form two king-sized strudels by rolling a 6-foot [1¾-m.] sheet of dough around a filling and halving the roll *(right, top)*. Or you can cut the dough into smaller strips and produce several dozen individual pastries *(right, bottom)*.

In either case, preliminary preparations are the same: The stretched dough is allowed to rest for five to 10 minutes at room temperature so that it firms slightly, becoming easier to roll. Then it is painted with melted butter to prevent it from drying and to keep the layers separate during baking. Many cooks also sprinkle the sheet with dry bread or cake crumbs before filling it to keep the layers from fusing as they bake. To absorb excess moisture so that the pastry will be crisp, the area that will hold the filling may be dusted with farina or semolina.

Fillings for strudel are numberless. Nuts, fruits and fresh cheese all can be used *(recipes, pages 150-152)*. In the top demonstration, for example, a custardy mixture of egg yolks, sugar, sour cream, flour and cottage cheese is enlivened with raisins and lemon peel, then aerated with beaten egg whites. The filling for the small strudels shown below also begins with a custard and ends with egg white. The flavoring, however, is poppy seeds, their musky taste tempered with grated apple. To soften them and develop flavor, the seeds are ground in a mortar or food processor, then simmered briefly.

Once the filling is added, small strudels are rolled by hand. Large strudels are unwieldy, however, and should be rolled with the aid of the cloth on which they were stretched *(Step 3, top)*. In either case, roll the dough loosely to leave room for the filling to expand.

Either type of strudel should be laid with the seam side down on buttered baking sheets. Otherwise, the seam will curl during cooking. To fit a large strudel on standard-sized sheets, cut it into two more manageable lengths and, if necessary, bend these into horseshoe shapes.

A Grandly Scaled Parcel for Cheese

1 **Making the filling.** Prepare strudel dough and leave it to rest for 30 minutes. Meanwhile, beat butter, vanilla sugar and egg yolks in a large bowl until foamy. Stir in sour cream, raisins, lemon peel, flour and salt. Let the mixture stand for about 15 minutes to thicken slightly. Sieve cottage cheese, then stir it into the mixture.

2 **Adding the filling.** Stretch the dough on a floured cloth and let it dry for five to 10 minutes. Brush the dough sheet with melted butter. Scatter dry bread crumbs over it. Sprinkle semolina in a strip 3 inches [8 cm.] wide and at least 3 inches from one edge of the sheet, leaving a margin at both ends. Fold stiffly beaten egg whites into the filling and spoon it over the semolina.

Small Rolls with a Poppy-Seed Filling

1 **Cooking the filling.** Make strudel dough and let it rest for 30 minutes. Beat vanilla sugar and egg yolks until foamy. Stir in flour, lemon peel, butter and hot milk. Pour the mixture into a pan and slowly bring it to a simmer. Stir in ground poppy seeds. When the mixture simmers, set it aside to cool.

2 **Adding the apples.** Stretch the strudel dough and allow the sheet to dry for five to 10 minutes. Meanwhile, grate a peeled, cored apple. Stir the apple and raisins into the cooled poppy-seed mixture.

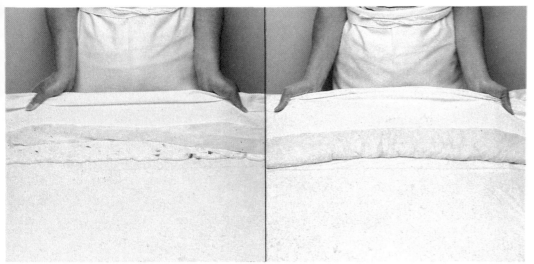

3 **Rolling the sheet.** If the filling is very soft, tuck in the sides of the sheet to prevent leakage during cooking. With both hands, gently lift the cloth so that the edge of the sheet flips over the filling (above, left). Pull the cloth — and the sheet — toward you and, at the same time, gently lift the cloth so that the sheet gradually rolls itself around the filling (right). Cut the strudel in two and tuck in the ends of the rolls — after removing a little of the filling from the ends if it is very soft. One at a time, tip the rolled strudels, seam side down, onto buttered baking sheets.

4 **Cooking and serving.** Brush the strudels with melted butter and bake them in a preheated 400° F. [200° C.] oven for about 40 minutes, or until they are crisp and golden. Remove the strudels from the oven and dust them with confectioners' sugar. You may serve them either warm or cooled.

3 **Cutting the sheet.** Brush the sheet with melted butter. Using a ruler, measure rectangular strips of the desired size — pieces 8 by 24 inches [20 by 60 cm.] are used here — and incise guidelines in the sheet with the tip of a knife. Cut out the strips with a sharp knife or pastry wheel.

4 **Filling.** Fold stiffly beaten egg whites into the poppy-seed mixture. Spread a 1-inch [2½-cm.] band of filling about 1 inch from the end of each strip of dough, leaving borders on both sides. Fold the end over the filling and loosely roll up each strudel. Place the strudels on buttered baking sheets.

5 **Baking.** Bake the strudels in a 400° F. [200° C.] oven for 30 minutes, or until crisp and golden. Cool them to lukewarm on a rack set on wax paper. Dip a fork in icing — here, a lemon-flavored fondant icing (recipe, page 167) — and trail it over the strudels. Top with sliced, toasted almonds.

Layering or Coiling Phyllo Assemblies

Phyllo dough, strudel's Middle Eastern progenitor, is kneaded and stretched until paper-thin in essentially the same way as its descendant *(pages 74-75)*. The ingredients differ, however, and traditional modes of shaping are distinct.

Phyllo should have as its base strong, gluten-rich bread flour—as is often the choice for strudel. The flour is mixed with water and oil to form a dough *(recipe, page 164)* that is kneaded, rested, then kneaded and rested again before being stretched. Because phyllo lacks the eggs that give strudel additional flexibility, phyllo is more difficult to manipulate—and many cooks compromise with tradition by adding an egg or two. Fresh and frozen phyllo is also available readymade in Middle Eastern food stores.

Phyllo pastries are not simple rolls, but assemblies formed by cutting the stretched sheet into pieces, each called a leaf—the Greek meaning of the word "phyllo"—then layering or folding the leaves around various fillings. These operations take time and demand precautions to keep the dough pliable. Freshly made phyllo leaves should be used immediately or stacked and tightly enclosed in plastic wrap to preserve their moistness; the leaves will keep up to four days in the refrigerator. Frozen commercial phyllo should be defrosted, still in its wrapper, overnight in the refrigerator.

During shaping, phyllo should be kept stacked and protected by a lightly dampened towel if the assembly process is a slow one. As the pastry is assembled, the phyllo is brushed, leaf by leaf, with melted butter to ensure that the multiple layers will crisp individually.

The most famous layered phyllo pastry is baklava *(top demonstration; recipe, page 154)*. It is made in a baking pan by interspersing the leaves—as few as 20 or as many as 50—with ground nuts and spices, and drenching the baked assembly in honey-flavored syrup. Because of its many layers, baklava may be made with imperfect leaves.

If the assembly consists of a single leaf enclosing a filling *(bottom demonstration; recipe, page 153)*, the leaf must be perfect to help keep the filling from leaking. Suitable fillings are firm, such as the semolina-stiffened custard shown here.

Leaves Stacked with Nuts and Honey

1 **Preparing the dough.** Prepare and stretch phyllo dough—about 2 pounds [1 kg.] is used here. Let the dough rest for 10 to 20 minutes. Cut the dough into rectangular pieces that will just fit in your baking pan. Stack these leaves on a baking sheet; to prevent sticking, sift a little cornstarch over each leaf as you proceed.

2 **Layering with nuts.** Place 10 phyllo leaves in a buttered baking pan one at a time, brushing each leaf with a little melted butter. Then add a layer of filling: in this case, a mixture of spices and walnuts. Cover with two buttered leaves. Alternate filling and phyllo until the filling is used up. Top with three or four buttered leaves.

Coils Filled with a Creamy Blend

1 **Preparing the dough.** Prepare semolina-thickened custard and cool it. Cut phyllo into 12-by-18-inch [30-by-46-cm.] leaves, stack them *(Step 1, top)* and cover them with a damp towel. Spoon the custard into a pastry bag fitted with a No. 6 plain tube. Brush one leaf with melted butter, fold it in half lengthwise and butter the top.

2 **Filling the pastry.** Pipe a band of filling along one of the long edges of the phyllo leaf, allowing 1-inch [2½-cm.] margins of dough along that edge and at both ends. Fold the ends over to seal in the filling. Fold the long edge over the filling and roll the leaf into a cylinder.

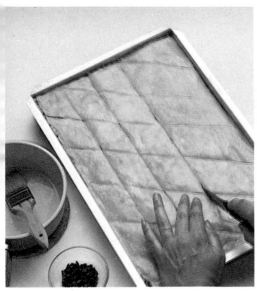

3 **Baking.** With a sharp knife, score diamonds in the pastry, cutting only through the top layers. Insert a clove into each diamond. Pour melted butter over the pastry. Sprinkle on a little water to prevent the leaves from curling. Bake the baklava in a preheated 325° F. [160° C.] oven for one and a half hours, or until golden brown.

4 **Adding the syrup.** While the baklava bakes, bring sugar, water, cloves, lemon juice and a lemon slice to a boil. Reduce the heat; boil gently for about 20 minutes, until syrupy. Remove the pan from the heat, discard the cloves and the lemon slice, and stir in honey. When the baklava is done, pour the cooled syrup over it.

5 **Serving.** Let the pastry rest at room temperature for four or more hours to absorb the syrup. Then divide the baklava into portions following the scored lines. With two forks or a narrow metal spatula, pry out an odd-shaped piece from the edge. Then, using a spatula, carefully lift out the diamond shapes one by one.

3 **Shaping coils.** Fold in one end of the cylinder, then coil the pastry around itself in a spiral *(left)*. Brush a little butter on the free end of the cylinder *(right)*, and gently press it against the coil. Put the finished pastries on a baking sheet. Brush the surface of each coil with melted butter. Bake in a preheated 350° F. [180° C.] oven for 45 minutes, or until golden. Remove the baking sheet from the oven and let the coils cool for about five minutes.

4 **Garnishing.** While the coils bake, prepare a sugar syrup — a lemon-flavored syrup is used here. When the pastries cool slightly, transfer them to a platter. Spoon a little syrup over each coil and sprinkle it with chopped nuts — in this case, walnuts.

Cannoli: Deep-fried Pipes of Wine-flavored Dough

Simple deep-fried pastries can be made from short-crust dough *(pages 16-17)* and chou paste *(pages 64-65)*. Complex molded forms such as the *cannoli* shown here *(recipe, page 158)* require special dough.

Cannoli are crisp, cylindrical pastry casings for creamy fillings (in Italian, the name means "small pipes"). They are formed by wrapping dough around tubular metal molds—available at kitchen-equipment shops—then deep frying and unmolding it. To keep its shape, the dough must be strong and flexible—characteristics acquired both from its ingredients and its manner of preparation. *Cannoli* dough contains a high proportion of flour to butter (melted, for even distribution). The liquid used is red wine, not only for color and flavor, but also because a generous amount of acid helps produce a supple gluten network in the flour. To develop the gluten network, *cannoli* dough is vigorously kneaded.

The firm dough that results must be fried at a high temperature to prevent it from absorbing oil. Therefore, the dough is rolled thin before it is molded, and the oil is heated to 390° F. [200° C.]. At this temperature the molded dough cooks in as little as one minute, emerging as a golden, bubble-covered tube.

Just-fried *cannoli* are still soft, and their metal molds are too hot to touch; completely cooled *cannoli* are brittle. For these reasons, allow *cannoli* to cool only slightly, until lukewarm but still flexible, before unmolding them.

The cooled pastries can be used at once or stored in an airtight container for several days at room temperature. In either case, fill the *cannoli* just before you serve them, to ensure their crispness. Most fillings are based on mild ricotta cheese flavored with sugar, liqueurs, chocolate, candied fruits or nuts. If you are unable to get the dry ricotta that is sold at Italian delicatessens, use the moist variety, but drain it beforehand *(Step 5)*.

1 Making dough. In a large bowl, stir together sifted flour, melted butter, salt and sugar. Pour in red wine, a little at a time, stirring with a fork to blend the ingredients. Continue adding the wine until a stiff dough forms.

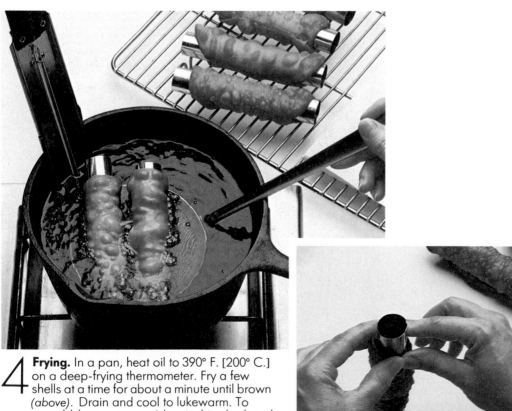

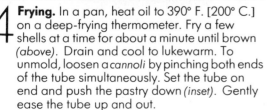

4 Frying. In a pan, heat oil to 390° F. [200° C.] on a deep-frying thermometer. Fry a few shells at a time for about a minute until brown *(above)*. Drain and cool to lukewarm. To unmold, loosen a *cannoli* by pinching both ends of the tube simultaneously. Set the tube on end and push the pastry down *(inset)*. Gently ease the tube up and out.

5 Preparing filling. Wrap moist ricotta in cheesecloth, suspend it from a wooden spoon set over a bowl and let it drain in the refrigerator overnight. Sieve the ricotta to eliminate lumps. Stir in sugar and orange liqueur. Add chopped candied orange peel and cherries, and chopped semisweet chocolate.

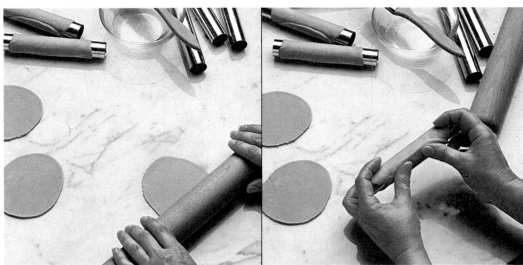

2 **Kneading the dough.** Place the dough on a flat, lightly floured surface and knead the dough for about 15 minutes, until it is smooth and satiny. Knead the dough into a ball. Cover it with plastic wrap and refrigerate it for an hour or two to relax the gluten.

3 **Shaping the cannoli.** Halve the dough and return one portion to the refrigerator. On a lightly floured surface, roll the other portion to a thickness of 1/16 inch [1½ mm.] and cut it into 4-inch [10-cm.] circles, using the rim of a large glass as a guide. Roll each circle into an oval *(left)*. Place an oiled *cannoli* tube lengthwise at the side of the oval and roll the tube to wrap the dough around it. Brush the seam in the dough with beaten egg white, then press the edges together to seal them *(right)*. Continue shaping *cannoli* until all of the dough is used up.

6 **Filling the pastry shells.** Holding a shell horizontally, spoon in the filling from both ends or pipe it in, as demonstrated above, using a pastry bag fitted with a No. 6 plain tube. Let the filling mound slightly at each end. For a finishing touch, dip the ends in grated chocolate or blanched, chopped pistachios, as here.

7 **Serving the cannoli.** Arrange the filled *cannoli* on a serving platter. With a dredger *(above)* or a small strainer, sprinkle a little confectioners' sugar over the *cannoli*. To prevent the shells from getting soggy, serve the pastries immediately.

Two Fryings to Make Pastry Petals

Combining a special dough and a special frying technique *(recipe, page 159)*, Argentine cooks are able to produce crisp-fried confections enthusiastically dubbed thousand-leaf pastries, but actually composed of 16 discrete, buttery layers. The dough is a strong one similar to strudel dough. Made of flour, butter and water, it also contains lemon juice and egg yolks, which contribute flexibility.

Once kneaded—to develop the gluten—and rolled out, the dough is repeatedly folded into layers. A thin film of butter brushed onto the dough before each folding helps to provide the steam that causes the layers to puff and separate to resemble flower petals as they cook. The film of melted butter is dusted with flour; this helps keep the layers of dough separate and prevents them from absorbing the liquid fat.

When folding is complete, the dough may be cut into small shapes such as crescents, triangles or the squares shown

here. The little shapes then may be deep fried as they are or, for a richer effect, sealed around a filling, which should be a fairly stiff, dry one that will not leak during frying. The pastries here, for instance, are filled with a thick mixture of quince paste—available at Latin American markets—and sweet wine.

Fried in the conventional manner at high heat, these pastries would not puff satisfactorily because the dough would harden immediately into a rigid, inflexible shell. Therefore, the pastries are first briefly fried at a very low heat so that the dough remains flexible enough to expand and unfold from the pressure of the steam that builds within it. Once they have puffed, the pastries are fried a second time at a high temperature so that they become crisp and brown.

As a finishing touch, pastries of this type could simply be dusted with sugar; in this demonstration, sugar syrup provides a translucent glaze.

1 **Mixing the dough.** Sift flour and salt into a large bowl and cut in chilled butter until the mixture looks like coarse meal. Make a well in the center and add lemon juice and beaten egg yolks, stirring the flour into them with a fork as you gradually add water *(left)*. Knead the dough with your hands *(right)* until it is smooth and elastic.

4 **Cutting and filling.** Using a ruler and a pastry wheel or knife, cut the large square into thirty-six 2½-inch [6-cm.] squares. Prepare a filling—here, quince paste and muscatel—and, using a pastry bag fitted with a No. 4 plain tube, pipe about a teaspoonful of filling into the centers of half of the small squares.

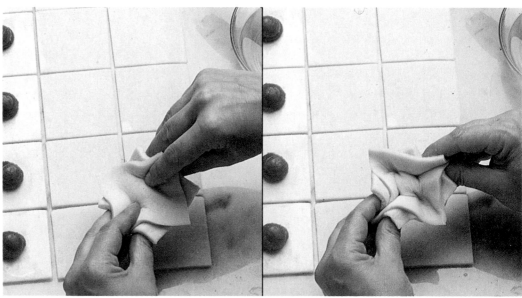

5 **Shaping the pastries.** Brush the surface of a filled square with a little water. Cover with a plain square set at an angle to form an eight-pointed star, and press the edges together to seal them. To produce a decorative grooved effect, pick up the pastry in both hands, resting your forefingers on opposing corners of the top square. With your thumbs and middle fingers, gently pinch the dough together around your forefingers *(left)*; lift your forefingers off the dough and pinch again to sharpen the crease. Repeat for the two remaining corners of the top square *(right)*.

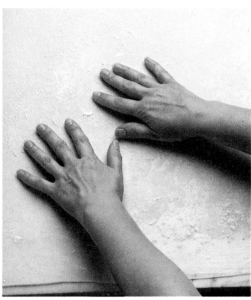

2 **Rolling out.** For easy handling, chill the dough for two or three hours. Then, on a lightly floured surface, roll it into a 32-inch [80-cm.] square about ¹⁄₁₆ inch [1½ mm.] thick. Trim the edges to form a perfect square. Brush the surface of the dough lightly with melted butter, then dust with flour. Gently rub the flour into the butter until the dough looks dry.

3 **Folding the dough.** Fold the square in half to form a rectangle. Butter and flour the top surface as in Step 2, then fold the rectangle in half to form a 16-inch [40-cm.] square (above), and butter and flour the dough again. Fold the dough in half again, butter and flour the surface, then fold the dough to produce an 8-inch [20-cm.] square. Chill the dough for 30 minutes to relax it. Roll out the dough (inset) to form a 16-inch square about ⅛ inch [3 mm.] thick. To eliminate uneven edges, trim the dough into a perfect 15-inch [38-cm.] square.

6 **Frying the pastries.** Pour 3 inches [8 cm.] of oil into a heavy skillet. Heat the oil to 175° F. [80° C.] on a deep-frying thermometer. Fry two or three pastries at a time for three minutes, or until the layers begin to puff and separate; do not brown them. Lift out the pastries with a skimmer, drain them on paper towels and set on a wire rack to cool.

7 **Completing the cooking.** When all of the pastries have been cooked, raise the temperature of the oil to 375° F. [190° C.]. Cook the pastries, two or three at a time, for one minute on each side to brown them. Drain the pastries and set them aside to cool.

8 **Glazing.** While the pastries cool, prepare sugar syrup (page 8) flavored with vanilla. Using tongs, dip the cooled pastries one at a time into the syrup to coat them lightly. Arrange the pastries on a platter and set them aside for five to 10 minutes before serving, to allow the glaze to harden slightly and lose its stickiness.

Crumb Crust: A Container with a Unique Texture

Compared with other types of pastry—even with the plainest short crust—a crumb crust is a model of simplicity: Cake, cracker, bread or cookie crumbs are moistened with melted butter, flavored and used to line a piepan *(recipe, page 165)*. Chilling hardens the butter so that it binds the crumb particles together, forming a crunchy crust.

Only a few general precepts govern the formation of the crust. The crumbs can be produced by rolling brittle crackers or cookies between sheets of wax paper. More easily, these or softer ingredients such as cake or bread can be pulverized in a blender or food processor. Either way, the crumbs should be shaken in a sieve to sift out fine, dusty particles and ensure a uniform texture for the finished crust.

Crumb crusts may be flavored with sugar for sweetness, spices such as cinnamon and cloves, or melted chocolate. For ease of mixing, dry ingredients are combined with the ground-up crumbs. Then the crumbs are mixed with melted butter—using about a quarter as much butter as crumbs—and flavorings. In this demonstration, melted chocolate enlivens a bland, bread-crumb base.

The best pan for a crumb crust is one with sloping sides: Straight-sided pans create sharp angles in the brittle mixture, increasing its chance of crumbling when sliced. Shaping the crust is simply a matter of pressing the crumbs evenly into the pan *(Step 2)*.

The molded crumb crust may simply be chilled to harden the butter, but best results are obtained by baking it, thus drying out excess moisture in the crumbs and preventing sogginess. Because it is highly porous, a crumb crust is blind-baked: If cooked with a filling, it will absorb liquid and may even disintegrate.

Once it is baked and cooled, the crust may be filled with ice cream, sherbet or precooked mixtures such as puddings and custards *(recipes, pages 160-161 and 166)*. Often, the pastry is garnished in a way that advertises its contents. Here, a chocolate Bavarian cream—a light custard sauce enriched with whipped cream and stiffened with gelatin *(recipe, page 161)*—is topped with whipped cream and decorated with scrolls scraped from a bar of barely softened chocolate *(Step 6)*.

1 **Preparing the crumbs.** Trim the crusts from slices of firm white bread, and toast the slices for 30 minutes in a 275° F. [140° C.] oven. Reduce the bread to fine crumbs in a blender or food processor. Mix the crumbs and sugar in a bowl. Melt butter and stir melted chocolate *(page 11)* into it; stir in the bread-crumb mixture.

2 **Forming the crust.** Turn two thirds of the crumb mixture into a buttered piepan or a glass pie plate, and press it into a ¼-inch [6-mm.] layer on the bottom with a spoon. Press the remaining crumb mixture onto the sides, working up from the bottom. Bake for 10 minutes in a 325° F. [160° C.] oven—300° F. [150° C.] for glass. Let the crust cool while you prepare the filling.

4 **Adding cream.** Add the dissolved gelatin and the chocolate to the hot custard and stir until the chocolate melts. Set the bowl in a larger, ice-filled bowl and whisk the custard until it is cool and thick. Whip heavy cream, stir a little into the custard to lighten it, then gently fold in the remaining cream.

5 **Filling the shell.** Pour the Bavarian-cream mixture into the cooled crust right away—before the mixture begins to firm. Quickly smooth the surface with a rubber spatula and chill for at least two hours to set the Bavarian cream.

3 **Making custard.** Beat egg yolks until foamy, then beat in sugar. When the yolks form a ribbon *(page 12)*, gradually stir in milk simmered with a vanilla bean. Over simmering water, stir until the custard coats the spoon, and a finger drawn through it leaves a clean path *(above)*. Strain it into a large bowl *(right)*. Dissolve gelatin in water; chop unsweetened chocolate.

6 **Scraping chocolate scrolls.** At serving time, set a bar of semisweet chocolate in a warm place (75° to 80° F. [about 25° C.]) until the chocolate begins to develop a slightly oily film — none should come off when you touch it with your finger. Run a knife blade along the top of the bar; the chocolate will peel off in thin curls. Transfer the curls to a chilled plate with the knife and refrigerate for five minutes to firm them.

7 **Serving.** Spread a thin layer of sweetened whipped cream over the pie with a spatula. Using a pastry bag, pipe a decorative border around the edge — here, a No. 6 star tube produced a shell design. Arrange the chocolate scrolls on the cream. To serve, cut a wedge, then slide a sharp knife under the crust to loosen it before lifting out the first piece with a pie server or spatula.

Snowy Shells Created from Meringue

Crisp meringue shells, wonderfully light and white, are shaped by one of two methods. The meringue can be piped from a pastry bag into decorative forms *(right)* or spread in a piepan or pie plate *(box, below)*. Whether the meringue is to be freestanding or supported, the shells must be made with molding meringue, prepared with ¼ cup [50 ml.] of sugar to each egg white *(page 45)*.

In either case, the shells are baked the same way—in a very slow oven, which prevents browning, and for a very long time, so that their moisture evaporates and they become crisp and firm. Once baked and cooled, meringue shells are ready for filling, but will also keep for as long as three days if they are stored in airtight containers.

Crisp meringue shells are a fine textural foil for custardy cream fillings. The shells' whiteness sets off brightly colored fruits. And many fillings combine both custards and fruits.

1 Making the shells. Fill a pastry bag, fitted with a No. 6 star tube, with molding meringue. Pipe a coiled disk of meringue onto a paper-covered baking sheet *(left)*. Lift the bag to pipe rings of meringue around the disk *(right)*. Bake in a preheated 250° F. [120° C.] oven for one and a half hours; turn off the heat and cool the shells in the oven.

2 Coating with chocolate. Holding one strawberry at a time by the leaves, dip it into melted semisweet chocolate *(page 11)*. Place the berries on parchment paper for 15 minutes to let the chocolate harden. Meanwhile, brush the interiors of the cooled meringue shells with melted chocolate. Let the lining set until it is no longer sticky.

A Swirled Foundation

Fashioning a pie shell. Make molding meringue. Coat a pie plate with oil and spread a ⅓-inch [1-cm.] layer of meringue on the bottom of the plate. Spoon dollops of meringue around the rim. With a spatula, spread each dollop toward the center, using a downward, sweeping motion. Bake and cool the shell *(Step 1)*.

3 Filling the shells. Fill the meringue shells with pastry cream *(page 12)*, in this case, made with orange-flavored liqueur. On top of the cream, spoon a layer of sliced strawberries; the ones shown in this demonstration were marinated in liqueur for half an hour.

4 Garnishing the pastry. Using a pastry bag fitted with a No. 6 star tube, pipe a swirl of lightly sweetened whipped cream over the strawberries. Put the pastries on individual serving dishes and garnish each of them with a chocolate-covered strawberry.

Anthology
of Recipes

Drawing upon the cooking traditions and literature of more than 17 countries, the editors and consultants for this volume have selected 201 published recipes for the Anthology that follows. The selections range from the familiar to the exotic—from 13 variations of apple pie to an unusual 17th Century recipe for a tart filled with salt pork and almonds, pounded together, bonded with eggs, and flavored with cinnamon and rose water.

Many of the recipes were written by world-renowned exponents of the culinary art, but the Anthology also includes selections from rare and out-of-print books and from works that have never been published in English. Whatever the sources, the emphasis in these recipes is always on fresh, natural ingredients that blend harmoniously.

Since many early recipe writers did not specify amounts of ingredients, sizes of pans, or even cooking times and temperatures, the missing information has been judiciously added. In some cases, instructions have been expanded or clarifying introductory notes have been supplied in italics. Modern terms have been substituted for archaic language, but to preserve the character of the original recipes and to create a true anthology, the authors' texts have been changed as little as possible.

Most of the recipes for pies, tarts, tartlets and turnovers are categorized according to their fillings. For easy reference, recipes for puff, chou, phyllo and strudel pastries are grouped separately—as are recipes for fried pastries and for fillings that can be used interchangeably in a variety of assemblies.

Recipes for standard preparations—basic pastry doughs and fondant icing, among them—appear at the end of the Anthology. Unfamiliar cooking terms and uncommon ingredients are explained in the combined General Index and Glossary.

Apart from the primary components—dough elements and any filling elements specifically mentioned in recipe titles—all ingredients are listed within each recipe in order of use, with both the customary United States measurements and the new metric measurements provided. The metric quantities reflect the American practice of measuring such solid ingredients as flour by volume rather than by weight, as in Europe.

To make the quantities simpler to measure, many of the figures have been rounded off to correspond to the gradations on metric spoons and cups. (One cup, for example, equals 237 milliliters; however, wherever practicable in these recipes, a cup's equivalent appears as a more readily measurable 250 milliliters—¼ liter.) Similarly, the weight, temperature and linear metric equivalents have been rounded off slightly. Thus the American and metric figures do not precisely match, but using one set or the other will produce the same good results.

Fruit Pies

Apple Tart

A *pâte sablée*—crumbly cookie-like pastry—is also the usual base for jam tarts, made by replacing the apples in this recipe with a thin layer of jam and pressing a decorative latticework of pastry strips on top. Any fairly thick puréed jam or fruit butter may replace the apricot jam as a glaze in this recipe—I usually use a wild-plum jam.

To make one 12-inch [30-cm.] tart

2 cups	flour	½ liter
3 tbsp.	sugar	45 ml.
4 tbsp.	butter, softened	60 ml.
	salt	
1	egg	1
4	medium-sized apples	4
	sugar	
	puréed apricot jam	

Combine the dough ingredients in a bowl, stirring and mashing with a fork until the dough is fairly smooth; then work it with your finger tips until it forms a coherent mass. Transfer the dough to a floured pastry marble or board, and knead it for a couple of minutes. Gather the dough together in a ball and begin again—it will, at this point, be soft and sticky; wrap it in plastic wrap or wax paper, and refrigerate it for at least a couple of hours.

Lightly butter a large baking sheet. Roll out the dough as rapidly as possible, being certain that it is always lightly coated with flour. Turn over the dough two or three times while rolling it into a circular sheet approximately 14 inches [35 cm.] in diameter.

Fold the sheet and transfer it to the baking sheet; then unfold the sheet. (The dough is extremely fragile; if it should tear, don't worry—patch it up.) Roll up the edges to form a border, pressing all around with the tines of a fork.

Halve the apples. Core and peel them. Slice each of the halves crosswise into ⅛- to ¼-inch [3- to 6-mm.] thicknesses and arrange the slices, starting just inside the border of the pastry, in concentric overlapping rings. Sprinkle with sugar and bake in a preheated 350° F. [180° C.] oven for about one hour, checking progress regularly after 45 minutes.

Using a pastry brush, paint the surface of the apple slices with the puréed jam, or simply dribble on the jam with a teaspoon, then smear it with the back of the spoon over the surface of each apple slice. Slip the tart onto a large flat, round platter. Serve hot, tepid or cold.

RICHARD OLNEY
SIMPLE FRENCH FOOD

Grandmother's Apple Tart

Tarte aux Pommes Grand-Mere

To make one 9-inch [23-cm.] tart

½ lb.	short-crust dough *(recipe, page 162)*	¼ kg.
1½ lb.	apples, peeled, cored and sliced	¾ kg.
3 to 4 tbsp.	sugar	45 to 60 ml.
1	egg	1
3 tbsp.	heavy cream	45 ml.
	kirsch	

Line a tart pan with the dough and arrange the apple slices on top. Sprinkle them with 2 to 3 tablespoons [30 to 45 ml.] of the sugar. Bake in a preheated 350° F. [180° C.] oven for 15 minutes, or until the pastry is firm but not brown.

Whisk together the egg, 1 tablespoon [15 ml.] of sugar, the cream and a few drops of kirsch. Pour this mixture over the apples and continue to bake the tart for 15 minutes, or until the cream mixture has set. Serve hot.

FELIX BENOIT AND HENRY CLOS JOUVE
LA CUISINE LYONNAISE

Upside-Down Apple Tart

Tarte des Demoiselles Tatin

To make one 8-inch [20-cm.] tart

½ lb.	short-crust dough *(recipe, page 162)*	¼ kg.
1 lb.	tart apples, peeled, cored and quartered	½ kg.
¼ cup	sugar	50 ml.
4 tbsp.	butter, melted	60 ml.

Thickly butter a 2-inch-deep [5-cm.] tart pan, preferably one of tinned copper, and sprinkle the bottom with a little of the sugar. Fill the pan with the apples. Sprinkle the top with the remaining sugar and pour in the melted butter. Cover the apples with the dough, rolled out ⅛ inch [3 mm.] thick.

Bake in a preheated 425° F. [220° C.] oven for about 30 minutes, or until the caramel syrup coating the apples looks golden brown when you tip the pan to check its color. Let the tart rest at room temperature for 30 minutes before serving. Then turn it upside down onto a serving plate so that the apples are on top. The tart can be eaten hot or cold.

CURNONSKY
RECETTES DES PROVINCES DE FRANCE

Apple Tart Mapie

Tarte aux Pommes Mapie

To make one 9-inch [23-cm.] tart

1	unbaked tart shell, made from ½ lb. [¼ kg.] short-crust dough (recipe, page 162)	1
2	apples, peeled, cored and diced	2
8 tbsp.	butter	120 ml.
1¼ cups	sugar	300 ml.
4	eggs	4
3 tbsp.	flour	45 ml.
	confectioners' sugar	

Heat the butter over low heat until it turns a light brown color. Place the sugar in a bowl and pour the butter over it, stirring well. Add the eggs, one by one, beating after each addition. Add the flour and mix well. Put the apples in the bottom of the tart shell and cover them with the egg mixture. Bake in a preheated 400° F. [200° C.] oven for 30 minutes, or until a knife inserted in the center comes out clean. Serve the tart warm or cold, sprinkled with confectioners' sugar.

MAPIE, THE COUNTESS DE TOULOUSE-LAUTREC
LA CUISINE DE FRANCE

Glazed Apple Tart

To prepare apple jelly for glazing the tart, cook the cores, seeds and peelings of the apples in enough water to cover them. When soft, drain the apple mixture through dampened muslin or a double layer of cheesecloth without pressing on the solids. Add an equal volume of sugar to the resulting apple juice and boil over medium heat until this jelly is syrupy.

To make one 10-inch [25-cm.] tart

2 cups	flour, sifted	½ liter
7 tbsp.	butter, softened and cut into small pieces	105 ml.
⅓ cup	sugar	75 ml.
	salt	
3 tbsp.	water	45 ml.
3	egg yolks	3
Apple filling		
6	apples, peeled, cored, and quartered or sliced	6
4 tbsp.	sugar	60 ml.
	apple jelly (optional)	

To make the dough, heap the flour on a board. Make a well in the center of the heap, and into this put the butter, the sugar,

a pinch of salt, the water and the egg yolks. Knead these ingredients together with your finger tips to make a smooth dough. Form the dough into a ball, cover it and let it rest for 20 minutes in the refrigerator.

Roll out the dough with a rolling pin and use it to line a flan ring placed on a baking sheet. Cut off the edges of the dough level with the top of the ring; crimp the edges. Fill this pastry shell with the apples. Sprinkle the top with 2 tablespoons [30 ml.] of the sugar and bake in a preheated 425° F. [220° C.] oven for 10 to 15 minutes. Then reduce the temperature to 375° F. [190° C.] and bake for a further 15 minutes, or until the edges of the pastry are golden and the apples are tender.

Serve the tart hot, sprinkled with the remaining sugar or glazed with an apple jelly made from the boiled peelings.

J. B. REBOUL
LA CUISINIÈRE PROVENÇALE

Apple Pie

To make one 9-inch [23-cm.] pie

1 lb.	short-crust dough (recipe, page 162)	½ kg.
2 lb.	tart apples, peeled, cored and sliced	1 kg.
1¼ to 1½ cups	sugar	300 to 375 ml.
⅛ tsp.	salt	½ ml.
¾ tsp.	ground cinnamon	4 ml.
½ tsp.	grated nutmeg	2 ml.
2 tbsp.	flour	30 ml.
½ tsp.	grated lemon peel	2 ml.
1 tbsp.	fresh lemon juice (optional)	15 ml.
1 to 2 tbsp.	butter	15 to 30 ml.

Line a piepan with two thirds of the dough. Cover the remaining dough with plastic wrap to keep it moist. In a large bowl, mix together the sugar, salt, cinnamon, nutmeg and flour. Add the sliced apples and mix well so that the apples are coated with the other ingredients. Place the apple slices in the piepan, laying slices first along the outside and then working toward the center until the bottom of the pastry shell is covered.

Continue layering the slices in the same way until the shell is filled up. Sprinkle the apples with the lemon peel and the juice, if desired, and dot with butter. Moisten the edge of the shell. Cover the pie with the remaining dough and trim the edge to ½ inch [1 cm.] larger than the piepan. Press the edges firmly together, flute, and then slash vents in the center of the top of the pie. Bake in a preheated 375° F. [190° C.] oven for 30 to 40 minutes, until the apples are tender and the crust is golden brown.

LETHA BOOTH
THE WILLIAMSBURG COOKBOOK

Apple or Fruit Turnovers

To make 6 turnovers

10 oz.	short-crust dough or puff-pastry dough *(recipes, pages 162 and 164)*	300 g.
⅔ cup	stewed apples or other fruit, or ½ cup [125 ml.] fruit jam	150 ml.
3 tbsp.	superfine sugar	45 ml.

Roll out the dough thin and cut it into 4-inch [10-cm.] rounds. Place the rounds on a floured baking sheet. Put a little of the fruit or jam in the center of each round. Carefully fold the round from three sides so that they meet in the center to form a triangle. Moisten the edges of the dough and pinch them tightly together to seal them. Brush the top of each pastry with a little water, then sprinkle the top with superfine sugar. Bake in a preheated 350° F. [180° C.] oven for about 35 minutes, or until lightly browned.

COUNTESS MORPHY
SWEETS AND PUDDINGS

Nona's Apple Pie

The author suggests that if the apples used are not tart, the sugar should be reduced to ⅔ cup [150 ml.], and 2 tablespoons [30 ml.] of lemon juice plus 1 teaspoon [5 ml.] of grated lemon peel should be sprinkled between the layers of apples.

To make one 9-inch [23-cm.] pie

1 lb.	short-crust dough *(recipe, page 162)*	½ kg.
5 or 6	medium-sized tart apples (about 2 lb. [1 kg.]), peeled, cored and quartered	5 or 6
5 tbsp.	butter	75 ml.
1 cup	sugar, white, brown or mixed	¼ liter
¼ cup	applejack, Calvados or other apple brandy	50 ml.
2 tbsp.	flour	30 ml.
1 tsp.	ground cinnamon	5 ml.
½ tsp.	grated nutmeg	2 ml.
1 or 2 tbsp.	fine dry bread crumbs	15 or 30 ml.

Cut each apple quarter into three slices. Heat the butter in a heavy frying pan. Stir in the sugar and cook, stirring, until melted. (If white sugar is used, cook until it turns golden.) Add the apple slices. Cook over medium heat, lifting the slices gently with a spatula, until all slices are coated with the sugar mixture and are one-quarter to one-half cooked. Cooking time depends on the apples, but do not overcook them since the pie will be baked later. Pour the brandy into a ladle, warm and ignite it, and pour it over the apples.

Roll out the dough and line a piepan with half of it. Mix the flour, cinnamon and nutmeg; set aside. Sprinkle the

bread crumbs over the bottom of the pie shell; this will keep it from getting soggy. Layer the apples in the pie shell, sprinkling the flour-spice mixture between the layers. Pour any apple syrup remaining in the frying pan over the apples. Cover the pie with the remaining rolled dough, crimping the edges by pinching them with your fingers or the tines of a fork, and make a few slits in the top to allow steam to escape while baking. Bake in a preheated 400° F. [200° C.] oven for about 30 minutes, or until the crust is golden brown. Do not overbake the already partially cooked apples.

NIKA HAZELTON
AMERICAN HOME COOKING

Sheet Pie Filled with Apples

Almás Pite

To make twelve 4-inch [10-cm.] squares

1¾ cups	flour	425 ml.
16 tbsp.	butter	240 ml.
¼ tbsp.	salt	4 ml.
¾ cup	confectioners' sugar	175 ml.
3	egg yolks	3
1 tbsp.	sour cream	15 ml.
Apple and walnut filling		
9	medium-sized, firm baking apple	9
2 oz.	walnuts, ground in a nut grinder, or in a food processor operated at short spurts	60 g.
2 tbsp.	flour	30 ml.
4 tbsp.	butter, melted	60 ml.
½ cup	vanilla sugar	125 ml.
¼ cup	raisins, soaked in warm water for 15 minutes and drained	50 ml.
1 tbsp.	fresh lemon juice	15 ml.

Mix together the butter and flour until the mixture forms crumbs. Then mix the salt and confectioners' sugar into it. Make a well in the center, put in two of the egg yolks and the sour cream; if the sour cream is very thick, add an extra teaspoon [5 ml.]. Knead the dough and chill it for one hour.

Divide the dough into two pieces, one slightly larger than the other. The larger piece will be used for the bottom crust and it must overlap the edges of the top crust slightly. Roll out each piece between two pieces of floured wax paper to make a thin sheet of dough.

To make the filling, first peel and core the apples, then grate them through the coarse holes of a box grater. Add the flour and melted butter, ground walnuts, vanilla sugar, raisins and lemon juice. Mix well with your hands.

Line a baking pan 12 by 8 inches [30 by 20 cm.] with the larger sheet of dough. Spread the apple mixture evenly on top of this bottom crust. Cover with the smaller sheet of dough, evening it out with your hand. Beat the remaining egg yolk with 1 teaspoon of water and spread this egg-yolk glaze over the top crust. Prick the top crust with a fork at intervals of 2 or 3 inches [5 or 8 cm.].

Bake in a preheated 375° F. [190° C.] oven for 45 minutes. When cool, cut the pie into 4-inch [10-cm.] squares.

GEORGE LANG
THE CUISINE OF HUNGARY

Apple, Apricot and Walnut Tart

La Tarte à la Bréalaise

To make the fruit purées for this recipe, each fruit—cores or pits removed—is first quartered and cooked with sugar to taste, until reduced to a thick pulp; then it is puréed through a sieve or food mill. The combined purées can be bound with a beaten egg. You may substitute ⅔ cup [150 ml.] of apricot jam for the apricot purée. For a demonstration of the turning technique required for the pastry, see pages 48-49. The techniques of shaping lattices are shown on pages 26-29.

To make two 7-inch [18-cm.] tarts

4 cups	flour, sifted	1 liter
2	eggs	2
25 tbsp.	butter (¾ lb. [⅓ kg.]), cut into small pieces and chilled	375 ml.
	salt	
1 tbsp.	sugar	15 ml.
¾ cup	cold milk	175 ml.

Apple, apricot and walnut filling

1¼ cups	apple purée	300 ml.
1¼ cups	apricot purée	300 ml.
6 to 8	walnuts, shelled and quartered	6 to 8

Heap the flour onto a board and make a well in the center. Put in the eggs, 8 tablespoons [120 ml.] of the butter, a pinch of salt and the sugar. Work together with your finger tips, gradually adding the milk to the dough as the flour is absorbed. Knead briefly, wrap the dough in plastic wrap and let it rest in the refrigerator for one hour. Roll out the dough and enclose the remaining butter in it as for puff pastry, then give the dough three turns. Refrigerate and allow it to rest again for one hour, then roll it out and use about two thirds of the dough to line two tart pans.

Meanwhile, in a saucepan, blend the apple purée and 1 cup [¼ liter] of the apricot purée. Cook over medium heat, stirring until the mixture holds its shape in a spoon.

Fill the tart shells with the fruit mixture. Crisscross the top of each tart with strips of the remaining rolled dough. Bake in a preheated 425° F. [220° C.] oven for about 30 minutes, turning the heat down to 375° F. [190° C.] after the first 10 minutes. The tarts are finished when the pastry is crisp and golden.

When the tarts are cold, place a walnut quarter in each of the spaces between the lattice strips. Cook the remaining apricot purée until it is reduced to a syrupy consistency and use it to glaze the tarts.

ÉDOUARD NIGNON
LES PLAISIRS DE LA TABLE

Apricot Pastry

Tort Morelowy Krakowski

To make one 4-layer, 8-inch [20-cm.] pastry

2 cups	flour, sifted	½ liter
14 tbsp.	butter	210 ml.
7 tbsp.	superfine sugar	105 ml.
3	egg yolks	3
1 tbsp.	vinegar	15 ml.

Apricot filling

1 cup	apricot jam, melted	¼ liter
5 tbsp.	sugar	75 ml.
5	egg whites, stiffly beaten	5

Apricot glaze

⅓ cup	apricot jam, sieved	75 ml.
1 cup	superfine sugar	250 ml.
1 tbsp.	fresh lemon juice	15 ml.
½ cup	halved or chopped blanched almonds (optional)	125 ml.

To make the dough, cut the butter into the sifted flour until the mixture is crumbly. Add the sugar, egg yolks and vinegar. Quickly work the mixture on a board and, when it forms a smooth dough, cover it and refrigerate for two hours.

Divide the dough into four parts, roll out each part very thin and fit each part into a separate round cake pan. Bake in a preheated 350° F. [180° C.] oven for 20 minutes, or until golden brown. Cool.

For the filling, gradually beat the sugar and then the warm melted jam into the beaten egg whites. Continue beating until the mixture is stiff and fluffy. Spread this filling between the rounds of pastry.

Mix all of the glaze ingredients until smoothly blended, then glaze the top of the pastry with this mixture. Decorate the top with the halved or chopped almonds.

Z. ZAWISTOWSKA
Z. NASZEJ KUCHNÍ

Banana Tart

Tarte aux Bananes

To make one 9-inch [23-cm.] tart

2½ cups	sifted cake flour	625 ml.
1 cup	sifted all-purpose flour	¼ liter
9 tbsp.	unsalted butter	135 ml.
¼ cup	sugar	50 ml.
1	egg	1
⅛ tsp.	salt	½ ml.

Banana filling

7	ripe bananas	7
6 tbsp.	sugar	90 ml.
4½ tbsp.	rum	67 ml.
⅔ cup	apricot jam, melted	150 ml.

Soften the butter over extremely low heat and stir in the sugar with a wooden spoon. The mixture should have a creamy consistency. Mix the flours well and heap them on a working surface. Fashion a well in the center and into it put the egg, the butter-sugar mixture and the salt. Work with your finger tips only long enough to blend the ingredients.

Roll out the mixture very carefully, because it is crumbly. Both the working surface and rolling pin must be well floured. Let the dough rest for 30 minutes.

Slice three of the bananas, and place them in a bowl with 2 tablespoons [30 ml.] of the sugar and 3 tablespoons [45 ml.] of the rum. Let the mixture stand for 10 minutes.

Roll out the dough and with it line a buttered tart pan. Prick the dough well with a fork. In another bowl, crush the remaining four bananas with a fork, and stir in the remaining rum and sugar. Mix well and spread the mixture in the tart shell. Over this arrange the sliced bananas in concentric circles. Cut a circle of parchment paper ¼ inch [6 mm.] smaller than the diameter of the pan and lightly place it over the banana slices. Bake the tart in a preheated 400° F. [200° C.] oven for 20 minutes, or until the pastry is golden brown.

As soon as the tart is baked, lift off the paper and paint the surface of the banana slices with melted apricot jam.

MAPIE, THE COUNTESS DE TOULOUSE-LAUTREC
LA CUISINE DE FRANCE

Sour-Cream Blackberry Pie

To make one 8-inch [20-cm.] pie

1	unbaked pie shell, made from ½ lb. [¼ kg.] short-crust dough(recipe, page 162)	1
1 cup	sour cream	¼ liter
3 cups	ripe blackberries	¾ liter
1 tbsp.	flour	15 ml.
½ cup	sugar	125 ml.
1 tbsp.	fresh lemon juice	15 ml.
	freshly grated nutmeg	

Mix together the sour cream, flour and sugar. Spread the blackberries in the pie shell, sprinkle the lemon juice over the blackberries and cover the berries with the sour-cream mixture. Grate a sprinkling of nutmeg over the top. Bake in a preheated 425° F. [220° C.] oven for 10 minutes, then reduce the heat to 325° F. [160° C.] and bake for 40 minutes, or until the berries are soft, juicy and bubbling.

MARILYN KLUGER
THE WILD FLAVOR

Stillmeadow Berry Pie

To make one 9-inch [23-cm.] pie

6	egg whites, at room temperature	6
¼ tsp.	salt	1 ml.
2 cups	sugar	½ liter
1 tsp.	vanilla extract	5 ml.
1 tbsp.	vinegar	15 ml.
about 2 cups	berries, sweetened and partially crushed	about ½ liter
	heavy cream, whipped	

Beat the egg whites with the salt until stiff. Add 1 cup [¼ liter] of the sugar gradually, beating constantly, then add the vanilla extract. Add the remaining cup of sugar bit by bit, alternating the piecemeal addition of this sugar with the vinegar—adding the vinegar ½ teaspoon [2 ml.] at a time.

Pile the meringue in a greased, lightly floured pie plate, preferably made of ovenproof glass, building up the center into a dome. Bake for one and a half hours in a preheated 275° F. [140° C.] oven. Increase the oven temperature to 300° F. [150° C.] and bake for 30 minutes more. As it bakes the meringue will puff up, then crack and fall in the center.

Cool the shell well, but do not refrigerate. Fill the hollow with the berries and top them with whipped cream.

GLADYS TABER
STILLMEADOW KITCHEN

Deep-Dish Blueberry Pie

To make one 8-inch [20-cm.] pie

½ lb.	short-crust dough (recipe, page 162)	¼ kg.
4 cups	blueberries	1 liter
1 cup	sugar	¼ liter
3 tbsp.	flour	45 ml.
1 tbsp.	fresh lemon juice	15 ml.
2 tbsp.	butter, cut into small pieces	30 ml.
	tart cream, whipped cream or vanilla ice cream (optional)	

In a deep pie dish, toss the berries with the sugar and flour. Sprinkle with the lemon juice and dot with the butter. Cover with the rolled dough. Bake in a preheated 400° F. [200° C.] oven for 10 minutes, then reduce the heat to 325° F. [160° C.] and continue baking for 15 to 20 minutes. Serve warm—either plain, with cream or with vanilla ice cream.

THE EDITORS OF AMERICAN HERITAGE
THE AMERICAN HERITAGE COOKBOOK

Latticed Blueberry Pie

The techniques of shaping lattices appear on pages 26-29.
When baking berry pies, it is wise to line the shelf below with foil to catch any overflow.

To make one 9-inch [23-cm.] pie

1 lb.	short-crust dough (recipe, page 162)	½ kg.
4 cups	blueberries	1 liter
¾ cup	sugar	175 ml.
¼ cup	flour	50 ml.
1 tsp.	grated lemon peel	5 ml.
2 tsp.	fresh lemon juice	10 ml.
1 tbsp.	gin (optional)	15 ml.
2 tbsp.	butter, cut into small pieces	30 ml.

Divide the dough into halves. Roll out one half. Line a deep piepan with the dough and trim off the edge of the dough about ½ inch [1 cm.] outside the rim of the pan. Fill the pie shell with the blueberries. Mix together the sugar and flour, and sprinkle them over the berries. Sprinkle the top with the lemon peel, lemon juice and gin, if used. Dot with the butter.

Roll out the remaining dough and cut it into ½-inch strips with a knife or a fluted pastry wheel. Moisten the edge of the shell with water. Crisscross the pastry strips over the blueberries to make a lattice pattern. Fold the ½-inch overhang around the shell over the ends of the strips. Press the edges together and flute them with your fingers or a fork.

Bake in a preheated 425° F. [220° C.] oven for 35 to 45 minutes, or until the crust is golden and the filling begins to bubble. Cool before serving.

NIKA HAZELTON
AMERICAN HOME COOKING

Fresh Deep-Dish Cherry Pie

The techniques of covering a deep-dish pie with dough are demonstrated on pages 24-25.

To make one 8-inch [20-cm.] pie

½ lb.	short-crust dough (recipe, page 162)	¼ kg.
4 cups	red sour cherries	1 liter
¾ cup	sugar	175 ml.
3 tbsp.	cornstarch	45 ml.
⅛ tsp.	salt	½ ml.
½ cup	water	125 ml.

Pit the cherries and combine them with the sugar, cornstarch, salt and water. Pour the mixture into a square baking dish. Cover with the rolled dough. Make slits in the dough. Bake in a preheated 425° F. [220° C.] oven for 40 to 45 minutes, or until the crust is brown.

MARGUERITE DODD
AMERICA'S COOK BOOK

Cherry Turnover

Pirogui aux Cerises Anglaises

To make one 8-inch [20-cm.] pastry

1 lb.	rich short-crust dough (recipe, page 162), made with 1 tsp. [5 ml.] grated lemon peel	½ kg.
1 to 1¼ lb.	sour pie cherries, pitted (about 3 cups [¾ liter])	½ to ⅔ kg.
1 cup	heavy cream	¼ liter
½ cup	superfine sugar	125 ml.

Roll out the dough and place it in a buttered piepan, allowing the sides of the dough to overhang the edge. Fill the lined pan with the cherries. Pour in the cream, then sprinkle the top with the sugar. Fold up the edges of the dough above the filling, sealing them where they peak in the center and trimming them to give the pastry a neat shape. Prick the top of the pastry in several places with a knife tip or fork.

Bake in a preheated 350° F. [180° C.] oven for 30 minutes, or until the pastry is lightly browned.

H. WITWICKA AND S. SOSKINE
LA CUISINE RUSSE CLASSIQUE

Alsatian Black-Cherry Tart

Tarte aux Cerises Noires à l'Alsacienne

To make one 9-inch [23-cm.] tart

1	unbaked tart shell, made from ½ lb. [¼ kg.] short-crust dough *(recipe, page 162)*	1
1 lb.	black cherries, pitted	½ kg.
4 tbsp.	unsalted butter, melted	60 ml.
½ cup	sugar	125 ml.
⅓ cup	ground almonds	75 ml.
4	eggs, the yolks separated from the whites	4
1 tsp.	ground cinnamon	5 ml.
3	soft dinner rolls, torn into small pieces, soaked in 1 cup [¼ liter] milk for 5 minutes and squeezed almost dry	3

Combine the butter with 6 tablespoons [90 ml.] of the sugar, the almonds, egg yolks and cinnamon. Mix well. Stir in the squeezed, soaked rolls.

Beat the egg whites and add the remaining sugar to keep them from falling. Gradually and gently fold the egg whites into the butter-almond mixture. Fold in the cherries.

Pour the filling into the pie shell and bake in a preheated 300° F. [150° C.] oven for 45 minutes.

MAPIE, THE COUNTESS DE TOULOUSE-LAUTREC
LA CUISINE DE FRANCE

Cherry and Strawberry Tart

Tarte Nouvelle

To make one 9-inch [23-cm.] tart

½ lb.	rich short-crust dough *(recipe, page 162)*	¼ kg.
½ lb.	cherries, pitted (about 1½ cups [375 ml.])	¼ kg.
½ lb.	strawberries, hulled (about 2 cups [½ liter])	¼ kg.
¼ cup	sugar	50 ml.
½ cup	water	125 ml.
¼ cup	kirsch	50 ml.
2 cups	pastry cream *(recipe, page 166)*	½ liter
½ cup	raspberry jelly, melted	125 ml.

Dissolve the sugar in the water. Bring this syrup to a simmer and gently poach the cherries in it for about 10 minutes.

Drain them. Sprinkle the strawberries with the kirsch and allow them to macerate for about 30 minutes.

Roll out the dough and use it to line a buttered tart pan. Cover the dough with a piece of parchment paper and weigh down the shell with dried beans. Bake the tart shell in a preheated 400° F. [200° C.] oven for 30 minutes. Remove the beans and paper, and let the shell cool.

Fill the cooled shell with the pastry cream. Cover the cream with alternating rings of cherries and strawberries. Glaze the tart with the melted raspberry jelly.

MADAME ELISABETH
500 NOUVELLES RECETTES DE CUISINE

Cherry Pie à la Fulton's Farm

The techniques of shaping lattices appear on pages 26-29.

To make one 9-inch [23-cm.] pie

2 cups	flour	½ liter
½ tsp.	salt	2 ml.
1 tsp.	baking powder	5 ml.
⅔ cup	vegetable shortening	150 ml.
6 to 8 tbsp.	ice water	90 to 120 ml.
Cherry filling		
2 quarts	cherries, pitted	2 liters
1½ cups	sugar	375 ml.
3 tbsp.	flour	45 ml.

Sift together the flour, salt and baking powder. Rub in the shortening, using a fork or pastry blender. When the mixture is thoroughly blended, add just enough ice water—a little at a time—to make a stiff dough. Turn the ball of dough onto a floured board and roll lightly until about ⅛ inch [3 mm.] thick. Line the pan with the dough, trim off the edges and save them to roll out again.

For the filling, mix together the sugar and flour. Add the mixture to the pitted cherries. Mix with a fork and then fill the pie shell with the fruit.

Roll out the scraps of dough ⅛ inch thick. Cut the dough into strips ½ inch [1 cm.] wide, and place the strips crisscross over the pie, pinching the edges of the strips into the dough at the edges of the pie. Bake in a preheated 450° F. [220° C.] oven for 20 minutes, then reduce the heat to 350° F. [180° C.] and bake for 20 minutes longer.

CLAIRE SUGDEN
THE ROMANTIC AND PRACTICAL SIDE OF COOKERY

Cantaloupe Tart

Tarte au Melon

Although this dessert must be well chilled before serving, it must be eaten the same day it is prepared; otherwise the tart shell will become soggy and the melon balls will become soft. For the techniques of fully baking an empty tart shell, see the demonstration on pages 42-43.

To serve 4		
1¾ cups	flour	425 ml.
6 tbsp.	butter, cut into small pieces and softened	90 ml.
½ cup	sugar	125 ml.
¼ tsp.	salt	1 ml.
4	egg yolks	4
2 tbsp.	water	30 ml.
Cantaloupe filling		
3	cantaloupes, about 1⅓ lb. [700 g.] each, 2 quartered, seeded and the pulp removed, 1 halved and seeded	3
2 tsp.	fresh lemon juice	10 ml.
2 tbsp.	sugar	30 ml.
2 tbsp.	unflavored powdered gelatin, dissolved in ¾ cup [175 ml.] cold water	30 ml.

Place the flour in a bowl and make a well in the center. Mix the softened pieces of butter with the sugar and salt. Cut the butter mixture into the flour. Add the egg yolks, two at a time, thinning each addition with 1 tablespoon [15 ml.] of the water. Gradually work the flour into the egg yolks and butter. When you are satisfied that they are sufficiently blended, knead the dough twice. Wrap the dough in a plastic bag and, before using, chill it well in the refrigerator.

Prepare the tart shell and bake it completely. Cool.

Using a melon-ball cutter, form 24 (or more) balls from the halved melon and refrigerate them to use later for decoration. Remove the remaining pulp, avoiding any rind, and pass the pulp through a food mill or sieve into a bowl. Add the lemon juice and chill the purée.

Put the pulp from the two quartered melons, with the sugar, in a heavy casserole. Stirring frequently with a wooden spoon, cook the mixture until most of the water evaporates (about 30 minutes). Then add the softened gelatin and make sure that it is thoroughly dissolved. Remove the casserole from the stove and, when the mixture has cooled, add the uncooked melon purée.

Cover the bottom of the baked tart shell with the melon mixture and chill it for at least two hours in the refrigerator. Before serving, decorate with the ice-cold melon balls.

JEAN & PIERRE TROISGROS
THE NOUVELLE CUISINE OF JEAN & PIERRE TROISGROS

Cranberry Pie

To make one 9-inch [23-cm.] pie		
1 lb.	short-crust dough (recipe, page 162)	½ kg.
2 cups	cranberries	½ liter
½ cup	molasses	125 ml.
¼ cup	sugar	50 ml.

Line a piepan with half of the dough, then fill it with the cranberries; add the molasses and sugar. Cover with an upper crust made from the remaining dough and bake in a preheated 400° F. [200° C.] oven for 30 minutes.

MRS. GRACE TOWNSEND
IMPERIAL COOK BOOK

Eccles Cakes

The original version of this recipe, from Eccles in Lancashire, England, dates from 1904.

To make about 12 cakes		
½ lb.	short-crust dough (recipe, page 162), made with lard	¼ kg.
1 cup	dried currants, soaked in warm water for 15 minutes and drained	¼ liter
¼ cup	finely chopped mixed candied fruit peel	50 ml.
½ tsp.	mixed ground allspice and grated nutmeg	2 ml.
¼ cup	granulated sugar	50 ml.
2 tbsp.	butter	30 ml.
	superfine sugar	

Put the currants, candied peel, spices, granulated sugar and butter into a pan. Heat for a few minutes, stirring to blend, then turn the mixture into a bowl to cool.

Roll out the dough about ¼ inch [6 mm.] thick. Cut the dough into 6-inch [15-cm.] rounds. Place a good tablespoonful [15 ml.] of the filling on each round. Gather up the edges all around, and fold them toward the center. Press with the rolling pin into flat cakes; make a hole in the center of the top crust of each cake.

Place the cakes on a baking sheet and bake in a preheated 425° F. [220° C.] oven for 10 to 15 minutes, or until lightly browned. Sprinkle the superfine sugar over the cakes when they are cooked.

FLORENCE WHITE (EDITOR)
GOOD THINGS IN ENGLAND

Gooseberry Meringue Tart

To make one 8-inch [20-cm.] pie

½ lb.	short-crust dough (recipe, page 162)	¼ kg.
5 cups	gooseberries, topped and tailed	1¼ liters
2	egg yolks, beaten	2
4 tbsp.	butter, cut into small pieces	60 ml.
2 tbsp.	fresh bread crumbs	30 ml.
	sugar	
1	egg white, lightly beaten with 1 tsp. [5 ml.] sugar	1

Meringue

2	egg whites, stiffly beaten	2
4 tbsp.	sugar	60 ml.

Place the gooseberries in an ovenproof container, cover, set in a preheated 300° F. [150° C.] oven for 30 minutes or until quite soft, then rub the berries through a sieve into a bowl. Add the egg yolks, butter, bread crumbs and sugar to taste.

Line a piepan around the sides and rims (not on the bottom) with the dough and glaze the edges with the egg-white-and-sugar mixture. Put in the gooseberries. Bake in a preheated 350° F. [180° C.] oven until the pastry is lightly browned, about 45 minutes. For the meringue, beat the sugar into the egg whites. Spread it over the gooseberries, return to the oven for 10 minutes, or until just set, and serve.

MAY BYRON
PUDDINGS, PASTRIES, AND SWEET DISHES

Fresh Fig Pie

To make one 9-inch [23-cm.] pie

1	9-inch graham-cracker pie shell (recipe, page 165)	1
2 cups	diced but unpeeled ripe figs	½ liter
2 tbsp.	unflavored powdered gelatin	30 ml.
¼ cup	water	50 ml.
2	eggs, the yolks separated from the whites	2
6 tbsp.	sugar	90 ml.
⅛ tsp.	salt	½ ml.
¾ cup	milk	175 ml.
1 tbsp.	grated orange peel	15 ml.
2 tbsp.	orange liqueur	30 ml.
½ cup	heavy cream, whipped	125 ml.

Sprinkle the gelatin on the water and stir to blend. Beat the egg yolks with 4 tablespoons [60 ml.] of the sugar and the salt. Scald the milk in a heavy saucepan or the top of a double boiler. Add 2 tablespoons [30 ml.] of the scalded milk to the egg yolks and blend; then stir the egg mixture into the remaining scalded milk and blend thoroughly. Cook over very low heat or over hot water, stirring constantly, until the mixture thickens and coats a spoon. Add the gelatin and stir until it is dissolved. Remove from the heat, and stir in the orange peel and orange liqueur. Cool the custard until it has the consistency of thick egg whites, or until it begins to jell. Beat the egg whites with the remaining 2 tablespoons of sugar until stiff. Fold the figs, whipped cream and egg whites into the cooled custard. Turn the mixture into the pie shell and refrigerate until set.

NIKA HAZELTON
AMERICAN HOME COOKING

Lemon-Lime Sky-High Pie

To make one 9-inch [23-cm.] pie

1	fully baked pie shell, made from ½ lb. [¼ kg.] short-crust dough (recipe, page 162)	1
⅓ cup	fresh lemon juice	75 ml.
⅓ cup	fresh lime juice	75 ml.
1 tsp.	grated lemon peel	5 ml.
1 tsp.	grated lime peel	5 ml.
1 tbsp.	unflavored powdered gelatin	15 ml.
1¼ cups	sugar	300 ml.
¼ tsp.	salt	1 ml.
6	eggs, the yolks separated from the whites	6
⅓ cup	water	75 ml.
½ tsp.	cream of tartar	2 ml.
	whipped cream	
	lime peel	

In the top of a double boiler mix together the gelatin, ½ cup [125 ml.] of the sugar and the salt. Beat the egg yolks with the water, lemon and lime juices. Stir the egg mixture into the gelatin mixture. Place the pan over boiling water and cook, stirring constantly, until the gelatin dissolves and the mixture thickens slightly, about six minutes. Add the lemon and lime peels. Cool, stirring constantly, until the mixture mounds lightly when dropped from a spoon.

Beat the egg whites with the cream of tartar until stiff. Fold in the gelatin mixture. If necessary, chill until the filling will mound firmly. Turn the filling into the pie shell, piling it high in the center. Chill until firm: several hours or overnight. Before serving, garnish with whipped cream and a twist of lime peel.

GLENN MC CULLOUGH (EDITOR)
GEORGIA RECEIPTS

Angie Earl's Lemon Pie

The techniques of baking blind tartlet shells are demonstrated on pages 42-43.

To make twelve 2 ½-inch [6-cm.] tartlets

2 cups	flour, sifted	½ liter
1 tsp.	salt	5 ml.
1 tsp.	sugar	5 ml.
¾ cup	lard, chilled	175 ml.
2 tsp.	butter, chilled	10 ml.
about ½ cup	ice water	about 125 ml.

Lemon filling

¼ tsp.	lemon extract	1 ml.
½ cup	fresh lemon juice	125 ml.
3	eggs, the yolks separated from the whites	3
1 ½ cups	sugar	375 ml.
1 ½ cups	water	375 ml.
1 ½ tsp.	butter	7 ml.
⅛ tsp.	salt	½ ml.
¼ cup	cornstarch, dissolved in ½ cup [125 ml.] water	50 ml.
	whipped cream	

To prepare the dough, sift together the flour, salt and sugar. With your finger tips, break the lard into ½-inch [1-cm.] bits and add them to the flour. Then break in the butter, making the pieces half the size of the lard bits. With a knife, cut in the ice water, adding only a little at a time. When the dough forms into a ball, turn it onto a floured board and knead just enough to have a smooth dough. Wrap the dough in wax paper and allow the dough to stand in the refrigerator overnight or longer.

Roll out the dough. Use it to cover the backs of 12 tartlet tins. Bake the shells in a preheated 375° F. [190° C.] oven for 15 to 20 minutes.

First beat the egg yolks until they are lemon-colored and frothy. In a separate bowl, beat the egg whites with ½ cup [125 ml.] of the sugar and the lemon extract. Combine the lemon juice, water, the remaining 1 cup [¼ liter] of sugar, the butter and salt, and bring to a boil. Stir the dissolved cornstarch into the boiling mixture. Cook for two minutes. Beating constantly, pour part of the lemon mixture slowly over the egg yolks, then add the yolks to the lemon mixture. Take the mixture from the stove immediately and fold it into the stiffly beaten egg whites. When the lemon mixture is cool, fill the tartlet shells and top them with whipped cream.

MARIAN TRACY
FAVORITE AMERICAN REGIONAL RECIPES

Key Lime Pie

Key limes, introduced to the Florida Keys in 1838 from Mexico, are a distinctively sweet variety with a thin skin and a greenish yellow flesh.

To make one 8-inch [20-cm.] pie

1	partially baked pie shell, made from ½ lb. [¼ kg.] short-crust dough (recipe, page 162)	1
¼ cup	Key lime juice	50 ml.
4	eggs, the yolks separated from the whites	4
14 oz.	sweetened condensed milk	420 ml.
¼ cup	sugar	50 ml.

Beat the egg yolks. Add the condensed milk and mix well. Slowly add the lime juice and beat until the filling mixture resembles custard. Pour the filling into the pie shell. Bake in a preheated 350° F. [180° C.] oven for 10 to 15 minutes, or until the filling is firm. Allow to cool. Beat the egg whites until stiff, adding the sugar gradually while beating. Put this meringue on top of the pie. Increase the oven temperature to 450° F. [230° C.] and bake until golden brown on top, about 10 minutes.

THE JUNIOR LEAGUE OF GAINESVILLE, FLORIDA
GATOR COUNTY COOKS

Pear Cream Pie

Picanchagne

To make one 9-inch [23-cm.] pie

1 lb.	short-crust dough (recipe, page 162)	½ kg.
1 ½ lb.	pears, peeled, cored and sliced	¾ kg.
½ cup	sugar	125 ml.
2 ¼ cups	heavy cream or tart cream (recipe, page 166)	550 ml.
¼ tsp.	freshly ground pepper (optional)	1 ml.
1	egg yolk, lightly beaten	1

Roll out the dough to a thickness of ⅛ inch [3 mm.] and use two thirds of it to line a piepan. Mix the pear slices with the sugar and cream, and add the pepper, if desired. Fill the pie shell with this mixture and cover with the remaining rolled dough. Glaze with the egg yolk and make a small hole in the middle for the steam to escape during cooking. Bake in a preheated 350° F. [180° C.] oven for about 50 minutes, or until the top is browned.

LES DESSERTS DE NOS PROVINCES

Orange and Anise Tart

Millas

To make one 9-inch [23-cm.] tart

1	partially baked tart shell, made from ½ lb. [¼ kg.] short-crust dough (recipe, page 162)	1
2 tsp.	orange-flower water	10 ml.
2 tsp.	anisette	10 ml.
4	egg yolks	4
½ cup	sugar	125 ml.
8 tbsp.	butter, softened	120 ml.
⅓ cup	sifted flour	75 ml.
½ tsp.	salt	2 ml.
1	whole egg, lightly beaten	1
2 cups	milk	½ liter

Beat together the egg yolks and the sugar until the mixture is very thick and white. Then beat in the softened butter, the flour, salt and whole egg. Flavor the mixture with the orange-flower water and anisette. Beating constantly, gradually add the milk. Pour this custard into the tart shell. Bake on the lowest shelf of a preheated 325° F. [160° C.] oven for about 30 minutes, or until the custard is set.

RAYMOND OLIVER
LA CUISINE

Marmalade Pie

The techniques of shaping lattices appear on pages 26-29.

This pie may be served plain, or with a topping made by whipping 1 cup [¼ liter] of heavy cream with 2 tablespoons [30 ml.] of confectioners' sugar and 2 teaspoons [10 ml.] of grated orange peel.

To make one 9-inch [23-cm.] pie

1 lb.	short-crust dough (recipe, page 162)	½ kg.
2	medium-sized oranges	2
1¼ cups	sugar	300 ml.
1 tbsp.	fresh lemon juice	15 ml.
½ cup plus 1 tsp.	water	130 ml.
2½ tbsp.	cornstarch	37 ml.
4 tbsp.	butter, softened	60 ml.
3	eggs	3
2 tbsp.	orange liqueur	30 ml.

Wash and dry the oranges. Peel off the paper-thin, outer layer of the skin with a vegetable peeler and chop it very fine. Separate the oranges into sections, cutting between the membranes. Put the orange sections in a saucepan and squeeze any extra juice that remains in the membranes into the pan. Discard the membranes.

Add the chopped peel, ¼ cup [50 ml.] of the sugar, the lemon juice and ½ cup [125 ml.] of the water to the saucepan. Bring to a boil and boil gently for 15 minutes, uncovered. Cool the orange mixture to room temperature.

Mix the remaining sugar with the cornstarch in a bowl. Add the butter and beat until smooth and fluffy. Beat in the eggs, one at a time, reserving 1 teaspoon [5 ml.] of yolk.

Fold in the cooled marmalade mixture and the orange liqueur. Pour the filling into a piepan lined with dough. Roll the remaining dough into strips and arrange the strips in a lattice pattern over the top. Combine the reserved spoonful of egg yolk with the remaining teaspoon of water and brush the mixture over the pastry.

Bake in a preheated 425° F. [220° C.] oven for 10 minutes. Reduce the oven temperature to 350° F. [180° C.]; bake for 30 to 40 minutes longer, or until the pie is set. Cool.

JEAN HEWITT
THE NEW YORK TIMES LARGE TYPE COOKBOOK

Marsala Peach Pie

To make one 9-inch [23-cm.] pie

1	fully baked pie shell, made from ½ lb. [¼ kg.] short-crust dough (recipe, page 162)	1
¼ cup	Marsala	50 ml.
7 cups	peach slices, made from 6 to 8 large, very ripe freestone peaches, peeled, halved, pitted and sliced	1¾ liters
½ cup plus 1 tbsp.	sugar	140 ml.
2 tbsp.	cornstarch	30 ml.
1 tsp.	unflavored powdered gelatin	5 ml.
½ cup	fresh orange juice	125 ml.
½ cup	water	125 ml.
1 cup	heavy cream, whipped	¼ liter

In a small, heavy saucepan blend all but 1 tablespoon [15 ml.] of the sugar with the cornstarch and gelatin, pressing out any lumps. Stir in the orange juice and water, set over medium heat, and cook and stir until the mixture bubbles—three minutes. Remove from the heat and chill until the mixture becomes very syrupy.

Meanwhile, mix the peaches with the remaining tablespoon of sugar and the Marsala wine, and allow them to marinate until the gelatin mixture has thickened. Combine the peaches with the gelatin mixture, cover, and chill until the gelatin is almost set.

Spoon the filling into the baked pie shell and chill until the filling is set. Just before serving, frost the top with the whipped cream.

JEAN ANDERSON
THE GRASS ROOTS COOKBOOK

Orange and Apple Pie

The techniques of baking a blind pie shell are demonstrated on pages 40-41.

To make one 9-inch [23-cm.] pie

1 lb.	short-crust dough (recipe, page 162)	½ kg.
5	juice oranges, unpeeled but thinly sliced and seeds discarded	5
4	apples, peeled, cored and sliced	4
3 cups	water	¾ liter
1 cup	honey	¼ liter
1 tbsp.	strained fresh lemon juice	15 ml.
½ cup	brown sugar	125 ml.
⅛ tsp.	salt	½ ml.
¼ tsp.	ground cinnamon	1 ml.
⅛ tsp.	ground ginger	½ ml.
2 tbsp.	confectioners' sugar, dissolved in 1 tbsp. [15 ml.] rose water	30 ml.

Roll out two thirds of the dough and use it to line a 9-inch [23-cm.] piepan. Partially bake the blind pie shell and allow the shell to cool.

Combine the water, honey and lemon juice in a large saucepan. Bring to a boil and add the orange slices. Cover, reduce the heat and simmer for about two hours, or until the peel is limp and tender. Drain the orange slices and set them aside. In a bowl, combine the brown sugar, salt and spices. Add the apple slices and toss until they are evenly coated.

Place a layer of apple slices in the pie shell, then a layer of orange slices. Repeat these layers with the remaining fruit. Roll out the remaining dough and use it to cover the pie. Slash the lid in a few places to let steam escape. Paint the lid with the sugar-and-rose-water mixture. Bake for one hour at 350° F. [180° C.].

LORNA SASS
TO THE QUEEN'S TASTE

Orange Tart

La Tarte à l'Orange

To make one 10-inch [25-cm.] tart

½ lb.	short-crust dough (recipe, page 162)	¼ kg.
4	oranges, unpeeled but sliced thin and seeded	4
1 cup	apricot jam, melted	¼ liter
¼ cup	superfine sugar (optional)	50 ml.
2	egg whites, stiffly beaten (optional)	2

Butter a tart pan and line it with the rolled dough. With a brush, coat the pastry shell with some of the melted jam. Arrange the orange slices in the shell, overlapping them. Spread them with the remaining jam. Bake in a preheated 425° F. [220° C.] oven for 20 to 25 minutes, or until the edges of the pastry are golden brown.

If you wish, you may cover the tart with meringue: Sprinkle the sugar onto the egg whites and beat again until they are very stiff and glossy. Spread this meringue on the tart, and return it to the oven—the heat reduced to 325° F. [170° C.]—until the meringue is puffed and lightly browned, about 10 minutes.

JOSÉPHINE BESSON
LA MÈRE BESSON "MA CUISINE PROVENÇALE"

Green Mango Pie

The techniques of shaping lattices are shown on pages 26-29.

This recipe makes a very tart pie; for one less acid, use mangoes that are only partially ripe. Also, a filling consisting of half apples and half green mangoes makes an interesting flavor combination.

To make one 9-inch [23-cm.] pie

1 lb.	short-crust dough (recipe, page 162)	½ kg.
3 or 4	large green mangoes, peeled, halved, pitted and thinly sliced	3 or 4
2 cups	sugar	½ liter
1 tsp.	ground nutmeg	5 ml.
4 tbsp.	butter, cut into small bits	60 ml.

Roll out the dough and use half of it to line a pie plate. Fill the pie shell with the green mango slices. Mix together the sugar and nutmeg; spread over the mango slices. Dot the top with the butter. Top the mango slices with a solid or lattice-type crust; if using a solid-crust top, make several small slits in it to let the steam escape.

Bake for 15 minutes in a preheated 425° F. [220° C.] oven. Reduce the temperature to 350° F. [180° C.] and bake for 45 minutes longer.

MARIAN TRACY
FAVORITE AMERICAN REGIONAL RECIPES

Pear Upside-Down Tart

Tarte aux Poires Renversée

The receptacle chosen to serve as a pie dish should be of a heavy material and able to support direct heat. It should be fairly deep in order to contain a sufficient quantity of wine during the first part of the cooking process. A frying pan with an ovenproof handle is perfect if your oven is large enough to accommodate the handle; a round enameled iron-ware gratin dish will serve equally well.

The tart may be served hot, tepid or cold, but should, in any case, be unmolded only just before serving to prevent the pastry's being soaked in the cooking juices.

To make one 10-inch [25-cm.] tart

½ lb.	short-crust dough *(recipe, page 162)*	¼ kg.
7	firm, slightly underripe pears, halved, cored and peeled	7
½ cup	sugar	125 ml.
½ tsp.	ground cinnamon	2 ml.
2½ cups	red wine	625 ml.

Lay the pear halves in the pan chosen for baking the tart, arranging them with cored surfaces facing upward, the wide ends of each half pressed against the side of the pan, and the tips pointing in toward the center so that the ungarnished areas form a fairly symmetrical star shape. Split the remaining pear halves and fill the empty spaces, tips pointing out, ends meeting in the center so that, when unmolded, the body of pears will form a neat geometric pattern.

Sprinkle the sugar and cinnamon over the pears, pour in enough red wine to cover them, bring to a boil, cover, and cook at a simmer for an hour or so, or until the pears are tender — lending no resistance to the tip of a sharp knife, but still firmly intact. Drain all of the liquid into a saucepan, holding the lid firmly against the pears' surface so as not to displace them. Reduce the cooking liquid over high heat, stirring from time to time, until only about ½ cup [125 ml.] of syrupy liquid remains. Dribble this syrup over the pears.

Roll out a round of dough to the exact dimensions of the pan or slightly larger; prick the dough four or five times with a knife tip; roll up the edges and crimp them either with the floured side of your thumb or with fork tines. Gently lay the pastry upside down over the pears. Bake in a preheated 375° to 400° F. [190° to 200° C.] oven for about 40 minutes, or until the pastry is golden and crisp.

Unmold with care. If you have used a frying pan, the handle will keep the tart from being unmolded onto the center of the platter: Place the platter upside down over the pan, its edge pressed to the handle's point of attachment, then turn everything over and ease the tart into the middle of the platter. The pears often spread slightly in the unmolding — push them gently back into place, pressing all around the outside with the back of a tablespoon or a spatula.

RICHARD OLNEY
SIMPLE FRENCH FOOD

Indiana Persimmon Pie

Sometimes I add a tablespoon [15 ml.] of orange juice to the pie filling and garnish with candied orange peel.

To make one 8-inch [20-cm.] pie

1	fully baked pie shell or 4 tartlet shells, made from ½ lb. [¼ kg.] short-crust dough *(recipe, page 162)*	1
2 cups	persimmon pulp	½ liter
5 tbsp.	confectioners' sugar	75 ml.
1 cup	heavy cream, whipped	¼ liter
	ground cinnamon	

Blend 2 tablespoons [30 ml.] of the confectioners' sugar into the whipped cream. In a bowl, combine the persimmon pulp with the remaining confectioners' sugar. Fold in half of the whipped cream. Turn the filling into a baked pastry shell or into four baked tartlet shells. Spread the remaining whipped cream over the top of the pie and sprinkle lightly with cinnamon. Chill thoroughly before serving.

MARILYN KLUGER
THE WILD FLAVOR

Plum Pie

Zwetschkeweihe

To make one 8- or 9-inch [20- or 23-cm.] pie

½ lb.	short-crust dough *(recipe, page 162)*	¼ kg.
1½ lb.	small blue plums	¾ kg.
1	egg	1
½ cup	heavy cream	125 ml.
	salt	
¼ cup	sugar	50 ml.
1 tsp.	grated lemon peel	5 ml.

Roll out the dough and fit it into a pie plate. Halve the plums and discard the pits. Arrange the plum halves in concentric circles on the pastry. Bake on the bottom shelf of a preheated 400° F. [200° C.] oven for 20 minutes. Beat together the egg, cream, a pinch of salt, the sugar and lemon peel. Pour the mixture over the plums. Reduce the oven temperature to 350° F. [180° C.] and continue baking for another 20 minutes. Let cool. Serve in the pie plate.

MADELEINE KAMMAN
THE MAKING OF A COOK

Damson Pie

To make eight 3-inch [8-cm.] tartlets

8	unbaked tartlet shells, made from 1 lb. [½ kg.] short-crust dough *(recipe, page 162)*	8
1 cup	damson plum preserves	¼ liter
5	eggs, the yolks separated from the whites, and the whites stiffly beaten	5
1½ cups	sugar	375 ml.
½ cup	butter, softened	125 ml.
1 tbsp.	flour	15 ml.
⅛ tsp.	salt	½ ml.
	whipped cream (optional)	

Beat the egg yolks until light. While beating, slowly add ¾ cup [175 ml.] of the sugar. Beat the other ¾ cup of sugar into the softened butter. Combine the two mixtures and add the flour and salt to them. Now add the preserves. Last, fold in the beaten egg whites. Spoon into the tartlet shells. Bake the tartlets in a preheated 350° F. [180° C.] oven for about 30 minutes or until set. Rich as it is, damson pie is sometimes served with a topping of whipped cream.

MARIAN TRACY
FAVORITE AMERICAN REGIONAL RECIPES

Prune Tart

La Tarte aux Pruneaux à la Crème

To make one 12-inch [30-cm.] tart

1	fully baked tart shell, made from 1 lb. [½ kg.] rich short-crust dough *(recipe, page 162)*	1
1 lb.	pitted, dried prunes	½ kg.
½ cup	sugar	125 ml.
1	vanilla bean	1
1¼ cups	water	300 ml.
2½ cups	pastry cream *(recipe, page 166)*	625 ml.
¾ cup	blanched almonds, halved	175 ml.

Make a syrup by boiling the sugar and the vanilla bean in the water for about five minutes. Over low heat, poach the prunes in this syrup for 30 minutes, or until they are plump and tender. Drain the prunes. Remove the vanilla bean from the syrup, and cook the syrup until it is thick and reduced by at least half.

Fill the pastry shell with the pastry cream. Arrange the prunes on the cream and put an almond half on top of each prune. Glaze the tart with the reduced syrup.

ÉDOUARD NIGNON
LES PLAISIRS DE LA TABLE

Stewed Prune Tart

Aleanentorte aus Wisch

To make one 9-inch [23-cm.] tart

2 cups	flour, sifted	½ liter
8 tbsp.	butter	125 ml.
¼ cup	sugar	50 ml.
1	egg yolk	1
	salt	
1 tbsp.	rum	15 ml.

Prune-cream filling

1½ lb.	pitted, dried prunes (about 6 cups [1½ liters])	¾ kg.
2 cups	milk	½ liter
¾ cup	sugar	200 ml.
9	eggs, the yolks separated from the whites, the yolks lightly beaten, and the whites stiffly beaten	9
3 tbsp.	strained fresh lemon juice	45 ml.
2 tsp.	freshly grated lemon peel	10 ml.
½ cup	heavy cream, whipped	100 ml.

Put the flour onto a board and make a well in the center. Put the butter, sugar, egg yolk, a pinch of salt and the rum into the well. Blend the mixture together with your finger tips to make a smooth dough. Form the dough into a ball, wrap, refrigerate and let it rest for 30 minutes.

Put the prunes into a saucepan with 2 cups [½ liter] of water and simmer gently for 30 minutes, or until they are soft. Let them cool.

Meanwhile, roll out the dough and fit it into a springform pan; bake in a preheated 350° F. [180° C.] oven for 20 minutes or until golden. Strain the prunes, cut them into quarters and arrange them in the tart.

Bring the milk to a boil. Remove it from the heat and stir in the sugar. Cool slightly, then stir in the beaten egg yolks. Bring slowly to a boil, stirring constantly and taking care that the yolks do not curdle. Allow the mixture to cool to room temperature. Fold in the lemon juice and peel, and the beaten egg whites.

Pour the mixture onto the prunes and bake in a preheated 400° F. [200° C.] oven for about 40 minutes, or just until the topping is set and brown. Cool the tart completely before removing the sides of the pan. Before serving, decorate the top with whipped cream.

JUTTA KÜRTZ
DAS KOCHBUCH AUS SCHLESWIG-HOLSTEIN

Prune Pastry

Galette Béarnaise

To make one 10-inch [25-cm.] pastry

2 cups	flour, sifted	½ liter
2 tsp.	orange-flower water	10 ml.
1	egg	1
½ tsp.	salt	2 ml.
1 tsp.	Cognac or fruit brandy	5 ml.
10 tbsp.	butter, cut into small pieces	150 ml.

Prune filling

1½ cups	dried prunes	375 ml.
2 cups	cold water	2 liters
½ cup	sugar	125 ml.
2 tbsp.	butter	30 ml.

Put the prunes in a saucepan with 2 cups [½ liter] of cold water and 5 tablespoons [75 ml.] of the sugar. Bring slowly to a boil and cook over low heat for 20 to 25 minutes, or until the prunes are very tender. Drain the prunes, cut them in half and pit them.

To make the dough, pour the flour onto a pastry board and make a well in the center. Put in the orange-flower water, egg, salt, Cognac or fruit brandy, and the pieces of butter. Work all of the ingredients together with your hands until a smooth dough is formed. Roll out the dough, fold it in quarters and roll it out again as thin as possible.

Cut a round of dough just big enough to line the bottom and sides of a tart pan. Butter the pan and line it with the dough. Scatter some of the prune halves in the pie shell and cover the prunes with another thin round of dough. Continue alternating layers of prunes and dough until the pan is full.

Finish with a layer of dough and seal it to the bottom crust by moistening the edges. Sprinkle the top with the remaining sugar, dot with the butter, and bake in a preheated 325° F. [170° C.] oven for one hour, or until golden brown.

LES DESSERTS DE NOS PROVINCES

Mixed Fruit Turnovers

For a crunchy filling, you may add ⅔ cup [150 ml.] of chopped nuts—walnuts, pecans or almonds—to the dried fruit mixture. This recipe also can be used to make one large turnover as demonstrated on pages 34-35. For a large turnover, roll the dough and cut out a 14-inch [35-cm.] square, spread the filling on one half of the dough, fold the square in half to form a rectangle, prick or slash the top, and bake the turnover at

425° F. [220° C.] for 20 minutes. Reduce the heat to 375° F. [190° C.] and continue baking for 15 minutes.

To make 14 small turnovers

1 lb.	short-crust dough (recipe, page 162)	½ kg.
⅔ cup	cooked dried prunes, chopped	150 ml.
⅓ cup	cooked dried apricots, chopped	75 ml.
¼ cup	sugar	50 ml.
1 tbsp.	cornstarch	15 ml.
¼ tsp.	salt	1 ml.
1 tbsp.	fresh lemon juice	15 ml.

Combine all of the ingredients for the filling and stir over low heat for five minutes. Roll out the dough ⅛ inch [3 mm.] thick and cut it into 4-inch [10-cm.] squares.

Place a spoonful [15 ml.] of filling on half of each square, moisten the edges and fold the dough to form triangles. Seal the edges by pressing them together with the tines of a fork, prick the top of each turnover to allow for the escape of steam, place the turnovers on a baking sheet, and bake in a preheated 425° F. [220° C.] oven for 15 minutes.

ANN SERANNE
THE COMPLETE BOOK OF HOME BAKING

Quince Tart

Torta de Marmelos

To make one 10-inch [25-cm.] tart

¾ lb.	short-crust dough (recipe, page 162)	⅓ kg.
2 lb.	unripe quinces, peeled, cored, quartered and scalded in boiling water	1 kg.
4 cups	sugar	1 liter
2 or 3	whole cloves	2 or 3
1	cinnamon stick	1
12	egg yolks	12

Over medium heat cook the quinces with 2½ cups [625 ml.] of the sugar, the cloves and the cinnamon stick until the mixture is thick and syrupy, about 30 minutes. Let it cool.

Beat the egg yolks with the remaining sugar, then stir over very low heat or in a double boiler, until the mixture is lightly thickened. Cool, stirring occasionally.

Roll out the dough and use it to line a tart pan. Put in the quince mixture, removing the cloves and cinnamon stick. Cover with the egg mixture.

Bake in a preheated 350° F. [180° C.] oven for 30 minutes, or until the pastry is lightly browned and the egg topping is puffed and golden. Serve warm.

ANTONIO DE MACEDO MENGO
COPA E COZINHA

Quince Tartlets

The original version of this 14th Century recipe reads in its entirety: "Make coffyrs of paaste and take quynces and pare and take out the core and take sugar ynugh (or ellse take hony in stede if thou maest more sugar) and if thou takest hony put thereto poudre pepor and ginger and fill the quynces and bake them ynugh." Dorothy Hartley, who adapted the recipe, determined that "coffyrs of paaste" refers to small tartlet shells and that the quinces were precooked.

To make twelve 3-inch [8-cm.] tartlets

1 lb.	short-crust dough *(recipe, page 162)*	½ kg.
6	quinces, peeled and cored	6
6 tbsp.	sugar or ¼ cup [50 ml.] honey	90 ml.
	pepper	
	ground ginger	
	ground allspice	

Put the quinces in a baking dish, and fill them with sugar or honey combined with a little pepper, ginger and allspice. Bake in a preheated 350° F. [180° C.] oven for 45 minutes, or until the quinces are soft but still hold their shape. Allow the quinces to cool and halve them.

Roll out the dough, cut it into rounds and use it to line small tartlet pans. Place a quince half in each pan and bake in a preheated 400° F. [200° C.] oven for 20 minutes, or until the edges of the pastry are lightly browned. Serve hot or cold.

DOROTHY HARTLEY
FOOD IN ENGLAND

Rhubarb and Strawberry Pie

An alternative way to prepare the fruits is shown on pages 26-27. If desired, this pie may be covered with a lattice top. The techniques of shaping lattices appear on pages 26-29.

To make one 9-inch [23-cm.] pie

1 lb.	short-crust dough *(recipe, page 162)*	½ kg.
2½ cups	thickly sliced rhubarb	625 ml.
2 cups	strawberries	½ liter
½ cup	sugar	125 ml.
¼ tsp.	salt	1 ml.
2½ tbsp.	quick-cooking tapioca	37 ml.
1 tsp.	grated lemon peel	5 ml.
1 tbsp.	water, mixed with 1 tsp. [5 ml.] molasses	15 ml.
	whipped cream	

Mix together the sugar, salt, tapioca and lemon peel, and combine them with the rhubarb slices. Let the mixture stand for 15 minutes. Drain the rhubarb, then add the strawberries. Line a piepan with half of the rolled dough. Place the fruit mixture in the shell, and cover with the top crust, making a few slits on top and brushing with the water-and-molasses mixture. Bake the pie for 10 minutes in a preheated 450° F. [230° C.] oven, then reduce the oven temperature to 350° F. [180° C.] and continue baking for 30 to 35 minutes longer, depending on the tenderness of the rhubarb. Serve cold with plain whipped cream.

LOUIS P. DE GOUY
THE PIE BOOK

Strawberry Tart

Flan de Fraises à la Tyrolienne

This tart is especially delicious made with wild strawberries: the French fraises des bois.

To make one 12-inch [30-cm.] tart

1	fully baked tart shell, made from 1 lb. [½ kg.] rich short-crust dough *(recipe, page 162)* flavored with a pinch of ground cinnamon	1
1 lb.	strawberries, hulled and halved, or sliced if large	½ kg.
⅔ cup	superfine sugar	150 ml.
¼ cup	kirsch	50 ml.
1 cup	heavy cream	¼ liter

In a bowl, sprinkle the strawberries with 7 tablespoons [105 ml.] of the sugar and half of the kirsch. Whip the cream with the remaining sugar and kirsch.

Spread a layer of the whipped cream in the tart shell, then mix the remaining cream with the strawberries and use this mixture to fill the shell. Serve immediately, before the pastry loses its crispness.

JEAN DE GOUY
LA CUISINE ET LA PATISSERIE BOURGEOISE

Fruit Tartlets

Tartelettes aux Fruits

The following recipe calls for apples to be used in half of the tartlets and strawberries in the other half. You can, if you wish, substitute other fresh fruits such as green grapes or raspberries, for example, using 1 ½ cups [375 ml.] of each. For green grapes or raspberries, the tartlet shells should be baked blind (pages 42-43), sprinkled with the bread-crumb mixture, filled with the fruit, then glazed and finished with a little confectioners' sugar. Use currant-jelly glaze for red fruits and apricot glaze for white fruits. Whichever tartlets you choose to make, keep them in their molds until serving time to protect the delicate shells.

To make 12 tartlets

1 lb.	short-crust dough *(recipe, page 162)*	½ kg.
2 cups	strawberries, hulled	½ liter
2	large eating apples, peeled, cored and halved	2
1 tsp.	grated lemon peel	5 ml.
2 tsp.	strained fresh lemon juice	10 ml.
½ cup	peach jam	125 ml.
¼ cup	dry bread crumbs	50 ml.
⅔ cup	sugar	150 ml.
½ tsp.	ground cardamom	2 ml.
	grated nutmeg	
4 tbsp.	unsalted butter, melted	60 ml.
2 tbsp.	confectioners' sugar	30 ml.
Currant and apricot glazes		
½ cup	currant jelly	125 ml.
1 tbsp.	*framboise*	15 ml.
½ cup	apricot jam	125 ml.
1 tbsp.	Cognac, brandy or sherry	15 ml.

Roll out the dough ¼ inch [6 mm.] thick. Set 12 round 3¼-inch [8½-cm.] tartlet molds in a cluster, touching each other. Carefully lift the sheet of dough on the rolling pin and lay it over the molds. Run the rolling pin over the dough to cut the correct size round for each mold. With your fingers, press the dough against the bottoms and sides of the molds. Brush the dough with a little melted butter.

Mix together the bread crumbs, 4 tablespoons [60 ml.] of the sugar, the cardamom and a pinch of grated nutmeg. Divide half of the mixture evenly among six of the pastry shells and put the other half aside, with the remaining six shells.

Prepare the apple filling by cutting two of the halves into tiny dice; sprinkle the dice with half of the lemon juice. Slice the other two halves into paper-thin slices and sprinkle with the remaining lemon juice. Mix the diced apple with the peach jam and the grated lemon peel. Fill the shells lined with bread crumbs with the diced apple and arrange the slices in a pinwheel pattern on top of each shell. Sprinkle with the remaining sugar.

Put the tartlets on a baking sheet and bake them in a preheated 375° F. [190° C.] oven for 25 minutes, or until the edges are golden brown. At the same time, blind-bake the other six pastry shells, also for 25 minutes.

While the tartlets are baking, prepare the glazes. In two separate saucepans and over low heat, melt the currant jelly with the *framboise*, and the apricot jam with the Cognac, brandy or sherry. Sieve the glazes separately into small bowls and allow them to cool a little.

Remove the tartlets from the oven. Put the apple tartlets under the broiler for a moment just to singe the edges of the sliced apple. Brush them with the apricot-jam glaze and let them cool in their molds.

When the blind-baked shells are partially cooled, sprinkle the remaining bread-crumb mixture into the shells. Fill them with strawberries, standing the berries hulled ends down. Brush the strawberries with the currant-jelly glaze and sprinkle confectioners' sugar around the edges.

DIONE LUCAS AND MARION GORMAN
THE DIONE LUCAS BOOK OF FRENCH COOKING

Viennese Walnut Strawberry Pastry

Wiener Walnuss Erdbeertorte

To make one 10-inch [25-cm.] pastry

1⅓ cups	flour, sifted	325 ml.
¼ cup	sugar	50 ml.
7 tbsp.	unsalted butter, cut into small pieces and chilled	105 ml.
1	egg yolk	1
1½ cups	walnuts, ground in a nut grinder, or in a food processor operated at short spurts	375 ml.
4 cups	whole strawberries, plus about 1½ cups [375 ml.] sliced strawberries	1 liter
Jellied currant glaze		
1 cup	currant jelly	¼ liter
1 tbsp.	unflavored powdered gelatin	15 ml.
2 to 3 tbsp.	water	30 to 45 ml.
	whipped cream (optional)	

Mix the flour and sugar on a pastry board. Make a well in the center and cut in the butter. Add the egg yolk. Cover with the ground walnuts. Combine the mixture with your finger tips and work it quickly into a smooth dough: until the pastry board and your hands are clean of all ingredients. Form the dough into a ball. Wrap the ball in wax paper. Refrigerate for about 30 minutes.

Place the ball between two sheets of wax paper. Flatten it out slightly with your hands. Roll out the ball evenly to 1 inch [2½ cm.] larger than the spring-form pan you intend to use. Place the rolled dough on cardboard or a flat pot cover. Refrigerate it.

When the dough is almost firm, remove the top sheet of wax paper. Remove the outer ring of the spring-form pan. Place the rolled-out dough on the bottom of the pan. Gently remove the second sheet of wax paper. Attach the outer ring. Press the dough firmly into the pan to remove air pockets. With a knife, press down the sides to form an even border slightly thicker than the bottom. Prick the border and bottom several times with a fork. Bake the shell in a preheated 350° F. [180° C.] oven for 20 to 35 minutes, until golden. Cook the shell completely.

A few hours before serving, place the gelatin in a small saucepan, sprinkle it with the water and add ¼ cup [50 ml.] of the currant jelly. Dissolve completely over low heat. Remove the mixture from the heat, combine with the remaining jelly and blend until smooth. When this currant glaze is nearly firm, coat the bottom of the pastry shell with about half of it. Refrigerate.

When firm, cover the glaze with the sliced strawberries, then arrange the whole strawberries on top of the sliced berries according to size, starting with the largest one in the center. Spoon or brush the remaining currant glaze over the berries. Refrigerate.

Before serving, sprinkle the border lightly with confectioners' sugar. Serve with whipped cream.

LILLY JOSS REICH
THE VIENNESE PASTRY COOKBOOK

Tangerine Pie

To make one 9-inch [23-cm.] pie

1	fully baked pie shell, made from ½ lb. [¼ kg.] short-crust dough (recipe, page 162)	1
1 cup	fresh tangerine juice	¼ liter
2 tbsp.	julienned tangerine peel	30 ml.
3 tbsp.	flour	45 ml.
3	eggs, the yolks separated from the whites, and the whites stiffly beaten	3
2 tbsp.	fresh lemon juice	30 ml.
½ tsp.	grated orange peel	2 ml.
½ cup	sugar	125 ml.

In the top of a double boiler, combine the tangerine juice, flour, egg yolks, lemon juice, orange peel and sugar. Stirring constantly, cook over simmering water until thickened—about five minutes. Remove from the heat and cool. Fold in

the stiffly beaten egg whites, then pour the mixture into the baked pie shell. Sprinkle the top with finely julienned tangerine peel. Brown in a preheated 400° F. [200° C.] oven for 10 minutes. Chill before serving.

RALPH H. REESE (EDITOR)
THE FLAVOR OF PITTSBURGH

Linzer Tart with Almonds

Linzertorte (mit Mandeln)

The techniques of shaping lattices appear on pages 26-29.

To make one 11 ½-inch [28-cm.] tart

2 cups	flour, sifted	½ liter
½ lb.	blanched almonds, ground in a nut grinder, or in a food processor operated at short spurts	¼ kg.
16 tbsp.	butter (½ lb. [¼ kg.]), softened and cut into pieces	240 ml.
2	egg yolks	2
1 cup	sugar	¼ liter
2 tsp.	kirsch	10 ml.
¼ tsp.	ground cloves	1 ml.
2 tsp.	ground cinnamon	10 ml.
½ tsp.	grated lemon peel	2 ml.
1 tbsp.	cocoa powder	15 ml.
½ cup	raspberry or strawberry jam	125 ml.
1	egg, lightly beaten	1

Put the flour onto a board. Put the almonds, butter, egg yolks, sugar, kirsch, spices, lemon peel and cocoa on top. Knead the mixture with your finger tips to form a smooth dough. Let it stand wrapped in plastic wrap for one hour.

Roll out two thirds of the dough and use it to line a round cake pan. Spread it with the jam. Roll out the rest of the dough, cut it into strips and decorate the top of the tart with a lattice pattern. Brush the rim of the pastry and the lattice with the beaten egg, and bake in a preheated 350° F. [180° C.] oven for 35 minutes, or until the pastry is light brown. Serve hot or cold.

HERMINE KIEHNLE AND MARIA HÄDECKE
DAS GROSSE KIEHNLE-KOCHBUCH

Banbury Tarts

To make about 36 tarts

1½ lb.	short-crust dough *(recipe, page 162)*	¾ kg.
1 cup	raisins, soaked in warm water for 15 minutes and drained	¼ liter
1 cup	sugar	¼ liter
1	egg, lightly beaten	1
1	soda cracker, rolled into fine crumbs	1
3 tbsp.	fresh lemon juice	45 ml.
1 tsp.	grated lemon peel	5 ml.

Chop the raisins; add the sugar, egg, cracker crumbs, lemon juice and lemon peel. Roll the dough ⅛ inch [3 mm.] thick, and cut pieces 3½ inches [9 cm.] long by 3 inches [8 cm.] wide. Put 2 teaspoons [10 ml.] of the raisin mixture on each piece. Moisten the edges with cold water halfway round, fold over, and press the edges together with a three-tined fork, first dipped in flour. Bake the tarts for 20 minutes in a preheated 300° F. [150° C.] oven.

FANNIE MERRITT FARMER
THE ORIGINAL BOSTON COOKING-SCHOOL COOK BOOK

Stuffed Monkey

To make one 8-inch [20-cm.] pastry

1½ cups	flour	375 ml.
½ tsp.	ground cinnamon	2 ml.
8 tbsp.	butter, softened and cut into pieces	120 ml.
1	egg, the yolk separated from the white, and the white lightly beaten	1
½ cup	brown sugar	125 ml.
Candied fruit filling		
½ cup	chopped mixed candied fruit peel	125 ml.
3 tbsp.	butter	45 ml.
2 tbsp.	superfine sugar	30 ml.
¼ cup	almonds, ground in a nut grinder	50 ml.
1	egg yolk	1

Sift the flour and cinnamon into a bowl, rub in the butter, add the egg yolk and sugar, and knead to a pliable dough. For the filling, melt the butter and mix in the candied peel, sugar, almonds and egg yolk. Butter a round cake pan. Roll out the dough into two rounds. Put one round into the pan, spread with the filling and cover with the other round. Brush with the egg white and bake in a preheated 350° F. [180° C.] oven for 30 minutes, or until light brown. Cool in the pan.

FLORENCE GREENBERG
JEWISH COOKERY

Yorkshire Mint Pasty

To make one large pasty

½ lb.	short-crust dough *(recipe, page 162)*	¼ kg.
¼ cup	finely chopped mint leaves	50 ml.
¾ cup	dried currants	175 ml.
1 cup	raisins, soaked in warm water for 15 minutes and drained	¼ liter
½ cup	finely chopped mixed candied fruit peel	125 ml.
¼ cup	brown sugar	50 ml.
2 tbsp.	butter	30 ml.
½ tsp.	grated nutmeg or ground allspice	2 ml.

Roll out the dough about ¼ inch [6 mm.] thick and trim it into a large round. Put the rolled dough onto a baking sheet. On one half of the round, place a layer of half of the currants, raisins and candied peel. Sprinkle with the mint, then with the brown sugar. Make another layer of the remaining currants, raisins and peel. Dot with the butter and sprinkle on the nutmeg or allspice.

Wet the edges of the dough. Turn the plain half over to cover the fruit. Pinch the edges of the dough together. Bake in a preheated 350° F. [180° C.] oven for about 30 minutes or until browned. Serve hot or cold.

FLORENCE WHITE
GOOD THINGS IN ENGLAND

Jam Tart

Crostata di Frutta

The techniques of shaping lattices are shown on pages 26-29.

To make two 10-inch [25-cm.] tarts

5 cups	flour, sifted	1¼ liters
¼ cup	cornmeal	50 ml.
1 cup	superfine sugar	¼ liter
2 tbsp.	vanilla sugar	30 ml.
1 tsp.	salt	5 ml.
16 tbsp.	butter (½ lb. [¼ kg.]), softened and cut into pieces	240 ml.
1 tbsp.	olive oil	15 ml.
3	egg yolks	3
½ tsp.	freshly grated lemon peel	2 ml.
1⅓ cups	jam	325 ml.

Mix the flour and cornmeal together and pour onto a board. Sprinkle on the superfine sugar, vanilla sugar and salt.

Make a well in the center and put in the butter, oil, egg yolks and lemon peel. Work with your finger tips until the dough mixture holds together. Cover it with a cloth and let it rest for about one hour.

Divide the dough in half. Roll out each half into a large circle and use it to line a buttered tart pan, reserving the trimmings. Fill the tarts with the jam, then make a lattice top with strips of the leftover rolled dough. Bake in a preheated 350° F. [180° C.] oven for 35 minutes or until the pastry is golden brown. Allow the tarts to cool before removing them from the pans.

LUIGI VOLPICELLI AND SECONDINO FREDA
L'ANTIARTUSI: 1000 RICETTE

Custard and Cream Pies

Cream Tart

Farce de Cresme

Making a free-form tart from short-crust dough is shown on pages 36-37; a puff-pastry tart on pages 52-53.

To make one 10-inch [25-cm.] tart

½ lb.	short-crust or puff-pastry dough (recipes, pages 162 and 164)	¼ kg.
1 cup	milk	¼ liter
2	eggs	2
¼ cup	flour	50 ml.
2 tbsp.	butter	30 ml.
	salt	
½ cup	sugar	125 ml.
	rose water	

Mix one of the eggs into the flour. When it is thoroughly incorporated, beat in the remaining egg. Bring the milk to a boil over medium heat and, stirring constantly with a wooden spatula, gradually add the flour and eggs. Stir in the butter and a pinch of salt. Still stirring constantly, cook the mixture for six or seven minutes, or until it thickens to a stiff paste. Pour the mixture into a bowl and let it cool before covering and refrigerating it. The mixture will keep for about one week.

To use the cream, work in about ¼ cup [50 ml.] of sugar with the wooden spatula. Roll out the dough to any shape desired and press strips of the dough onto the edges to form borders. Spread the surface with the cream filling, sprinkle the top with 2 tablespoons [30 ml.] of the sugar and bake in a preheated 375° F. [190° C.] oven for about 30 minutes, or until lightly browned. When the tart is baked, sprinkle it with the remaining sugar and a few drops of rose water.

NICOLAS DE BONNEFONS
LES DELICES DE LA CAMPAGNE

Cream Custard Tarts

Babeczki Smietankowe

To make 12 tartlets

1⅔ cups	flour, sifted	400 ml.
14 tbsp.	unsalted butter	200 ml.
½ tsp.	baking soda	2 ml.
½ cup	superfine sugar	125 ml.
1	egg	1
2	egg yolks	2
2	hard-boiled egg yolks, sieved	2

Cream custard filling

½ cup	heavy cream	125 ml.
3	egg yolks	3
⅔ cup	superfine sugar	150 ml.
½	vanilla bean, split lengthwise, seeds scraped out	½

To make the dough, cut the butter into the flour, then add the remaining ingredients and knead briefly but thoroughly. Wrap the dough in plastic wrap, refrigerate and allow it to rest for at least one hour.

For the custard filling, put the egg yolks in a saucepan, and stir in the sugar, cream and vanilla bean. Cook over low heat, stirring constantly, until the mixture thickens. Remove from the heat and put the saucepan in a shallow pan of cold water to stop the cooking. Cool the custard, stirring occasionally. Discard the vanilla bean.

Roll out the dough and line buttered tartlet pans with it. Fill the pastry shells with the custard and cover with rounds cut from the remaining rolled dough. Crimp the edges together to seal, then bake the tartlets in a preheated 350° F. [180° C.] oven for 30 minutes, or until lightly browned. Cool before unmolding.

I. PLUCINSKA
KSIAZKA KUCHARSKA

Chess Pie

To make one 9-inch [23-cm.] pie

1	unbaked pie shell, made from ½ lb. [¼ kg.] short-crust dough (recipe, page 162)	1
3	eggs	3
1½ cups	sugar	375 ml.
½ cup	light cream	125 ml.
2 tbsp.	flour	30 ml.
2 tsp.	cornmeal	10 ml.
5 tbsp.	butter, melted	75 ml.
½ tsp.	vanilla extract	2 ml.
	grated nutmeg	

Beat the eggs until thick and lemon-colored. Add the sugar, cream, flour, cornmeal, melted butter and vanilla extract. Mix thoroughly and pour the filling into the unbaked pie shell. Sprinkle freshly grated nutmeg on top. Bake in a preheated 300° F. [150° C.] oven for about one hour, or until a knife inserted in the center of the pie comes out clean.

SOUTHERN RAILWAY LADIES CLUB COOKBOOK

President Tyler's Puddin' Pie

If individual pies are to be baked, the recipe will make 12 small ones. Bake them for 15 to 20 minutes after the filling has been put in the precooked crusts.

To make one 9-inch [23-cm.] pie

1	partially baked pie shell, made from ½ lb. [¼ kg.] short-crust dough (recipe, page 162)	1
¾ cup	granulated sugar	175 ml.
¾ cup	brown sugar	175 ml.
8 tbsp.	butter	120 ml.
2	eggs	2
½ cup	heavy cream	125 ml.
½ tsp.	vanilla extract	2 ml.
	nutmeg	
	confectioners' sugar	

Cream together the granulated and brown sugars and butter. Add the eggs, cream and vanilla extract. Add the filling to the prepared pie shell and grate a dusting of nutmeg over the top. Bake the pie in a preheated 350° F. [180° C.] oven for about 35 to 40 minutes, or until the crust is golden brown and the filling is firm and trembles only slightly in the middle when the pie is shaken gently. (If cooked too long, the

filling will be granular or candied; it should be like a firm, transparent jelly when properly baked.) As soon as the filling no longer shakes all over, remove the pie from the oven, dust it with confectioners' sugar and let it cool slightly before removing from the pan.

MARION FLEXNER
OUT OF KENTUCKY HOMES

Cream Pie with Chocolate Meringue

To make one 9-inch [23-cm.] pie

1	fully baked pie shell, made from ½ lb. [¼ kg.] short-crust dough (recipe, page 162)	1
1 cup	sugar	¼ liter
4 tbsp.	cornstarch	60 ml.
4	extra large egg yolks	4
4 cups	milk	1 liter
2 tbsp.	butter	30 ml.
1 tsp.	vanilla extract	5 ml.
Chocolate meringue		
4	egg whites	4
4 tbsp.	sugar	60 ml.
2 oz.	unsweetened baking chocolate, melted	60 g.

In a heavy saucepan, combine the sugar and cornstarch, add the egg yolks, mix well, and stir in the milk, butter and vanilla extract. Stirring constantly, cook this custard filling over medium heat until thick—about 10 to 15 minutes. Pour the filling into the pie shell.

For the meringue, beat the egg whites until foamy. Gradually add the sugar and melted chocolate, and continue to beat until soft peaks are formed. Spread the chocolate meringue on the filling, being sure that the meringue meets the edges of the pie crust. Brown the meringue in a preheated 425° F. [220° C.] oven for five minutes.

THE EASTERN SHORE COOK BOOK

Huldah's Buttermilk Pie

In colonial days, and for a long time thereafter, buttermilk was not the prepared beverage we find in our supermarket dairy cases today, but the by-product of butter churning. Chilled in a convenient swift-running stream, it was valued as a thirst quencher and was used in cooking interchangeably with sour milk. Modern buttermilk is a cultured milk, made from the addition of a special bacterial culture. The culture produces the desirable acidity, body, flavor and aroma that characterize old-fashioned buttermilk.

	To make one 9-inch [23-cm.] pie	
1	unbaked pie shell, made from ½ lb. [¼ kg.] short-crust dough *(recipe, page 162)*	1
2 cups	buttermilk	½ liter
3	eggs, the yolks separated from the whites, the yolks beaten, and the whites beaten into stiff peaks	3
1 cup	sugar	¼ liter
¼ tsp.	salt	1 ml.
3 tbsp.	flour	45 ml.
4 tsp.	butter, melted	20 ml.
1 tsp.	vanilla extract	5 ml.

Beat the buttermilk into the egg yolks. Combine the sugar, salt and flour. Stir the sugar mixture into the buttermilk mixture and blend well. Stir in the butter and vanilla extract. Fold the stiffly beaten egg whites into the buttermilk mixture. Pour the filling into the pie shell. Bake in a preheated 450° F. [230° C.] oven for 10 minutes. Reduce the heat to 350° F. [180° C.] and bake for 30 to 35 minutes, or until the pie is set. The pie will get very brown on top.

HYLA O'CONNOR
THE EARLY AMERICAN COOKBOOK

Jeff Davis Pie

	To make one 9-inch [23-cm.] pie	
1	partially baked pie shell, made from ½ lb. [¼ kg.] short-crust dough *(recipe, page 162)*	1
1¾ cups	sugar	425 ml.
1 tbsp.	flour	15 ml.
½ cup	butter, softened	125 ml.
1 cup	heavy cream	¼ liter
6	eggs, the yolks of 4 eggs separated from the whites	6
	salt	

In the top of a double boiler, blend together 1¼ cups [300 ml.] of the sugar, the flour and butter. Mix in the cream, the two whole eggs and four egg yolks.

Set over simmering—*not* boiling—water. Cook and stir for 10 to 12 minutes, or until thickened and smooth—about the consistency of a stirred custard. Remove from the heat.

Beat the four egg whites with a pinch of salt and the remaining ½ cup [125 ml.] of sugar for about five minutes

until thick and silvery; because of the high proportion of sugar, the egg whites will not froth up into a meringue. Slowly fold the egg whites into the custard mixture until no streaks of white or yellow remain.

Pour the filling into the baked pie shell and bake in a preheated 325° F. [160° C.] oven for about 35 minutes, or until puffed and a rich caramel brown on top. Cool the pie to room temperature, then allow it to chill in the refrigerator for approximately an hour, or until the filling is firm. Cut into small wedges and serve.

JEAN ANDERSON
THE GRASS ROOTS COOKBOOK

Butterscotch Cream Pie

	To make one 9-inch [23-cm.] pie	
1	unbaked pie shell, made from ½ lb. [¼ kg.] short-crust dough *(recipe, page 162)*	1
1 cup	brown sugar	¼ liter
½ cup	flour	125 ml.
½ tsp.	salt	2 ml.
2 cups	milk	½ liter
3	egg yolks, lightly beaten	3
2 tbsp.	butter	30 ml.
½ tsp.	vanilla extract	2 ml.
	Meringue topping	
2	egg whites	2
¼ tsp.	cream of tartar	1 ml.
3 tbsp.	granulated sugar or 4 tbsp. [60 ml.] confectioners' sugar	45 ml.
½ tsp.	vanilla extract	2 ml.

In the top of a double boiler, combine the brown sugar, flour and salt. Add the milk. Stir and cook over—not in—boiling water for 10 minutes, or until the mixture thickens. Remove from the heat. Stirring well, pour half of the hot mixture into the beaten egg yolks. When smooth, return the egg yolks to the rest of the hot mixture and cook until thickened. Remove from the heat, and add the butter and vanilla extract. Cool slightly before turning the mixture into the pie shell.

Whip the egg whites until frothy. Add the cream of tartar. Whip until the egg whites are stiff, but not dry—until they stand in peaks that lean over slightly when the beater is removed. Beat in the sugar, 1 tablespoon [15 ml.] at a time, until stiff peaks form. Do not overbeat. Beat in the vanilla extract. Spread this meringue on the pie and bake in a preheated 350° F. [180° C.] oven for 10 to 15 minutes, or until the meringue is lightly browned.

IRMA S. ROMBAUER AND MARION ROMBAUER BECKER
JOY OF COOKING

Lemon Chess Pie

To make one 9-inch [23-cm.] pie

1	unbaked pie shell, made from ½ lb. [¼ kg.] short-crust dough *(recipe, page 162)*	1
¼ cup	fresh lemon juice	50 ml.
2 tbsp.	grated lemon peel	30 ml.
8 tbsp.	butter	120 ml.
2 cups	sugar	½ liter
1 tbsp.	cornstarch	15 ml.
4	eggs	4
	sweetened whipped cream	

Cream the butter until fluffy. Mix the sugar with the cornstarch, add to the butter, and cream together until the mixture is light and fluffy. Add the eggs, one at a time, beating well after each addition. Add the lemon juice and grated lemon peel. (The mixture will look curdly.) Pour the filling into the pie shell and bake in a preheated 350° F. [180° C.] oven for 35 to 45 minutes, or until it bakes to a thick custard. Do not overbake. The filling will be soft, but will firm up after it cools. Remove the pie from the oven and let it cool on a wire rack. Serve with slightly sweetened whipped cream.

GLENN MC CULLOUGH (EDITOR)
GEORGIA RECEIPTS

Apulian Baked Sweet Ravioli

Bocconotti

To make about 80 ravioli

4 cups	flour, sifted	1 liter
3 tbsp.	sugar	45 ml.
	salt	
¼ cup	mild olive oil	50 ml.
1 cup	sweet white wine	¼ liter
	black-cherry jam	
1	egg, lightly beaten	1
Custard cream filling		
5	egg yolks	5
⅔ cup	sugar	150 ml.
¼ cup	flour	50 ml.
2 cups	milk	½ liter
	vanilla extract	
1	thin strip lemon peel	1

To prepare the custard, beat the egg yolks and sugar until well mixed. Blend in the flour. Mix the milk with vanilla

extract to taste, and gradually add it to the egg mixture. Pour the mixture into the top of a double boiler, add the lemon peel and cook over hot water, stirring constantly, until the custard is very thick. Remove the lemon peel. Pour the custard cream into a bowl and refrigerate it until quite cold.

To make the ravioli dough, sift the flour, sugar and a pinch of salt onto a pastry board or into a large bowl. Make a well in the center, add the oil and enough wine to make a firm, pliable dough. Knead well and roll out into a very thin square or rectangular sheet.

Arrange a neat row of teaspoonfuls of custard cream about 4 inches [10 cm.] apart and 2½ inches [6 cm.] from the edge of the dough. Top each mound with a teaspoonful of cherry jam. Fold the nearest edge of the dough over the row of filling and press down firmly between each little mound to seal it completely. Cut out the squares with a pastry wheel or a sharp knife. Continue in this manner until all of the pastry and filling are used. Brush each square with beaten egg.

Grease a baking sheet with oil and arrange the squares on it in rows. Bake in a preheated 375° F. [190° C.] oven for 15 to 20 minutes, or until golden brown. Serve warm or cold.

ADA BONI
REGIONAL ITALIAN COOKING

Osgood Pie

To make one 9-inch [23-cm.] pie

1	unbaked pie shell, made from ½ lb. [¼ kg.] short-crust dough *(recipe, page 162)*	1
1 cup	raisins, soaked in warm water for 15 minutes, drained and chopped	¼ liter
½ cup	chopped pecans or walnuts	125 ml.
8 tbsp.	butter, softened	120 ml.
1½ cups	sugar	375 ml.
1 tsp.	ground cinnamon	5 ml.
1 tsp.	grated nutmeg	5 ml.
3	eggs, the yolks separated from the whites	3
2 tsp.	vinegar	10 ml.

Cream together until fluffy the butter, 1¼ cups [300 ml.] of the sugar, the cinnamon and nutmeg. Beat in the egg yolks and vinegar. Stir in the raisins and the pecans or walnuts. Beat the egg whites until foamy throughout. Add the remaining sugar gradually and continue to beat until stiff but not dry. Fold the beaten egg whites into the raisin mixture. Turn the filling into the pie shell and bake on the lower shelf of a preheated 350° F. [180° C.] oven for 40 to 45 minutes, or until the top is golden. Cool before serving; the filling will fall slightly. Serve with whipped cream, if desired.

JEANNE A. VOLTZ
THE FLAVOR OF THE SOUTH

Japanese Fruit Pie

To make one 9-inch [23-cm.] pie

1	unbaked pie shell, made from ½ lb. [¼ kg.] short-crust dough *(recipe, page 162)*	1
½ cup	flaked coconut	125 ml.
½ cup	golden raisins, soaked in warm water for 15 minutes and drained	125 ml.
6 tbsp.	butter, melted	90 ml.
1 cup	sugar	¼ liter
⅛ tsp.	salt	½ ml.
2	eggs, beaten	2
½ cup	coarsely broken pecans	125 ml.
1 tsp.	vinegar	5 ml.

Blend together the butter, sugar, salt, eggs, coconut, raisins, pecans and vinegar. Pour the mixture into the pie shell. Bake in a preheated 350° F. [180° C.] oven for 40 minutes, or until golden brown and set. Serve warm or cold.

BETH TARTAN
THE GOOD OLD DAYS COOKBOOK

Date Chiffon Pie

To make one 8-inch [20-cm.] pie

1	fully baked pie shell, made from ½ lb. [¼ kg.] short-crust dough *(recipe, page 162)*	1
⅔ cup	chopped, pitted dates	150 ml.
1 tbsp.	unflavored powdered gelatin	15 ml.
½ cup	sugar	125 ml.
2	eggs, the yolks separated from the whites	2
½ cup	fresh orange juice	125 ml.
⅓ cup	fresh lemon juice	75 ml.
½ cup	light cream	125 ml.
	salt	

In a saucepan, thoroughly mix the gelatin and half of the sugar. In a mixing bowl, beat together the egg yolks, orange juice and lemon juice. Add the egg mixture to the contents of the saucepan and, over gentle heat, cook it, stirring constantly, until the gelatin dissolves and the mixture thickens slightly. Allow to cool. Stir in the cream.

In a mixing bowl, beat the egg whites together with a pinch of salt until they stand in soft peaks. Add the remain-

ing sugar and continue to beat until they stand in firm peaks. Fold a little of the egg-yolk custard into the egg whites; then fold all of the whites into the custard.

Fold in the dates, spoon the mixture into the pie shell and chill the pie for at least three hours before serving.

ROBERT ACKART
FRUITS IN COOKING

Lemon-Curd Meringue Pie

To make one 9-inch [23-cm.] pie

1	fully baked pie shell, made from ½ lb. [¼ kg.] short-crust dough *(recipe, page 162)*	1
3	eggs	3
⅞ cup	sugar	210 ml.
⅓ cup	fresh lemon juice	75 ml.
6 tbsp.	butter, cut into small pieces	90 ml.
1 tbsp.	grated lemon peel	15 ml.
Meringue		
3	egg whites	3
¼ cup	sugar	50 ml.

For the filling, beat the eggs and sugar in the top of a double boiler. Stir in the fresh lemon juice and add the butter. Place the mixture over hot water and cook, stirring steadily, until it is thickened and coats the spoon. Stir in the grated lemon peel and let this lemon-curd filling cool.

Pour the filling into the pie shell. To make the meringue, beat the egg whites until peaks form, then beat in the sugar, a tablespoon [15 ml.] at a time, and continue to beat until the mixture is stiff but not dry. Heap the meringue on the lemon filling, using a pastry bag, if you like; be sure that the meringue touches the crust all around. Bake in a preheated 400° F. [200° C.] oven for five minutes, or until the meringue is delicately browned. Cool.

MYRA WALDO
MYRA WALDO'S DESSERT COOKBOOK

The Perfect Lemon Meringue Pie

To make one 9-inch [23-cm.] pie

1	fully baked pie shell, made from ½ lb. [¼ kg.] rich short-crust dough *(recipe, page 162)*	1
⅓ cup	strained fresh lemon juice	75 ml.
7	eggs, the yolks separated from the whites	7
1 cup plus 2 tbsp.	sugar	¼ liter plus 30 ml.

For the filling, beat the egg yolks with a whisk in the top of a double boiler, off the heat. Add the 1 cup [¼ liter] of sugar and the lemon juice, and beat again briefly. Place over simmering water and cook, stirring constantly, until the mixture is quite thick. Remove from the heat and cool.

Beat the egg whites until they hold soft peaks. Using a spatula, fold about one third of the egg whites into the yolk-and-lemon mixture. Pour the filling into the baked crust. Add the remaining 2 tablespoons [30 ml.] of sugar to the remaining beaten egg whites one at a time, beating after each addition. When the egg whites are glossy but not overly stiff, pile them onto the lemon filling, covering it completely. You can do this by using a large spoon to scoop up the egg whites and drop them onto the filling. The meringue should look fluffy, like puffy clouds.

Place the pie in a preheated 350° F. [180° C.] oven for no more than 10 minutes, or until the meringue is light brown.

DORIS TOBIAS AND MARY MERRIS
THE GOLDEN LEMON

Nesselrode Chiffon Pie

To make one 9-inch [23-cm.] pie

1	fully baked, fluted pie shell, made from ½ lb. [¼ kg.] short-crust dough *(recipe, page 162)*	1
¾ cup	chopped mixed candied fruit	175 ml.
3 tbsp.	brandy	45 ml.
1 tbsp.	unflavored powdered gelatin, softened in ¼ cup [50 ml.] cold water	15 ml.
⅔ cup	sugar	150 ml.
2 tbsp.	cornstarch	30 ml.
1 cup	milk, scalded	¼ liter
6	egg yolks	6
1 cup	heavy cream, whipped	¼ liter
6	candied cherries	6

Place the gelatin, sugar and cornstarch in a deep saucepan; gradually add the scalded milk while stirring rapidly. Place

over low heat and bring the ingredients to a boil. Boil for approximately one minute. Remove from the heat. Beat the egg yolks until fluffy and pale in color. Add the brandy and mixed candied fruits. Stir the egg mixture rapidly into the hot-milk mixture. Blend all the ingredients well. Cool in the refrigerator or over a pan of cold water, stirring from time to time to accelerate cooling. When the mixture begins to set, fold in 1 cup [¼ liter] of the whipped cream.

Pour the mixture into the cooled pie shell and place it in the refrigerator for at least two hours, or until firm. Garnish with the remaining whipped cream and decorate with the candied cherries.

DOMINIQUE D'ERMO
THE CHEF'S DESSERT COOKBOOK

Pear and Almond Cream Tart

Tarte aux Poires Bourdaloue

To make one 9-inch [23-cm.] tart

½ lb.	short-crust dough *(recipe, page 162)*	¼ kg.
6	pears	6
3 cups	almond cream *(recipe, page 166)*	¾ liter
½ cup	apricot preserves, melted	125 ml.
6	almond macaroons, finely crumbled	6
Sugar syrup		
2 cups	sugar	½ liter
1 cup	water	¼ liter

Line a tart pan, or a flan ring placed on a baking sheet, with the rolled dough. Freeze the tart shell or chill it thoroughly. Spoon half of the almond cream into the tart shell. Bake the tart on the lowest shelf of a preheated 350° F. [180° C.] oven for about 35 minutes.

While the tart is baking, prepare the sugar syrup by stirring the sugar and water in a saucepan over medium heat until the sugar begins to dissolve. Increase the heat and boil without stirring for 10 minutes, or until the syrup reaches about 220° F. [110° C.] on a candy thermometer. (The temperature need not be exact in this instance.) Peel and core the pears and cut them into thin slices. Poach the pears in the sugar syrup over low heat for about five minutes, or until just tender; they should keep their shape. Drain the pears and cool them.

When the tart is baked and cooled, put the remaining almond cream into it. Arrange the pear slices in overlapping rows on the almond cream, spread them with the apricot preserves and sprinkle the tart with the macaroon crumbs.

RAYMOND OLIVER
LA CUISINE

Prune Custard Tart with Armagnac

La Tourte de Pruneaux à l'Armagnac

This recipe produces four times as much dough as the tart requires. The excess can be used for pies, tortes or cookies. The dough can be kept in the refrigerator for one week, but must be taken out 20 minutes before it is used. Or it can be kept in the freezer and taken out one hour in advance.

To make one 10-inch [25-cm.] tart

3½ cups	flour, sifted	875 ml.
¼ lb.	blanched almonds, ground to a powder in a nut grinder, or in a food processor operated at short spurts	125 g.
¼ tsp.	grated lemon peel	1 ml.
⅔ cup	superfine sugar	150 ml.
⅛ tsp.	salt	½ ml.
¾ lb.	butter, cut into large pieces and softened	⅓ kg.
1	egg	1
2	egg yolks	2
3 tbsp.	white rum	45 ml.

Prune custard filling

½ lb.	pitted, dried prunes, soaked in warm water for 15 minutes, drained and patted dry	¼ kg.
3 tbsp.	finely ground blanched almonds	45 ml.
¼ cup	vanilla sugar	50 ml.
2	eggs	2
5 tbsp.	heavy cream	75 ml.
2 tbsp.	orange-flower water	30 ml.
2 tbsp.	butter	30 ml.
¼ cup	Armagnac	50 ml.

Mix the flour, almonds, lemon peel, superfine sugar and salt. Make a well in the center of the mixture, and add the butter, egg, egg yolks and rum. Knead these ingredients together until they are all completely amalgamated, but do not work the dough beyond this stage. (If you have an electric mixer with a dough hook, use it at slow speed to knead the dough and stop as soon as the dough is blended.) Gather the dough into a ball, then divide it into four small balls weighing about 10 to 11 ounces [300 to 330 g.] each. Cover them with plastic wrap and store in the refrigerator or freezer.

To prepare the tart, sprinkle your work surface lightly with flour. Then, using a rolling pin, expand one ball of dough into a circle about 12 to 14 inches [30 to 36 cm.] in diameter. Lay the piece of dough over a round spring-form pan, pressing the dough lightly against the sides. The bottom and sides of the tart shell should be of the same thick-ness. Run the rolling pin across the top of the pan to cut off any excess dough. With the tines of a fork, prick the dough all over and refrigerate it thoroughly before baking.

To prepare the filling, put the ground almonds into a 2-quart [2-liter] mixing bowl along with the vanilla sugar, eggs, cream and orange-flower water. Using a wire whisk, beat the ingredients together until thoroughly incorporated. Over very low heat, melt the butter in a small saucepan, then stir it into the custard mixture.

Distribute the prunes evenly over the bottom of the tart shell. Then pour in the custard and bake the tart in a pre-heated 425° F. [220° C.] oven for 25 minutes. As soon as the tart is done, remove it from the oven and, while it is very hot, saturate the surface with the Armagnac. Serve lukewarm.

ROGER VERGE
CUISINE OF THE SOUTH OF FRANCE

Tangerine Chiffon Pie

To make one 9-inch [23-cm.] pie

1	fully baked pie shell, made from ½ lb. [¼ kg.] short-crust dough (recipe, page 162)	1
2	tangerines, peeled, sectioned, all white membrane removed and each section seeded	2
1 cup	tangerine juice	¼ liter
1 tbsp.	grated tangerine peel	15 ml.
1 tbsp.	unflavored powdered gelatin	15 ml.
½ cup plus ⅓ cup	sugar	125 ml. plus 75 ml.
	salt	
4	eggs, the yolks separated from the whites	4
¼ cup	fresh lemon juice	50 ml.
1 cup	heavy cream, whipped and flavored with 3 tbsp. [45 ml.] orange-flavored liqueur	¼ liter

In the top of a double boiler, combine the gelatin, the ½ cup [125 ml.] of sugar and a dash of salt. In a bowl, beat together the egg yolks, lemon juice and tangerine juice. Add the egg mixture to the contents of the double boiler and, over gently boiling water, cook, stirring constantly, until the gelatin and sugar dissolve and the mixture coats the spoon. Remove the pan from the heat. Stir the tangerine peel into the egg-yolk custard. Chill the custard, stirring it occasionally, until it is partially set. Beat the egg whites until frothy. Gradually add the ⅓ cup [75 ml.] of sugar, beating until the egg whites stand in stiff peaks. Fold the egg whites into the chilled custard. Spoon the mixture into the pie shell. Chill the pie for at least three hours, or until it is set. Garnish the pie with the whipped cream and the tangerine sections.

ROBERT ACKART
FRUITS IN COOKING

Raspberry Chiffon Pie

To make one 9-inch [23-cm.] pie

1	fully baked pie shell, made from ½ lb. [¼ kg.] short-crust dough (recipe, page 162)	1
1½ cups	crushed raspberries	375 ml.
¼ cup	sugar	50 ml.
½ cup	hot water	125 ml.
1 tsp.	grated lemon peel	5 ml.
¼ tsp.	salt	1 ml.
1 tbsp.	unflavored powdered gelatin, soaked in ¼ cup [50 ml.] cold water	15 ml.
½ cup	heavy cream, whipped	125 ml.
	Boiled meringue topping	
2	egg whites, stiffly beaten	2
2 tbsp.	cold water	30 ml.
½ tbsp.	light corn syrup	7 ml.
½ cup	sugar	125 ml.
¼ tsp.	vanilla extract	1 ml.
¼ tsp.	fresh lemon juice	1 ml.

Combine the sugar, hot water, raspberries, grated lemon peel and salt, and bring the mixture to the boiling point, stirring frequently. As soon as the boiling point is reached, remove at once from the heat and add the softened gelatin. Stir until the gelatin is dissolved and the mixture is thoroughly blended. Cool until the mixture begins to congeal, then fold in the whipped cream. Taste, and add more sugar if necessary. Spoon the filling into the pie shell and chill it thoroughly.

To make the boiled meringue, place the water, corn syrup and sugar in a saucepan; stir until the sugar is dissolved and the syrup blended. Boil over high heat, without stirring, until the syrup reaches 238° F. [115° C.]—or, if you have no thermometer, until the syrup reaches the soft-ball stage, indicated when a small ball of syrup dropped in ice water can be flattened out between your fingers.

Remove from the heat immediately, and pour the syrup over the stiffly beaten egg whites, in a threadlike stream, beating briskly and constantly until all of the syrup is used. Stir in the vanilla extract and fresh lemon juice.

Spread the topping over the raspberry-chiffon filling and return the pie to the refrigerator. Serve very cold.

LOUIS P. DE GOUY
THE PIE BOOK

Frangipane Pie

Tourte de Frangipane

A 16th Century cook named Frangipani is said to have created the almond filling that gives this pie its name. La Varenne, on the other hand, can take full credit for the unusual puff pastry that surrounds the almond cream. His idea of rolling out thin sheets of dough and layering them in a pie plate has been abandoned today by French cooks, whose method of making puff pastry is more complicated—although not superior, in this case—than the technique developed by La Varenne three centuries ago.

To make one 9-inch [23-cm.] pie

1¾ cups	flour	425 ml.
5	egg whites	5
16 tbsp.	butter, softened	240 ml.
	Almond-pistachio filling	
½ cup	blanched almonds	125 ml.
½ cup	blanched pistachios	125 ml.
6 tbsp.	flour	90 ml.
2 cups	milk	½ liter
	orange-flower water (optional)	
⅓ cup	sugar	75 ml.
	salt	
5	egg yolks	5

For the almond cream, first mix the flour with several teaspoons of the milk. Place the remaining milk in a pot. Add the flour mixture. Cook for 10 minutes over low heat, stirring constantly. Remove from the heat and cool.

Pound the almonds and pistachios in a mortar until a fine paste is formed. (A few drops of orange-flower water can be sprinkled on the nuts to prevent them from losing their oil.) Mix the pounded nuts with the sugar and salt. Stir the egg yolks, one by one, into the cool flour-and-milk mixture. Stir in the nut mixture.

For the pastry, place the flour in a bowl. Mix with the egg whites until the dough is smooth and can be formed into a ball. Leave the dough in the bowl and cover it with a cloth. Let stand for two hours before using.

Butter a piepan with 1 tablespoon [15 ml.] of the butter. Divide the dough into two equal parts. Take the first part and divide it into six pieces. Take one of these small pieces and, with your hands or a rolling pin, flatten it until it is paper-thin (almost transparent) and the size of the pan. Place it in the piepan.

Divide the remaining butter into 11 equal parts. Spread one part of the butter over the dough in the pan. Flatten another small piece of dough and place it over the first. Spread with another part of the butter. Repeat this operation until you have six layers of dough. Spread the almond cream over the sixth layer of dough.

With the second half of the dough make six more layers. Place these over the almond cream, separating each layer by a layer of butter. Butter the top of the pie.

Bake in a preheated 400° F. [200° C.] oven for 35 minutes, or until golden brown. Serve either warm or cold.

CELINE VENCE AND ROBERT COURTINE
THE GRAND MASTERS OF FRENCH CUISINE

Grasshopper Pie

A Texas version of a Southern favorite, this pie is best made the day before it is served. To make chocolate curls, the square or block of baking chocolate should be at room temperature. Use a vegetable peeler with a long, narrow blade. Draw the peeler along the smooth surface of the square or block. For large curls, pull the peeler over the wide surface of the chocolate; for small curls, pull the blade along the narrow side. Refrigerate the curls until ready to use.

To make one 9-inch [23-cm.] pie

1½ cups	chocolate cookie crumbs, pressed through a sieve	375 ml.
4 tbsp.	butter, melted	60 ml.
⅛ tsp.	ground cinnamon	½ ml.
	Grasshopper filling	
¼ cup	green or white crème de menthe	50 ml.
¼ cup	crème de cacao	50 ml.
1½ tsp.	unflavored powdered gelatin	7 ml.
⅓ cup	milk	75 ml.
4	egg yolks	4
¼ cup	superfine sugar	50 ml.
1 cup	heavy cream, whipped	¼ liter
⅓ cup	shaved chocolate curls	75 ml.

Place the cookie crumbs in a bowl, and stir in the melted butter and cinnamon. Press the crumbs onto the bottom and sides of a generously buttered deep piepan; the crumb shell should be thin.

In a small heatproof bowl, sprinkle the gelatin over the milk and mix. Stand the bowl in a saucepan of boiling water and heat until the gelatin is completely dissolved. Beat the egg yolks until thick. Gradually beat in the sugar, crème de menthe and crème de cacao, beating well after each addition. Stir in the gelatin and mix well. Chill until the mixture begins to thicken. Fold in the whipped cream. Turn the filling into the cookie-crumb shell. Smooth the surface and chill the pie overnight. At serving time, sprinkle the top with the chocolate curls.

NIKA HAZELTON
AMERICAN HOME COOKING

Sugar Tart

Zuckerwähe

To make one 7-inch [18-cm.] tart

½ lb.	short-crust dough (recipe, page 162)	¼ kg.
½ cup	superfine sugar	125 ml.
4	eggs	4
6 tbsp.	butter, melted	90 ml.
½ tsp.	ground cinnamon	2 ml.

Line a cake pan with the rolled dough. Beat the eggs with 1 tablespoon [15 ml.] of the sugar, and pour the egg mixture into the pastry shell. Pour 4 tablespoons [60 ml.] of the melted butter over the eggs and bake in a preheated 350° F. [180° C.] oven for 45 minutes, or until the pastry is golden and the custard filling is set. Blend the remaining butter with the remaining sugar and the cinnamon, and sprinkle the mixture over the top of the filling. Return the tart to the oven just until the topping has melted a little.

ANNE MASON
SWISS COOKING

Whiskey Cream Pie

To make one 9-inch [23-cm.] pie

1	fully baked pie shell, made from ½ lb. [¼ kg.] short-crust dough (recipe, page 162)	1
½ cup	bourbon or Irish whiskey	125 ml.
2 cups	heavy cream, whipped	½ liter
¾ cup	sugar	175 ml.
7	egg yolks	7
3 tbsp.	fresh lemon juice	45 ml.
1 tbsp.	finely grated lemon peel	15 ml.
4 tsp.	unflavored powdered gelatin, softened in 2 tbsp. [30 ml.] cold water	20 ml.
3 tbsp.	boiling water	45 ml.
4	egg whites, at room temperature	4

Set aside 3 tablespoons [45 ml.] of the sugar; beat the rest gradually and thoroughly into the egg yolks. Add the lemon juice and peel. Dissolve the softened gelatin in the boiling water and add the mixture to the egg yolks. Pour in the whiskey and stir to blend. Reserve one quarter of the whipped cream and fold in the rest. In a separate bowl, beat the egg whites to the soft-peak stage. Add the reserved sugar and beat until the whites are stiff. Fold them into the yolk mixture. Spread the filling in the pie shell and refrigerate until firm. Top with the remaining whipped cream.

CHARLOTTE ADAMS & DORIS MC FERRAN TOWNSEND
THE FAMILY COOKBOOK: DESSERT

Red Wine Tart

Tourte de Vin Vermeil

To produce currant juice, squeeze fresh currants through a sieve. If fresh currants are not obtainable, use strained orange juice flavored with 1 tablespoon [15 ml.] grapefruit juice.

To make one 8-inch [20-cm.] tart

1	partially baked pie shell, made from ½ lb. [¼ kg.] short-crust dough (recipe, page 162)	1
½ cup	port or red wine	125 ml.
½ cup	currant juice	125 ml.
2	almond macaroons, crumbled	2
4	egg yolks, lightly beaten	4
	salt	
¼ cup	sugar	50 ml.
1 tbsp.	finely chopped candied lemon peel	15 ml.
1 tbsp.	butter, softened	15 ml.
	orange-flower water	

In a saucepan, mix the wine and currant juice with the macaroons, egg yolks, salt to taste and the sugar. Stirring constantly, cook over very low heat until the mixture thickens slightly. Off the heat, stir in the candied lemon peel and the butter. Line a tart pan with the dough and pour in the wine mixture. Bake the tart in a preheated 350° F. [180° C.] oven for 30 minutes, or until the filling is firm to the touch. Sprinkle the top with orange-flower water before serving.

L'ÉSCOLE PARFAITE DES OFFICIERS DE BOUCHE

Carolina Sugar and Pepper Pie

To make one 9-inch [23-cm.] pie

1	partially baked pie shell, made from ½ lb. [¼ kg.] short-crust dough (recipe, page 162)	1
2 cups	dark brown sugar	½ liter
¼ tsp.	freshly ground pepper	1 ml.
	salt	
1 tbsp.	sifted flour	15 ml.
2	eggs	2
2 tbsp.	butter, melted	30 ml.
¼ cup	dark corn syrup	50 ml.
2 tsp.	vanilla extract	10 ml.
2 cups	heavy cream, 1 cup [¼ liter] whipped	½ liter

Combine the sugar, a pinch of salt and the flour in a large bowl. Stir in the eggs, melted butter, dark corn syrup, pep-

per, vanilla extract, and unwhipped heavy cream; mix well. Pour the filling into the pie shell.

Bake for 10 minutes in a preheated 425° F. [220° C.] oven. Reduce the oven heat to 325° F. [160° C.] and bake for 40 minutes longer. Cool completely on a wire rack. Just before serving, spread the pie with whipped cream.

BERT GREENE
BERT GREENE'S KITCHEN BOUQUETS

Rum Cream Pie

To make one 8- or 9-inch [20- or 23-cm.] pie

2½ cups	chocolate-wafer crumbs, made by crushing the wafers with a rolling pin or pulverizing them in a blender	625 ml.
6 tbsp.	butter, melted	90 ml.
Rum-cream filling		
½ cup	light rum	125 ml.
2½ cups	heavy cream, whipped	625 ml.
6	egg yolks	6
1 cup	sugar	¼ liter
1 tbsp.	unflavored powdered gelatin, softened for 5 minutes in ¼ cup [50 ml.] cold water	15 ml.
	grated sweet chocolate	

To make the crust, mix the chocolate crumbs with the butter, and press the mixture firmly and evenly against the bottom and sides of a spring-form pan. Bake for 10 minutes in a preheated 350° F. [180° C.] oven. Chill the crust until firm.

For the filling, beat the egg yolks with the sugar—using a wire whisk or rotary beater—until the yolk mixture is very thick and pale in color.

Stir the softened gelatin over hot water (the easiest way is just to set the measuring cup into some hot water) until completely dissolved. Add the melted gelatin to the yolk mixture and beat briskly. Now, using a rubber spatula, fold the whipped cream thoroughly into the yolk mixture. Fold in the rum. Pour the filling into the prepared crust and chill for at least four hours.

Before serving, remove the spring-form side of the pan and grate some sweet chocolate over the top.

DIANA AND PAUL VON WELANETZ
THE PLEASURE OF YOUR COMPANY

Coffee Pie

To make one 8- or 9-inch [20- or 23-cm.]
pie or eight 2-inch [5-cm.] tartlets

1	fully baked pie shell or 8 tartlet shells, made from ½ lb. [¼ kg.] short-crust dough (recipe, page 162)	1
2 cups	extra-strong hot coffee	½ liter
2 tbsp.	unflavored powdered gelatin, softened for 5 minutes in ½ cup [125 ml.] cold water	30 ml.
2	eggs, the yolks separated from the whites	2
⅔ cup	sugar	150 ml.
	salt	
1 tsp.	vanilla extract	5 ml.
1 cup	heavy cream, whipped	¼ liter

Add the softened gelatin to the freshly brewed hot coffee and stir until dissolved. In the top of a double boiler set over hot water, mix the egg yolks with ⅓ cup [75 ml.] of the sugar. Beat with a whisk until the yolks begin to thicken. Then beat in the coffee mixture. Cook and stir over hot water until the mixture thickens. Remove from the heat; stir in a pinch of salt and the vanilla extract; cool.

When the filling begins to set, whip it with a rotary beater until light and foamy. Whip the egg whites until frothy, then whip in the remaining ⅓ cup of sugar, a spoonful at a time, until the whites stand in soft peaks. Fold the egg whites into the filling, then fold in the whipped cream. Spoon the filling into the baked pie shell and chill until set.

EVE BROWN
THE PLAZA COOKBOOK

Vinegar Meringue Pie

This unusual pie might be called "mock lemon pie," for it tastes surprisingly like lemon meringue pie.

To make one 8-inch [20-cm.] pie

1	fully baked pie shell, made from ½ lb. [¼ kg.] short-crust dough (recipe, page 162)	1
¼ cup	cider vinegar	50 ml.
1⅓ cups	sugar	325 ml.
3 tbsp.	flour	45 ml.
3	large eggs, the yolks separated from the whites	3
1 cup	water	¼ liter
2 tbsp.	butter	30 ml.

Blend 1 cup [¼ liter] of the sugar and the flour in a small saucepan, pressing out all lumps. Add the egg yolks and water, and stir briskly; drop in the butter. Set over low heat and cook, stirring constantly, until smooth and thick—about eight to 10 minutes. Remove from the heat and add the vinegar in a slow stream, beating all the while.

Spoon the vinegar filling into the baked pie shell. Prepare the meringue by beating the egg whites with the remaining sugar until stiff peaks form. Spread the meringue on top of the pie, making sure that the meringue touches the pastry rim all around. For a more attractive meringue, swirl it into peaks and valleys, using a spatula or table knife.

Bake in a preheated 350° F. [180° C.] oven for eight to 10 minutes, or until the meringue is lightly browned. Cool the pie to room temperature before serving.

JEAN ANDERSON
THE GRASS ROOTS COOKBOOK

Wet-Bottom Pennsylvania Dutch Shoofly Pie

To make two 9-inch [23-cm.] pies

2	unbaked pie shells, made from 1 lb. [½ kg.] short-crust dough (recipe, page 162)	2
1 cup	dark molasses	¼ liter
1 cup	hot water	¼ liter
1 tsp.	baking soda	5 ml.
3	eggs, lightly beaten	3
	Crumb topping	
4 cups	flour	1 liter
1 cup	brown sugar	¼ liter
½ tsp.	mixed ground spices — nutmeg, ginger, cloves, cinnamon, mace and salt	2 ml.
½ cup	shortening	125 ml.

For the filling, stir together the dark molasses, hot water, baking soda and eggs; let cool. For the topping, combine in a bowl the flour, brown sugar, mixed spices and shortening. Using a pastry blender or two knives, cut the shortening into the dry ingredients until the mixture has the consistency of fine, moist bread crumbs.

Pour the syrup filling into the two pie shells, dividing it equally. Sprinkle the crumb topping over the syrup mixture, also dividing the topping equally between the two shells. Leave a little exposed filling in the center of each pie to allow for expansion and to prevent the mixture from boiling over. Bake in a preheated 350° to 375° F. [180° to 190° C.] oven for one hour to one hour and 10 minutes, or until the filling thickens into a custard.

AMISH DUTCH COOKBOOK

Pixie Pie

To make one 9-inch [23-cm.] pie

1	fully baked pie shell, made from ½ lb. [¼ kg.] short-crust dough (recipe, page 162)	1
2 tbsp.	unflavored powdered gelatin	30 ml.
⅔ cup	sugar	150 ml.
¼ tsp.	salt	1 ml.
¾ cup	light cream	175 ml.
¾ cup	water	175 ml.
2 oz.	unsweetened baking chocolate	60 g.
3	eggs, the yolks separated from the whites, and the yolks lightly beaten	3
1 tsp.	vanilla extract	5 ml.
	whipped cream	

In a saucepan, mix together thoroughly the gelatin, ⅓ cup [75 ml.] of the sugar and the salt. Add the light cream, water and chocolate. Stir over medium heat until the chocolate is melted and the gelatin is dissolved; do not boil. Blend evenly with an egg beater. Stirring constantly, pour the mixture slowly over the egg yolks. Return the mixture to the saucepan, cook and stir until thickened (about three minutes). Cool for 15 minutes. Beat the egg whites until foamy. Gradually add the remaining sugar, beating to stiff peaks. Blend in the chocolate mixture. Add the vanilla extract. Spoon the filling into the cool pie shell. Chill until firm. Garnish the pie with whipped cream.

WILLIAM I. KAUFMAN AND SISTER MARY URSULA COOPER
THE ART OF CREOLE COOKING

Devastating Chocolate Fudge Pie

To make one 9-inch [23-cm.] pie

1	unbaked pie shell, made from ½ lb. [¼ kg.] short-crust dough (recipe, page 162)	1
3 oz.	unsweetened baking chocolate	90 g.
8 tbsp.	butter	120 ml.
4	eggs	4
3 tbsp.	light corn syrup	45 ml.
1½ cups	sugar	375 ml.
¼ tsp.	salt	1 ml.
1 tsp.	vanilla extract	5 ml.

In the top of a double boiler over boiling water, heat the chocolate and butter, stirring until melted and blended; al-

low the mixture to cool slightly. Beat the eggs; blend in the corn syrup, sugar, salt and vanilla extract. Add the chocolate mixture; blend well. Pour the mixture into the pie shell. Bake in a preheated 400° F. [200° C.] oven for five minutes. Reduce the temperature to 350° F. [180° C.] and continue baking for 30 minutes, or until the pie is almost, but not quite, firm when shaken.

BETH TARTAN
THE GOOD OLD DAYS COOKBOOK

Latticed Chocolate One-Crust Tart

Rácsos csokoládés

The techniques of shaping lattices appear on pages 26-29.

To make one 8-by-10-inch [20-by-25-cm.] pie

5 cups	flour	1¼ liters
12 tbsp.	butter	180 ml.
1½ cups	confectioners' sugar	375 ml.
	salt	
1 tsp.	grated lemon peel	5 ml.
3 tbsp.	fresh lemon juice	45 ml.
4	egg yolks	4
Chocolate filling		
¼ lb.	unsweetened chocolate, grated	125 g.
4	egg whites	4
1 cup	granulated sugar	¼ liter
½ lb.	blanched almonds, ground in a nut grinder, or in a food processor operated at short spurts	¼ kg.
2-inch	piece vanilla bean, ground in a nut grinder, or in a food processor operated at short spurts	5-cm.
¼ cup	apricot jam	50 ml.
1	egg yolk, beaten with 1 tsp. [5 ml.] water	1

Mix the butter and flour together until they form crumbs. Then mix in the confectioners' sugar, salt, lemon peel, lemon juice and egg yolks.

Take two thirds of the dough and pat it down on the bottom of a buttered, shallow 8-by-10-inch [20-by-25-cm.] baking pan. Make sure that the sides are also covered. Bake in a preheated 400° F. [200° C.] oven for 10 minutes. Set aside to cool.

To make the filling, first make a very stiff froth with the egg whites and granulated sugar, then very gently, so as not to break the froth, mix in the almonds and chocolate. Add the ground vanilla bean.

Spread the jam on top of the cooled half-baked pastry. Spread the filling on top of the jam.

Roll out the rest of the dough into a thin sheet and cut it into thin strips. Form a diamond-shaped lattice on top of the filling. Brush the lattice with the beaten egg yolk and water to glaze it. Return the pan to the oven for an additional 30 to 35 minutes, or until it is properly baked.

GEORGE LANG
THE CUISINE OF HUNGARY

Black-Bottom Pie

To make one 9-inch [23-cm.] pie

1	fully baked pie shell, made from ½ lb. [¼ kg.] short-crust dough *(recipe, page 162)*	1
1 cup	sugar	¼ liter
1 tbsp.	cornstarch	15 ml.
	salt	
2 cups	milk	½ liter
4	eggs, the yolks separated from the whites, and the yolks beaten	4
1 tbsp.	unflavored powdered gelatin, softened in ¼ cup [50 ml.] cold water	15 ml.
2 oz.	unsweetened baking chocolate, melted	60 g.
1 tsp.	vanilla extract	5 ml.
1 tsp.	rum	5 ml.
⅛ tsp.	cream of tartar	½ ml.
1 cup	heavy cream, whipped	¼ liter

Mix ½ cup [125 ml.] of the sugar, the cornstarch and a dash of salt in a medium-sized saucepan. Stir in the milk. Stirring constantly, cook over low heat until this custard mixture thickens. Stir the hot custard mixture into the beaten egg yolks. Remove from the heat and add the softened gelatin. Strain the custard into a 4-cup [1-liter] measure. Spoon 1 cup [¼ liter] of the custard back into the saucepan; blend in the melted chocolate and the vanilla extract. Pour the chocolate custard into the pie shell. Chill.

Meanwhile, stir the rum into the remaining custard. When the rum custard is cool, beat the egg whites with cream of tartar and the remaining sugar. Fold the beaten egg whites into the rum custard. Spoon the rum-custard mixture over the chocolate custard in the shell. Chill for two hours. Top with whipped cream.

FAVORITE RECIPES OF AMERICA: DESSERTS

Super Chocolate Pie

To make one 9-inch [23-cm.] pie

3	egg whites	3
	salt	
¼ tsp.	cream of tartar	1 ml.
⅔ cup	sifted sugar	150 ml.
½ tsp.	vanilla extract	2 ml.
⅓ cup	finely chopped walnuts or pecans	75 ml.

Chocolate cream filling		
5 oz.	semisweet chocolate	150 g.
1 cup	heavy cream	¼ liter
¼ cup	hot milk	50 ml.
1 tsp.	vanilla extract	5 ml.
	salt	

Cream topping		
¾ cup	heavy cream	175 ml.
2 tbsp.	confectioners' sugar	30 ml.
	chocolate curls	

For the pie shell, beat together the egg whites, salt and the cream of tartar until soft peaks form. Beat in the sugar, a little at a time, until a very stiff meringue is formed. Then beat in the vanilla.

Butter the bottom and sides of a glass pie plate. Spread the meringue over the bottom and sides, building up the sides as high as possible. Sprinkle the nuts over the bottom. Bake in a preheated 275° F. [140° C.] oven for one hour. (If after 10 minutes the sides start to sag, gently push them back into place.) Turn off the oven and allow the shell to cool in the oven for 30 minutes. Remove the shell from the oven and let it cool completely.

For the filling, melt the chocolate in the top of a double boiler over hot water. Add the milk, vanilla and salt. Stir until smooth. Cool.

Whip the cream until stiff and fold it into the cooled chocolate. Spread the filling in the cooled meringue shell. Refrigerate the pie for four hours.

No more than one and a half hours prior to serving, whip the cream for the topping with the confectioners' sugar; spread it over the top of the pie. Decorate the whipped cream with chocolate curls. Refrigerate the pie until serving time.

BERT GREENE
BERT GREENE'S KITCHEN BOUQUETS

Cheese Pies and Cheesecakes

Cottage-Cheese Raisin Pie

To make one 9-inch [23-cm.] pie

1	partially baked pie shell, made from ½ lb. [¼ kg.] short-crust dough (recipe, page 162)	1
1½ cups	creamed cottage cheese, small curd	375 ml.
½ cup	raisins, soaked in warm water for 15 minutes and drained	125 ml.
2 tbsp.	milk	30 ml.
2 tbsp.	sour cream	30 ml.
2	eggs, beaten	2
1 tbsp.	flour	15 ml.
½ cup	sugar	125 ml.
	salt	
1 tsp.	grated lemon peel	5 ml.
3 tbsp.	fresh lemon juice	45 ml.
¼ tsp.	vanilla extract	1 ml.
	grated nutmeg	

Mix together well the cottage cheese, milk, sour cream and eggs. In a separate bowl, mix together the flour, sugar and a pinch of salt, then combine them with the cheese mixture. Add the grated lemon peel and the fresh lemon juice, vanilla extract and raisins. Pour all into the pie shell. Sprinkle grated nutmeg on top. Bake in a preheated 350° F. [180° C.] oven for 30 minutes, or until a knife, inserted into the center of the pie, comes out clean.

ELINOR SEIDEL (EDITOR)
CHEFS, SCHOLARS & MOVABLE FEASTS

Blueberry Cheese Pie

To make one 9-inch [23-cm.] pie

1	baked crumb pie shell, made from graham crackers (recipe, page 165)	1
2 cups	blueberries	½ liter
2 cups	creamed cottage cheese	½ liter
2 tbsp.	cold water	30 ml.
2 tbsp.	fresh lemon juice	30 ml.
1 tbsp.	unflavored powdered gelatin	15 ml.
½ cup	milk, scalded	125 ml.
2	egg yolks	2
⅓ cup	sugar	75 ml.
½ cup	currant jelly	125 ml.

Place the cold water, lemon juice and gelatin in a blender container, cover and blend at low speed. Add the scalded milk. If the gelatin granules cling to the container, push them down into the milk with a rubber spatula. When the gelatin is dissolved, turn the control to high speed; add the egg yolks, sugar and cottage cheese. Blend until smooth. Pour the mixture into the prepared pie shell. Chill until firm, about two hours. Melt the currant jelly over low heat, stir until smooth and then let it cool. Add the berries to the cooled jelly and stir until they are coated. Spoon the berries into the pie. Chill until ready to serve.

JEAN HEWITT
THE NEW YORK TIMES LARGE TYPE COOKBOOK

Cream Cheese Pie

Tarte au Fromage Frais

To make one 9-inch [23-cm.] pie

1	partially baked pie shell, made from ½ lb. [¼ kg.] short-crust dough (recipe, page 162)	1
½ lb.	cream cheese, softened	¼ kg.
14 tbsp.	unsalted butter, softened	210 ml.
½ cup	superfine sugar	125 ml.
¼ tsp.	freshly grated nutmeg	1 ml.
2	eggs	2

With an electric mixer, blend together well the cream cheese, butter, sugar and nutmeg. Add the eggs and blend for another two minutes.

Pour the mixture into the partially baked pie shell and bake in a preheated 400° F. [200° C.] oven for five minutes.

Reduce the oven temperature to 325° F. [160° C.] and bake for approximately 20 to 25 minutes longer.

The cheese pie is done when it is puffed and browned on top, or when a knife inserted into the center comes out clean. This pie can be served hot or cold.

CHARLES VIRION
CHARLES VIRION'S FRENCH COUNTRY COOKBOOK

Lindy's Cheesecake

The techniques of lining a spring-form pan for cheesecake are demonstrated on pages 40-41.

To make one 9-inch [23-cm.] cake

1 cup	flour, sifted	¼ liter
¼ cup	sugar	50 ml.
1 tsp.	grated lemon peel	5 ml.
1	egg yolk	1
¼ tsp.	vanilla extract	1 ml.
8 tbsp.	butter, cut into small pieces	120 ml.

Cheese filling

2½ lb.	cream cheese, at room temperature	1¼ kg.
1¾ cups	sugar	425 ml.
3 tbsp.	flour	45 ml.
1½ tsp.	grated orange peel	7 ml.
1½ tsp.	grated lemon peel	7 ml.
¼ tsp.	vanilla extract	1 ml.
5	eggs	5
2	egg yolks	2
¼ cup	heavy cream	50 ml.

Prepare the dough by first combining the flour, sugar and lemon peel in a small bowl. Make a well in the center and place the egg yolk, vanilla extract and butter in it. Using your finger tips, mix the ingredients together until the dough comes away from the sides of the bowl and will form a ball. Wrap the dough tightly in foil and refrigerate it for about one hour.

To make the bottom crust, first lightly grease the base of a spring-form pan. Place half of the dough on a lightly floured board and roll it out ⅛ inch [3 mm.] thick. Place the dough on the base of the pan and trim the edges. Add the trimmings to the rest of the dough in the refrigerator. Place the bottom crust on the middle shelf of a preheated 400° F. [200° C.] oven and bake for about 20 minutes, or until the crust is pale gold.

Remove the pan from the oven and place it on a rack to cool. When the bottom crust is cool, grease the sides of the pan, set the sides around the base and lock it. Roll the remaining dough into two strips about ⅛ inch thick and long enough so that end to end they will line the sides of the pan. Fit the strips into the pan, pressing the ends together to seal. Trim and discard the excess dough. Increase the oven temperature to 450° F. [230° C.].

Beat the cream cheese with a wooden spoon. Blend in the sugar, flour, orange and lemon peel, and vanilla. Beat in the eggs, one at a time, and then the egg yolks. Stir in the cream. Pour the mixture into the assembled pastry and place the pan in the oven for 15 minutes. Reduce the temperature to 250° F. [120° C.] and bake the cake for one hour more.

Remove the cheesecake from the oven and place it on a rack to cool. Let it cool for at least two hours before removing the sides of the pan.

WORLD ATLAS OF FOOD

Cream Cheese and Honey Pie

To make one 8-inch [20-cm.] pie

½ lb.	short-crust dough *(recipe, page 162)*	¼ kg.
6 oz.	cream cheese, at room temperature	175 g.
4 tsp.	honey, warmed if stiff	20 ml.
⅔ cup	milk or light cream	150 ml.
4 tbsp.	sugar	60 ml.
1 tsp.	freshly grated lemon peel	5 ml.
1 tsp.	ground cinnamon	5 ml.
2	eggs, lightly beaten	2

Roll the dough into a ball, then spread it into a removable-base flan or tart pan, patting it into place with your fingers.

To make the filling, beat the cream cheese until smooth. Add the milk or cream gradually. Then stir in the sugar, lemon peel, cinnamon, honey and, lastly, the beaten eggs.

Pour this filling mixture into the pastry case, stand the flan ring or tart pan on a baking sheet, and cook in the center of a preheated moderately hot oven—375° F. [190° C.]—for about 45 minutes, or until the filling is set. After the first 15 to 20 minutes, look to see if the top is browning too fast. If so, cover with a round of buttered wax paper, which should be already prepared.

ELIZABETH DAVID
SPICES, SALT AND AROMATICS IN THE ENGLISH KITCHEN

Cheesecake

To make one 9-inch [23-cm.] cheesecake

1 cup	graham cracker crumbs	¼ liter
3 tbsp.	granulated sugar	45 ml.
½ tsp.	ground cinnamon	2 ml.
4 tbsp.	unsalted butter, melted and cooled to room temperature	60 ml.
	confectioners' sugar	

Cream-cheese filling		
1½ lb.	cream cheese, at room temperature	¾ kg.
1¼ cups	granulated sugar	300 ml.
6	eggs, the yolks separated from the whites	6
⅓ cup	flour	75 ml.
2 cups	sour cream	½ liter
2 tsp.	vanilla extract	10 ml.
1 tbsp.	grated lemon peel	15 ml.
2 tbsp.	fresh lemon juice	30 ml.

Place the graham cracker crumbs, granulated sugar, cinnamon and melted butter in a small bowl; using a wooden spoon, combine them until they are thoroughly blended. Measure off ¾ cup [175 ml.] of the crumb mixture to line the pan, and set the remainder aside for topping the baked cake.

Press the crumb mixture into the well-buttered bottom and sides of a spring-form pan, making the bottom crust twice as thick as that on the sides. Chill for 30 minutes.

For the filling, place the cream cheese in a large bowl. Using a wooden spoon or an electric mixer set on low speed, beat the cheese until it is soft. Add the sugar gradually, beating until the mixture is light and fluffy. One at a time, beat in the egg yolks. Using a wooden spoon, stir in the flour, then the sour cream, vanilla, lemon peel and lemon juice. Continue stirring until the texture is smooth.

Beat the egg whites until they hold stiff peaks. With a rubber spatula, add about one third of the whites to the cheese mixture, stirring them together thoroughly. Pour this mixture into the remaining egg whites; still using the rubber spatula, fold them together quickly and thoroughly, but with a light touch. Pour the filling into the chilled crust, using the spatula to get all of it. Place the pan on the middle shelf of a preheated 350° F. [180° C.] oven and bake for one hour and 15 minutes, or until the top is golden. Turn off the oven heat and let the cake continue to bake for one hour.

Remove the cheesecake from the oven to a wire rack. Let the cake, in its pan, cool to room temperature. Sprinkle the reserved crumb mixture over the top of the cake. Place the cake in the refrigerator to chill in its pan for at least three hours. Before serving, sift confectioners' sugar over the top.

JOHN CLANCY & FRANCES FIELD
CLANCY'S OVEN COOKERY

Cretan Turnovers

Skaltsounia

To make 36 turnovers

4 cups	flour	1 liter
½ tsp.	salt	2 ml.
½ cup	shortening	125 ml.
½ to 1 cup	cold water	125 to 250 ml.

Mint-cheese filling		
2 tbsp.	dried mint leaves, crushed	30 ml.
½ lb.	feta cheese, crumbled	¼ kg.
3 oz.	cream cheese, softened	90 g.
2	eggs, beaten	2
8 tbsp.	butter, softened	120 ml.
	oil or fat for deep frying (optional)	
	sugar or honey	

In a bowl, combine the cheeses and eggs, and whip until smooth. Add the mint and mix in the butter. Set aside.

To make the dough, first sift the flour and salt into a mixing bowl. Cut in the shortening with a pastry blender or two knives. Stir in enough water to make a firm dough that can be gathered together in a ball.

On a floured board, roll out the dough as thin as possible. Cut the dough into 3-inch [8-cm.] rounds. Place one heaping tablespoonful [20 ml.] of filling on each round, fold over the dough as in making turnovers, moisten the edges and seal.

You can fry the *skaltsounia* in olive oil or hot fat, until light brown on both sides. Drain, place them on a platter, and sprinkle them with sugar or dip them in honey. Or, if preferred, the *skaltsounia* may be placed on an ungreased baking sheet and baked in a preheated 350° F. [180° C.] oven for 15 to 20 minutes, or until golden, then sprinkled with sugar or dipped in honey.

WOMEN OF ST. PAUL'S GREEK ORTHODOX CHURCH
THE ART OF GREEK COOKERY

Corsican Cheese Pie

Strenna Corse

This pie takes its name —Corsican gift —from a New Year's Day tradition in the Corsican town of Vico, where the pie is presented to relatives who have come to offer their good wishes for the coming year. The original version of this recipe calls for brocciu, a fresh Corsican sheep's-milk cheese, not avail-

able in the United States. Taleggio or ricotta cheese makes a suitable substitute.

To make one 10-inch [25-cm.] pie		
2 cups	flour, sifted	½ liter
1	egg	1
1 tbsp.	lard, softened	15 ml.
⅔ to 1 cup	milk	150 to 250 ml.
2 tsp.	sugar	10 ml.
	Tart cheese filling	
½ lb.	*Taleggio* or ricotta cheese	¼ kg.
¼ cup	sugar	50 ml.
3	eggs, 1 lightly beaten	3
1 to 2 tsp.	grated orange or lemon peel	5 to 10 ml.

Prepare the dough by working the flour, egg, lard, ⅔ cup [150 ml.] of the milk, and the sugar together with your fingers until the mixture is smooth. If the dough is stiff, work in more milk by the spoonful.

Roll out the dough about ¼ inch [6 mm.] thick. Cut out two large circles. Use one to line a tart pan.

Place the cheese in a bowl and beat in the sugar, two of the eggs and the grated lemon or orange peel. Put the cheese mixture into the pie shell and cover with the second circle of dough. Moisten the edges and seal them together, forming a crimped rim. Brush the top with the beaten egg and bake in a preheated 425° F. [220° C.] oven for 35 minutes, or until the top is golden brown.

NICOLE VIELFAURE
FÊTES, COUTUMES ET GÂTEAUX

Mocha Ricotta Pie

To make one 8-inch [20-cm.] pie		
1	fully baked pie shell, made from ½ lb. [¼ kg.] short-crust dough (recipe, page 162)	1
1 tbsp. plus 1 tsp.	cocoa powder	20 ml.
1 tbsp.	instant coffee granules, preferably freeze-dried	15 ml.
1 cup	part skim-milk ricotta cheese	¼ liter
1¼ cups	water	300 ml.
1 tbsp.	unflavored powdered gelatin	15 ml.
2 tbsp.	sugar	30 ml.
1 tsp.	almond-flavored liqueur	5 ml.

Pour ¼ cup [50 ml.] of the water into a small bowl or cup, and sprinkle on the gelatin; put the remaining cup [¼ liter] of

water in a small pot and bring it to a boil. Meanwhile, measure 1 tablespoon [15 ml.] of the cocoa, the instant coffee, sugar and almond-flavored liqueur into a mixing bowl, pour on the boiling water and stir briefly. Immediately scoop in the softened gelatin and stir until it has completely dissolved. Put the mixture aside to cool.

Pour the mocha mixture into the blender and, with the motor running, add the ricotta cheese, a heaping tablespoonful at a time. After all of the ingredients have been thoroughly blended, give a final burst at high speed.

Refrigerate the filling until it thickens slightly, stirring several times. Pour the mocha mixture into the baked pie shell and refrigerate until the filling sets. Remove the pie from the refrigerator about 30 minutes before serving. Just before serving, put the remaining teaspoon [5 ml.] of cocoa in a small sieve and shake it over the surface of the pie.

CAROL CUTLER
THE WOMAN'S DAY LOW-CALORIE DESSERT COOKBOOK

Sweet Cheese Pie

Pizza Dolce di Ricotta

To make one 10-by-16-inch [25-by-40-cm.] pie		
1 lb.	short-crust dough (recipe, page 162)	½ kg.
2 cups	ricotta cheese	½ liter
1 cup	sugar	¼ liter
1	egg	1
3	egg yolks	3
2 tbsp.	grated orange peel	30 ml.
1 tsp.	grated lemon peel	5 ml.
	lard, melted	
	confectioners' sugar	

For the filling, beat the ricotta together with the sugar, egg and egg yolks, and the grated orange and lemon peel.

Divide the dough in half and roll out each half into a large rectangle. Place one rectangle on a buttered baking sheet, spread the filling over it, leaving a ¾-inch [2-cm.] border. Cover with the other rectangle of dough. Pinch the edges together and cut a slit in the top. Brush the surface with a little melted lard.

Bake in a preheated 425° F. [220° C.] oven for 25 to 30 minutes or until the pastry is golden brown. Sprinkle with confectioners' sugar as soon as the pie comes out of the oven. Serve hot or cold.

ADOLFO GIAQUINTO
I DOLCI IN FAMIGLIA

Ricotta Cheese Tart

Crostata di Ricotta

The techniques of shaping lattices are shown on pages 26-29.

	To make one 9-inch [23-cm.] pie	
3½ cups	sifted flour	875 ml.
5 tbsp.	lard	75 ml.
5 tbsp.	butter	75 ml.
2 cups	superfine sugar	½ liter
5	egg yolks	5
3	eggs, 1 egg beaten with a few drops of warm water	3

Brandied ricotta-cheese filling

¼ cup	brandy	50 ml.
1½ lb.	ricotta cheese, sieved	¾ kg.
2 tbsp.	chopped candied fruit	30 ml.
1½ tsp.	grated orange peel	7 ml.
¼ tsp.	grated lemon peel	1 ml.
½ cup	raisins, soaked in warm water for 15 minutes and drained	125 ml.
3 tbsp.	pine nuts	45 ml.
	ground cinnamon	
	vanilla sugar	

Make a dough, combining the flour with the lard and butter, 1¼ cups [300 ml.] of the superfine sugar, two of the egg yolks, and one whole egg. Allow this dough to rest for half an hour, wrapped in a cloth.

Marinate the candied fruit in the brandy. In a mixing bowl, combine the ricotta, the remaining sugar, one whole egg, the three remaining egg yolks, the grated orange and lemon peels, raisins, pine nuts and a pinch of cinnamon. Add the candied fruit, discarding the brandy marinade. Work the mixture with a fork until a smooth paste is obtained.

Roll out the dough and cut a 10-inch [25-cm.] round for lining a tart pan. Grease the pan with melted lard and lay the dough in it. Add the ricotta mixture. Cut the remaining dough into strips, and decorate the top of the tart with them in the usual crisscross manner and with the usual border. Lightly brush the border and strips of dough with the beaten egg; transfer the pan to a preheated 350° F. [180° C.] oven. The pastry strips will begin to brown after half an hour; at

that time, remove the pan from the oven and allow it to cool. Sprinkle the top with vanilla sugar.

LUIGI CARNACINA
LUIGI CARNACINA PRESENTS ITALIAN HOME COOKING

Country-Style Cheese Tart

Torta di Ricotta Campagnola

	To make one 10-inch [25-cm.] tart	
2½ cups	flour, sifted with 1 tsp. [5 ml.] baking powder	625 ml.
1	egg	1
1	egg yolk	1
10 tbsp.	butter, softened and cut into small pieces	150 ml.
⅔ cup	vanilla sugar	150 ml.
	salt	
2 tbsp.	grated lemon peel	30 ml.
2 tbsp.	milk (optional)	30 ml.

Ricotta-fruit filling

1¼ lb.	ricotta cheese, sieved	⅔ kg.
½ cup	chopped mixed candied fruit peel	125 ml.
½ cup	chopped candied cherries	125 ml.
1¼ cups	granulated sugar	300 ml.
5 oz.	semisweet chocolate, grated	150 g.
5	egg yolks	5
⅓ cup	anisette	75 ml.
3 tbsp.	dry bread crumbs	45 ml.

Meringue

3	egg whites	3
⅓ cup	superfine sugar	75 ml.
¼ cup	slivered blanched almonds	50 ml.

For the dough, place the flour on a board, make a well in the center, and put in the egg, egg yolk, butter, vanilla sugar, a pinch of salt and the grated lemon peel. Work all of the ingredients together rapidly with your finger tips. If necessary, add a little milk to make a smooth dough. Form the dough into a ball, dust it with flour, cover, and allow it to rest for at least one hour.

For the filling, mix the ricotta with the granulated sugar, then add the fruit, chocolate, egg yolks and anisette, and blend thoroughly.

Butter a tart pan and dust it with the bread crumbs. Roll out the dough and use it to line the pan. Put in the filling.

Bake in a preheated 350° F. [180° C.] oven for about 50 minutes, or until the filling is lightly browned.

Meanwhile, prepare the meringue. Beat the egg whites with the superfine sugar until stiff. When the tart is baked, spread it with the meringue and sprinkle the top with the almonds. Return to the oven for about 10 minutes, or until the meringue is lightly browned. Serve hot or cold.

MARIÙ SALVATORI DE ZULIANI
LA CUCINA DI VERSILLIA E GARFAGNANA

———————◆———————

Torte with Pot-Cheese Filling

Topfentorte

To make one 9-by-1 ½-inch [23-by-4-cm.] pastry

1⅓ to 1⅔ cups	flour, sifted	325 to 400 ml.
¼ cup	granulated sugar	50 ml.
1 tsp.	grated lemon peel	5 ml.
8 tbsp.	unsalted butter, cut into pieces and chilled	120 ml.
1	egg, the yolk separated from the white, and the white lightly beaten	1
	confectioners' sugar	
	Pot-cheese filling	
½ lb.	pot cheese	¼ kg.
⅓ cup	sugar	75 ml.
2	eggs, the yolks separated from the whites, and the whites stiffly beaten	2
1 cup	unblanched almonds, ground in a nut grinder, or in a food processor operated at short spurts	¼ liter
1 tbsp.	flour	15 ml.

Combine 1⅓ cups [325 ml.] of the flour, the granulated sugar and lemon peel on a pastry board. Make a well in the center, cut in the butter and add the egg yolk. With a table knife, quickly blend the ingredients together. Work into a smooth, medium-firm dough. If necessary, add more flour by the spoonful until the dough no longer sticks to your hands and the board. Form a ball. Cover with wax paper. Refrigerate for about 30 minutes.

Divide the dough into almost equal halves. Place the larger piece of dough on the removable bottom of the tart pan, cover with a sheet of wax paper and roll out the dough, adding 1½ inches [4 cm.] all around to form a rim. Remove the wax paper. Place the bottom inside the outer ring. Pat the dough into the pan to remove air pockets. Lightly press down the rim to even it out. With a fork or toothpick, prick the rim all around.

To form the top layer of the torte, roll the second piece of dough between two sheets of wax paper and, using the pan as a guide, cut it to the exact size of the bottom of the tart pan. Refrigerate the tart shell and round piece until almost firm.

To prepare the filling, first press the pot cheese through a food mill. Add the sugar and egg yolks, and blend. Fold the almonds into the mixture. Add the beaten egg whites and flour. Combine. Fill the tart shell with the cheese mixture. Remove the top sheet of wax paper from the refrigerated round of dough and fold it gently over the back of your hand. After carefully removing the second sheet of paper, place the round piece gently on top of the cheese mixture, securing it lightly against the rim. (Alternatively, you can place the round piece directly over the cheese filling and then gently remove the wax paper.) With a pointed knife, make four or five small incisions on top of the torte. Brush the torte with the lightly beaten egg white.

Bake the torte on the lowest shelf of a preheated 350° F. [180° C.] oven for 30 minutes. Move the torte to the center shelf and bake for 30 minutes more, or until the top is golden brown and the torte shrinks away from the sides of the pan.

Before serving, sprinkle the torte with confectioners' sugar. To make your torte look even more attractive, place a paper doily on top, then sprinkle with confectioners' sugar. Remove the doily, being careful not to disturb the design.

LILLY JOSS REICH
THE VIENNESE PASTRY COOKBOOK

———————◆———————

Yorkshire Cheese Cakes

To make two 7-inch [18-cm.] or twelve 3-inch [8-cm.] cakes

¾ lb.	short-crust dough (recipe, page 162)	⅓ kg.
2 cups	farmer or pot cheese	½ liter
8 tbsp.	butter	120 ml.
1 cup	sugar	¼ liter
2	eggs, lightly beaten	2
¼ tsp.	baking soda	1 ml.
	grated nutmeg	
	rum	

In a saucepan, melt the butter over low heat. Off the heat, stir in the sugar, eggs, baking soda and cheese. Beat well so that the ingredients combine to make a smooth mixture. Then grate in a little nutmeg. Line two layer-cake pans or 12 tartlet pans with the dough, fill them three quarters full with the cheese mixture, and bake in a preheated 350° F. [180° C.] oven for 30 minutes, or until the filling is set and lightly browned. While the tarts are still warm, put a drop or two of rum in each. Serve warm or cold.

PEGGY HUTCHINSON
OLD ENGLISH COOKERY

Nut, Vegetable and Meat Pies

Almond Tartlets

Petits Marcellins

To make about eighteen 2-inch [5-cm.] tartlets

2 cups	flour, sifted	½ liter
1	egg	1
about 2½ cups	confectioners' sugar (1½ cups [375 ml.] sifted)	about 625 ml.
4 tbsp.	butter, melted	60 ml.
1 tbsp.	rum or kirsch	15 ml.

Almond-orange liqueur filling

6 oz.	blanched almonds, ground in a nut grinder, or in a food processor operated at short spurts	170 g.
2 tbsp.	orange liqueur	30 ml.
1⅔ cups	sugar	400 ml.
2	eggs, the yolks separated from the whites, and the whites stiffly beaten	2
2 tbsp.	flour	30 ml.

To prepare the dough, first thoroughly beat together the egg and sifted confectioners' sugar, then add the melted butter, the rum or kirsch, and finally the flour. Mix until the dough is firm and roll it into a ball. Chill for several hours or overnight. On a floured surface, roll out the dough as thin as possible and cut it into 3-inch [8-cm.] circles. Put these into buttered tartlet pans and prick the bottoms with a fork.

To prepare the filling, mix the ground almonds with the orange liqueur and ⅔ cup [150 ml.] of the sugar. Beat the egg yolks with the remaining sugar until pale, then gradually combine the two mixtures and add the flour. When well mixed, fold in the stiffly beaten egg whites.

Fill the tartlet shells with the almond mixture, cover with a thick layer of confectioners' sugar and bake in a preheated 300° to 325° F. [150° to 160° C.] oven for about 30 minutes. The sugar top will harden into a light crust.

THEODORA FITZGIBBON
A TASTE OF PARIS

Cake Royal

Fyrestekake

To make one 9-by-12-inch [23-by-30-cm.] pastry

2 cups	flour, sifted with 2 tsp. [10 ml.] baking powder	½ liter
½ cup	superfine sugar	125 ml.
16 tbsp.	butter (½ lb. [¼ kg.])	240 ml.
1	egg, beaten	1

Almond-sweet wine filling

2 cups	finely chopped blanched almonds	½ liter
2 tbsp.	sweet white wine	30 ml.
2 cups	superfine sugar	½ liter
1	egg white	1

To make the dough, first cut the butter into the flour-and-baking-powder mixture. Add the superfine sugar and the whole egg, and mix well to form a dough. Divide the dough into two parts. Roll out one part and with it cover the bottom of a rectangular baking pan.

To make the filling, combine the almonds, sugar, egg white and wine. Spread the mixture over the layer of dough in the baking pan.

Roll out the remaining dough into another rectangle and, using a pastry wheel or knife, cut it into strips 1½ inches [4 cm.] wide. Place the strips side by side on top of the filling.

Bake in a preheated 375° F. [190° C.] oven for 30 to 35 minutes, or until lightly browned. Serve hot or cold.

BARBARA KRAUS (EDITOR)
THE COOKBOOK OF THE UNITED NATIONS

Almond Pie from Lyon

Tarte à la Mode de Lyon

To make one 8-inch [20-cm.] pie

½ lb.	rich short-crust dough (recipe, page 162)	¼ kg.
1¾ cups	blanched almonds, ground in a nut grinder, or in a food processor operated at short spurts	425 ml.
4	slices stale, firm-textured white bread	4
1 cup	milk, heated	¼ liter
½ cup	sugar	125 ml.
4	eggs, the yolks separated from the whites, and the whites stiffly beaten	4
¼ cup	kirsch	50 ml.

Soak the bread in the hot milk. When the bread is soft, put it through a food mill into a bowl and add to it the sugar, ground almonds, egg yolks and kirsch. Mix well. Fold in the beaten egg whites. Pour the mixture into a buttered piepan.

Roll out the dough to a thickness of ⅛ inch [3 mm.] and use it to cover the pie. Bake in a preheated 350° F. [180° C.] oven for 35 to 40 minutes, or until the top is browned. Let the pie cool completely before serving it.

LES DESSERTS DE NOS PROVINCES

Almond Tart

Tarte aux Amandes

To make one 7-inch [18-cm.] tart

1 cup	flour, sifted	¼ liter
8 tbsp.	butter	120 ml.
2 tbsp.	sugar	30 ml.
	milk	

Ground-almond filling

¾ cup	finely ground blanched almonds	175 ml.
2	eggs	2
7 tbsp.	sugar	105 ml.
⅓ cup	milk	75 ml.
	heavy cream (optional)	

Prepare the dough by mixing the flour, butter and sugar with two knives or with your finger tips until the mixture is crumbly. Add just enough milk to make the dough cohere. Roll out the dough and use it to line a buttered tart pan.

Beat together the ground almonds, eggs, 6 tablespoons [90 ml.] of the sugar and the milk until the mixture is smooth and the consistency of thick cream.

Prick the bottom of the pastry lining with a fork, pour in the ground-almond filling, and bake in a preheated 375° F. [190° C.] oven for about 15 minutes, or until the filling is set. Two minutes before the end of the cooking time, sprinkle the tart with the remaining sugar. Serve hot with cream, or cold.

X. MARCEL BOULESTIN
THE FINER COOKING

Almond and Pastry-Strip Tart

Torta di Mandorle e Tagliatelle

To make one 8-inch [20-cm.] square pastry

½ lb.	rich short-crust dough (recipe, page 162), using 1 egg yolk	¼ kg.
2 cups	chopped blanched almonds	½ liter
1¼ cups	sugar	300 ml.
20 tbsp.	butter, cut into small pieces	300 ml.

Roll out the dough and cut it into very thin strips or tagliatelle. Mix the chopped almonds with the sugar. Butter a

square baking pan and place a thin layer of the tagliatelle in it, then add a layer of the almond mixture. Dot with butter. Continue to make these layers until the ingredients are used up, ending with a layer of tagliatelle dotted with butter.

Place in a preheated 350° F. [180° C.] oven and bake for about 45 minutes, or until the top layer of tagliatelle has become slightly golden. Cool the pastry for about two hours, then place the pan over low heat to warm the base slightly and make it easier to remove the pastry from the pan. Turn the pastry onto a plate upside down, then invert the pastry onto another plate so that it is right side up.

RENZO DALL'ARA AND EMILIO FANIN
MANGIAR MANTOVANO

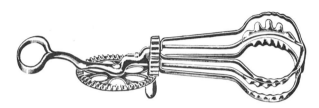

Maple Macadamia Pie

To prepare the coconut, see the editor's note for Saucer Cake (Saucy Kate), page 128.

To make one 8- or 9-inch [20- or 23-cm.] pie

½ lb.	short-crust dough (recipe, page 162)	¼ kg.
1 cup	maple syrup	¼ liter
1 cup	macadamia nuts, chopped or halved	¼ liter
1 cup	freshly shredded coconut	¼ liter
3	eggs, lightly beaten	3
¼ cup	sugar	50 ml.
¼ tsp.	salt	1 ml.
6 tbsp.	butter, melted and cooled	90 ml.
	whipped cream (optional)	

Line a pie plate with the dough, making a raised, crimped edge. Arrange the macadamias in one layer over the unbaked pie shell, covering as much of the pastry as you can. Sprinkle the shredded coconut over the nuts, and refrigerate the pie shell and its contents for 15 minutes.

In a large bowl, add to the beaten eggs the sugar, maple syrup, salt and melted butter. Mix thoroughly and pour into the chilled pie shell.

Bake the pie in a preheated 400° F. [200° C.] oven for 15 minutes. Reduce the heat to 350° F. [180° C.] and bake for an additional 20 or 25 minutes, or until the filling is custard-like. (If the top browns too quickly, cover it with a sheet of foil.) Insert a knife to test for doneness. The filling will rise substantially, but it will fall to the level of the pie plate as it cools. This pie is best served lukewarm with a dollop of ice-cold whipped cream.

JOE FAMULARO AND LOUISE IMPERIALE
THE FESTIVE FAMULARO KITCHEN

Maple Butternut Pie

To make one 9-inch [23-cm.] pie

1	unbaked pie shell, made from ½ lb. [¼ kg.] short-crust dough *(recipe, page 162)*	1
¾ cup	maple syrup	175 ml.
1½ cups	chopped butternuts, or substitute walnuts	375 ml.
3 tbsp.	butter	45 ml.
¼ cup	brown sugar	50 ml.
3	eggs	3
1 tsp.	vanilla extract	5 ml.
½ tsp.	salt	2 ml.
	freshly grated nutmeg	
	vanilla ice cream	

In the bowl of an electric mixer, cream the butter with the brown sugar. Add the eggs and beat well. Then add the maple syrup, vanilla extract and salt. Stir in the nuts and pour the filling into the pie shell. Grate a little nutmeg over the top of the pie.

Bake in a preheated 450° F. [230° C.] oven for 10 minutes; then reduce the temperature to 325° F. [160° C.] and bake for 25 minutes more, or until a knife inserted in the center of the pie comes out clean. Cool, and serve with vanilla ice cream.

MARILYN KLUGER
THE WILD FLAVOR

Coconut-Cream Pie

To prepare the coconut, see the editor's note for Saucer Cake (Saucy Kate), page 128.

To make one 9-inch [23-cm.] pie

1	fully baked pie shell, made from ½ lb. [¼ kg.] short-crust dough *(recipe, page 162)*	1
1 cup	freshly grated coconut	¼ liter
⅓ cup	flour	75 ml.
¾ cup	sugar	175 ml.
¼ tsp.	salt	1 ml.
2 cups	milk	½ liter
2	eggs, the yolks separated from the whites, the yolks lightly beaten, and the whites stiffly beaten	2
1½ tsp.	vanilla extract	7 ml.

Combine the flour, ½ cup [125 ml.] of the sugar and the salt, and add the milk. Stirring constantly, cook the mixture in the top of a double boiler until thickened. Pour a small amount of the mixture over the egg yolks, stirring vigorous-ly. Stir the yolks into the remaining milk mixture and cook for 10 minutes longer. Remove from the stove. Add the coconut and 1 teaspoon [5 ml.] of the vanilla extract. Cool.

Pour the coconut mixture into the pie shell. Fold the rest of the sugar into the beaten egg whites and add the remaining vanilla extract. Pile lightly on the coconut filling. Bake in a preheated 225° F. [110° C.] oven for 10 to 12 minutes, or until a delicate brown.

CLAIRE SUGDEN
THE ROMANTIC AND PRACTICAL SIDE OF COOKERY

Saucer Cake (Saucy Kate)

To open a coconut, drive an ice pick or a screwdriver into two of the dark "eyes" at the pointed end of the nut and pour out the fluid. Break the shell with a mallet, and pare off the skin and remove the flesh. Use the coarse side of a box grater to shred the flesh.

To make one 8-inch [20-cm.] pastry

4 cups	flour, sifted	1 liter
14 tbsp.	butter	210 ml.
6 tbsp.	superfine sugar	90 ml.
	salt	
1 cup	milk	¼ liter

Sweetmeat filling

2	coconuts, opened, drained and the flesh shredded	2
1 cup	sugar	¼ liter
1 tbsp.	slivered almonds	15 ml.
2 tbsp.	white raisins, soaked in warm water for 15 minutes and drained	30 ml.
2 tbsp.	dried currants, soaked in warm water for 15 minutes and drained	30 ml.
6	whole cardamoms, pods removed and seeds pounded to a paste	6

Melt 6 tablespoons [90 ml.] of the butter. Mix together the flour, superfine sugar, a little salt and the melted butter; add enough milk to make the flour mixture into a dough. Mix the shredded or flaked coconut with the sugar, almonds, white raisins, currants and cardamom paste. Divide the dough into four parts and roll out each piece of dough very thin. Put one layer in a piepan and sprinkle some of the sweetmeat filling over the rolled dough. Repeat the process—rolled dough and sweetmeat alternately—until there are seven layers.

With a knife, cut crossed lines, 2 inches [5 cm.] apart, not quite through the pastry layers. Put the remaining butter, in lumps, all over the surface of the cake. Bake in a preheated 400° F. [200° C.] oven for about 30 minutes, or until the crust is light brown.

MRS. J. BARTLEY
INDIAN COOKERY GENERAL FOR YOUNG HOUSEKEEPERS

Tropical Tart

To make coconut milk, grate ¼ cup [50 ml.] of fresh coconut into a bowl. Pour in ½ cup [125 ml.] of boiling water, let stand for five minutes and strain the liquid through a cloth. Squeeze the cloth hard to extract all of the coconut milk.

To make one 7-inch [18-cm.] tart

1	partially baked tart shell, made from ½ lb. [¼ kg.] short-crust dough (recipe, page 162)	1
1 cup	freshly grated coconut	¼ liter
¼ cup	sugar	50 ml.
1 tbsp.	butter	15 ml.
½ cup	coconut milk	125 ml.
½ tsp.	ground cinnamon	2 ml.
½ tsp.	grated nutmeg	2 ml.
½ tsp.	almond extract	2 ml.

Combine all the ingredients for the coconut filling. Pour the mixture into the shell and bake for 25 minutes in a preheated 450° F. [230° C.] oven, reducing the heat for the last few minutes if the coconut threatens to become too brown.

RUTH MAC NIVEN
MONTSERRAT COOKBOOK

Little Tea House Coconut-Cream Pie

For instructions on how to prepare coconut, see the editor's note for Saucer Cake (Saucy Kate), page 128.

To make one 9-inch [23-cm.] pie

1	fully baked pie shell, made from ½ lb. [¼ kg.] short-crust dough (recipe, page 162)	1
½ cup	freshly grated coconut	125 ml.
1¾ cups	milk	425 ml.
¾ cup	sugar	175 ml.
½ tsp.	salt	2 ml.
¼ cup	cake flour	50 ml.
2½ tbsp.	cornstarch	37 ml.
1	whole egg, plus 1 yolk	1
2	egg whites	2
1 tbsp.	butter	15 ml.
½ tsp.	vanilla extract	2 ml.
½ cup	cream, whipped	125 ml.

Mix 1¼ cups [300 ml.] of the milk, ½ cup [125 ml.] of the sugar and the salt, and bring the mixture to a boil. Pour the remaining ½ cup [125 ml.] of the milk into a bowl. Mix in the cake flour, cornstarch, the whole egg and yolk, and beat until smooth. Pour the mixture into the boiling ingredients very slowly, stirring until thick.

Remove the filling mixture from the heat, and add the butter and vanilla extract, stirring in well. Add half of the remaining sugar to the egg whites and beat until peaks form, then add the other half of the sugar and beat only until the sugar is dissolved. Fold the egg whites into the hot mixture and beat until thoroughly blended. Pour the filling into the baked pie shell and spread the top thickly with the coconut. Cool and cover with whipped cream.

SOUTHERN RAILWAY LADIES CLUB COOKBOOK

Walnut and Honey Pie

La Bonissima

To make the sugar syrup for this recipe, combine ¾ cup [175 ml.] of sugar with 3 tablespoons [45 ml.] of water in a saucepan. Let the mixture stand for 10 minutes, then cook over low heat until the sugar is completely dissolved. Bring to a boil and cook for about seven minutes, or until a candy thermometer placed in the syrup reaches 300° F. [149° C.], the hard-crack stage.

To make one 8-inch [20-cm.] pie

3½ cups	flour	875 ml.
⅔ cup	sugar	150 ml.
10 tbsp.	butter, softened and cut into pieces	150 ml.
1	egg, lightly beaten	1
½ tsp.	grated lemon peel	2 ml.
1 tbsp.	vanilla extract	15 ml.

Walnut and honey filling

2 cups	chopped walnuts	½ liter
1 cup	honey	¼ liter
¼ cup	rum	50 ml.
¼ lb.	semisweet baking chocolate, melted over hot water, or ½ cup [125 ml.] heavy sugar syrup	125 g.

For the dough, sift the flour and sugar together, and work in all of the remaining ingredients with your fingers. Roll out the dough and use about two thirds of it to line a piepan.

Mix together the honey, walnuts and rum. Pour the nut mixture into the pastry shell and cover it with the remaining dough, sealing the edges well. Bake in a preheated 350° F. [180° C.] oven for about 30 minutes, or until lightly browned.

Cool the pie, then cover it with the melted chocolate or sugar syrup. Let the topping set before serving the pie.

GIORGIO CAVAZZUTI (EDITOR)
IL MANGIARFUORI: ALMANACCO DELLA CUCINA MODENESE

Aromatic Stuffed Pastries, Cretan-Style

Patoudia

To make about forty-five 2-inch [5-cm.] squares

4 cups plus 2 tbsp.	flour, sifted	1 liter plus 30 ml.
¾ cup	mixed vegetable oil and olive oil	175 ml.
¼ cup	fresh orange juice	50 ml.
¼ cup	fresh lemon juice	50 ml.
¼ cup	water	50 ml.
¼ cup	granulated sugar	50 ml.
1 tsp.	salt	5 ml.
½ tsp.	baking soda	2 ml.
¾ cup	walnuts, ground in a nut grinder, or in a food processor operated at short spurts	175 ml.
¾ cup	blanched almonds, ground in a nut grinder, or in a food processor operated at short spurts	175 ml.
¾ cup	honey	175 ml.
⅓ cup	sesame seeds	75 ml.
about ⅓ cup	rose water	about 75 ml.
	confectioners' sugar	

In a large bowl, combine the vegetable and olive oils, orange and lemon juices, water and sugar. Mix thoroughly. Sift the flour with the salt and soda, and stir the mixture into the liquid ingredients. Knead the dough until smooth, then cover with plastic wrap and refrigerate for several hours, removing to room temperature one hour before rolling.

Meanwhile, in a medium-sized bowl, combine the walnuts, almonds, honey and sesame seeds to make a stiff filling. Set aside.

On a floured board, roll out the dough to a thin sheet, then with a sharp knife cut it into 3½-inch [9-cm.] squares. Place 1 teaspoon [5 ml.] of the filling in the center of each square, then dampen the edges of the square with water. Lift the corners of each square toward the center and press gently to seal. Set on a buttered cookie sheet until all are stuffed, then bake in a preheated 350° F. [180° C.] oven for 25 minutes, or until golden. Cool for 10 minutes, then dip each pastry into rose water and roll it in confectioners' sugar.

VILMA LIACOURAS CHANTILES
THE FOOD OF GREECE

Peanut Pie

To make one 9-inch [23-cm.] pie

1	unbaked pie shell, made from ½ lb. [¼ kg.] short-crust dough (recipe, page 162)	1
1 cup	salted, skinned peanuts	¼ liter
2	eggs	2
1 cup	dark corn syrup	¼ liter
1 cup	sugar	¼ liter
1 tsp.	vanilla extract	5 ml.
2 tbsp.	butter, cut into small pieces	30 ml.

In a mixing bowl, combine the eggs, corn syrup, sugar and vanilla extract. Stir in the peanuts and scrape the mixture into the pie shell. Dot with butter and bake in a preheated 350° F. [180° C.] oven for 45 to 50 minutes or until set.

JEAN HEWITT
THE NEW YORK TIMES LARGE TYPE COOKBOOK

Chocolate Pecan Pie

To make one 9-inch [23-cm.] pie

¾ lb.	short-crust dough (recipe, page 162)	⅓ kg.
2 oz.	semisweet baking chocolate	60 g.
1 cup	coarsely chopped pecans	¼ liter
1 cup	pecan halves	¼ liter
¼ cup	very strong coffee or espresso	50 ml.
2 tbsp.	unsalted butter, softened	30 ml.
4	eggs	4
½ cup	sugar	125 ml.
1 cup	light corn syrup	¼ liter
	unsweetened whipped cream	

Roll out the dough to an 11-inch [28-cm.] circle. Line a pie plate with the dough; trim the edges and flute them. Refrigerate until ready to use.

Melt the chocolate with the coffee in a heavy saucepan over low heat; stir until smooth. Remove from the heat; stir in the butter. Let the mixture stand to cool. In a medium-sized bowl, beat the eggs with the sugar and corn syrup until light and fluffy. Stir in the chocolate mixture; mix well. Stir in the chopped pecans.

Pour the mixture into the pastry shell. Arrange the pecan halves in a circle around the edge of the pie. Bake for 10 minutes in a preheated 425° F. [220° C.] oven. Reduce the oven temperature to 375° F. [190° C.] and bake until a toothpick inserted in the center comes out clean, about 20 to 30 minutes. Serve the pie with unsweetened whipped cream.

BERT GREENE
BERT GREENE'S KITCHEN BOUQUETS

Pecan Pie

To make one 9-inch [23-cm.] pie

1	unbaked pie shell, made from ½ lb. [¼ kg.] short-crust dough (recipe, page 162)	1
1 cup	coarsely chopped pecans	¼ liter
3	eggs	3
1 cup	dark brown sugar	¼ liter
¼ cup	light corn syrup	50 ml.
¼ tsp.	salt	1 ml.
¼ cup	dark rum	50 ml.
4 tbsp.	butter, melted	60 ml.
	Rum-cream topping	
3 tbsp.	dark rum	45 ml.
1 cup	heavy cream	¼ liter
1 tbsp.	sugar	15 ml.

Beat the eggs until light-colored and fluffy. Add the brown sugar, corn syrup, salt and rum. Stir until the ingredients are thoroughly mixed and the sugar is dissolved. Stir in the pecans and butter. Pour the mixture into the pie shell and bake in a preheated 375° F. [190° C.] oven for 40 to 45 minutes, or until a skewer inserted into the filling comes out clean. Cool the pie to room temperature. Whip the cream, then add the sugar and rum. Pass the topping in a bowl.

JOAN SMITH (EDITOR)
THE WOODLAWN PLANTATION COOKBOOK

Pecan Custard Pie

To make one 9-inch [23-cm.] pie

1	fully baked pie shell, made from ½ lb. [¼ kg.] short-crust dough (recipe, page 162)	1
1 cup	chopped pecans	¼ liter
1 tbsp.	unflavored powdered gelatin	15 ml.
½ tsp.	salt	2 ml.
¾ cup	dark brown sugar	175 ml.
4	eggs, the yolks separated from the whites, the yolks beaten	4
4 tbsp.	butter	60 ml.
1 cup	milk	¼ liter
1 tsp.	vanilla extract	5 ml.
½ cup	sugar	125 ml.
½ cup	heavy cream, whipped	125 ml.

Combine the unflavored powdered gelatin, salt and brown sugar in the top of a double boiler. Heat slightly over hot, not boiling, water. Stir in the egg yolks, 2 tablespoons [30 ml.] of the butter and the milk. Cook, stirring constantly, until slightly thickened. Remove the custard from the heat and add the vanilla extract. Allow to cool; then chill in the refrigerator, stirring occasionally.

Sauté the pecans in the remaining 2 tablespoons of butter, taking care not to burn the butter. Stir the nuts until brown, then drain them on paper towels. Beat together the egg whites and sugar until stiff. When the mixture in the refrigerator is thickened to the point where it mounds slightly when stirred with a spoon, fold in the egg whites and half of the pecans. Pour the mixture into the baked pie shell and chill until the custard is firm to the touch. Top with the whipped cream and sprinkle over the remaining pecans.

RALPH H. REESE (EDITOR)
THE FLAVOR OF PITTSBURGH

Chestnut Tart

To make the chestnut purée called for in this recipe, you will need 1 pound [½ kg.] of fresh chestnuts. Cut a cross through the shell on the flat side of each nut, parboil the nuts for 10 minutes, then shell and peel them. Cook the peeled chestnuts in simmering water for about 20 minutes, until they are tender. Drain, and force them through a food mill.

To make one 10-inch [25-cm.] tart

1	partially baked tart shell, made from ½ lb. [¼ kg.] short-crust dough (recipe, page 162)	1
3 cups	chestnut purée	¾ liter
⅔ cup	superfine sugar	150 ml.
⅔ cup	heavy cream	150 ml.
1 tbsp.	fresh orange juice	15 ml.
1 tbsp.	sweet sherry	15 ml.
2	egg yolks, well beaten	2
4 tbsp.	butter, cut into small pieces	60 ml.
	whipped cream	

Mix the chestnut purée with ½ cup [125 ml.] of the superfine sugar, the cream, orange juice, sherry and egg yolks. Let the tart shell cool for five minutes after baking it, then pour in the chestnut-filling mixture; do not let the filling overflow. If any filling is left over, make up some small tartlets. Dot the filling all over with small pieces of butter. Bake in a preheated 300° F. [150° C.] oven for about 20 minutes, or until just firm. Sprinkle the top with the remaining superfine sugar while the tart is still hot. Serve cold with whipped cream.

ELISABETH AYRTON
THE COOKERY OF ENGLAND

A Tender Tart

To make one 7-inch [18-cm.] tart

1¼ cups	flour, sifted	300 ml.
5 tbsp.	butter	75 ml.
1	egg yolk	1
	water	

Hazelnut-sugar filling

1 cup	finely chopped hazelnuts	¼ liter
2	eggs	2
1 cup	sugar	¼ liter
1 tsp.	vanilla extract	5 ml.

Blend the flour, butter and egg yolk with knives. Add only enough water to hold the dough together, knead lightly, then refrigerate the dough for 15 minutes.

Stir the eggs and sugar together; do not beat. Add the vanilla extract and hazelnuts.

Roll out a little more than half of the dough; place it in a tart pan with a detachable bottom. Fill this shell with the hazelnut mixture. Roll out the remaining dough and cover the tart; press the edges together so that the bottom and top crusts adhere. Bake in a preheated 350° F. [180° C.] oven for 40 minutes, or until the top is brown.

ALICE B. TOKLAS
THE ALICE B. TOKLAS COOKBOOK

Oatmeal Pie

To prepare the coconut called for in this recipe, see the editor's note for Saucer Cake (Saucy Kate), page 128.

To make one 9-inch [23-cm.] pie

1	unbaked pie shell, made from ½ lb. [¼ kg.] short-crust dough (recipe, page 162)	1
⅔ cup	rolled oats	150 ml.
3	eggs, beaten	3
⅔ cup	granulated sugar	150 ml.
1 cup	brown sugar	¼ liter
2 tsp.	butter, melted	10 ml.
⅔ cup	shredded coconut	150 ml.
1 tsp.	vanilla extract	5 ml.
½ cup	chopped nuts	125 ml.

Blend together the rolled oats, eggs, granulated sugar, brown sugar, melted butter, shredded coconut, vanilla extract and chopped nuts. Pour the mixture into the unbaked pie shell. Bake in a preheated 350° F. [180° C.] oven for 30 to 35 minutes, or until the filling is firm.

FAVORITE RECIPES OF THE GREAT PLAINS

Cream of Artichoke Tart

Tourte de Crème d'Artichaux du Sucre

If desired, the tart shell can be blind-baked partially (pages 38-39) before the filling is added. To prepare the artichoke bottoms, first break off the stem of each artichoke and snap off the large leaves. Slice off the top half, pare the bottom to remove the bases of the outer leaves, trim the top down to the central leaves, and scrape out the hairy choke with a teaspoon.

To make one 8-inch [20-cm.] tart

½ lb.	short-crust dough (recipe, page 162)	¼ kg.
3	artichoke bottoms, cooked, mashed to a paste and puréed through a nylon sieve	3
2 tbsp.	butter, melted and cooled	30 ml.
2	egg yolks, beaten	2
½ cup	heavy cream	125 ml.
1	almond macaroon, crumbled	1
	salt	
4 tbsp.	sugar	60 ml.
1 tbsp.	candied lemon peel, finely chopped	15 ml.
	orange-flower water	

Blend the artichoke purée with the butter, egg yolks, cream and macaroon crumbs. Season with salt; add the sugar and lemon peel. Roll out the dough and line a tart pan with it. Pour in the artichoke-cream mixture. Bake in a preheated 350° F. [180° C.] oven for 30 minutes, or until the cream is set. Sprinkle with sugar and glaze under the broiler for a few minutes. Sprinkle with orange-flower water before serving.

L'ESCOLE PARFAITE DES OFFICIERS DE BOUCHE

Avocado Tart

To make one 8-inch [20-cm.] tart

1	fully baked tart shell, made with ½ lb. [¼ kg.] short-crust dough (recipe, page 162)	1
2	large ripe avocados, peeled, halved, seeded and coarsely chopped	2
1½ tsp.	unflavored powdered gelatin	7 ml.
¼ cup	cold water	50 ml.
⅔ cup	fresh lemon juice	150 ml.
	salt	
14 oz.	sweetened condensed milk	420 ml.
	sweetened sour cream (optional)	

Soften the gelatin in the cold water and dissolve it in a double boiler over simmering water. In the container of an electric blender, combine the avocado and lemon juice. On medium speed, whirl them until the mixture is smooth. With the motor running, add to the contents of the blender the gelatin, a pinch of salt and—in a steady stream—the condensed milk. Pour the avocado mixture into the tart shell. Chill the tart for at least three hours, but remove it from the refrigerator 20 minutes before serving. The tart may be garnished with whipped cream or slightly sweetened sour cream.

ROBERT ACKART
FRUITS IN COOKING

Beet Tart

Tourte de Betteraves

If desired, the tart shell can be fully blind baked (pages 42-43) before adding the filling.

To make one 8-inch [20-cm.] tart

1	partially baked pie shell, made from ½ lb. [¼ kg.] short-crust dough (recipe, page 162)	1
2	large beets, baked until tender	2
1 cup	white wine	¼ liter
1 tbsp.	sugar	15 ml.
	salt	
1 tbsp.	finely chopped candied lemon peel	15 ml.
2 tbsp.	butter	30 ml.
	granulated sugar	
	orange-flower water	

Peel and cut up the beets, and cook them with the white wine until all of the wine is absorbed—about 20 minutes. Pound the mixture in a mortar together with the sugar and a pinch of salt, until it forms a smooth purée. Blend in the candied lemon peel and butter.

Bake the tart in a preheated 350° F. [180° C.] oven for 30 minutes, or until the filling is lightly browned. Sprinkle granulated sugar and orange-flower water over the top before serving.

L'ESCOLE PARFAITE DES OFFICIERS DE BOUCHE

Carrot Pudding

To make one 10-by-6-inch [25-by-15-cm.] tart

½ lb.	short-crust dough (recipe, page 162)	¼ kg.
1 cup	grated carrot	¼ liter
⅔ cup	fresh bread crumbs	150 ml.
2½ cups	hot milk	625 ml.
1 tsp.	grated lemon peel	5 ml.
½ cup	raisins, soaked in warm water for 15 minutes and drained	125 ml.
½ tsp.	mixed spices	2 ml.
2	eggs, beaten	2
½ cup	sugar	125 ml.
3 tbsp.	fresh lemon juice	45 ml.

Butter a 1½-quart [1½-liter] deep pie dish and line it with the rolled dough. Mix together the carrots and bread crumbs, then pour in the hot milk. Let the mixture cool, and add the grated lemon peel, raisins, mixed spices and eggs. Finally stir in the sugar and lemon juice, blending well before pouring into the pastry-lined dish. Bake in a preheated 325° F. [170° C.] oven for one and a half hours, or until set.

JOAN POULSON
OLD THAMES VALLEY RECIPES

Carrot Pie

To make one 9-inch [23-cm.] pie

1	unbaked pie shell, made from ½ lb. [¼ kg.] short-crust dough (recipe, page 162)	1
6	medium-sized carrots, boiled until tender, drained and puréed through a food mill (about 2 cups [½ liter])	6
2	eggs, beaten	2
2 cups	milk	½ liter
1 cup	brown sugar	¼ liter
1 tsp.	salt	5 ml.
½ tsp.	ground ginger	2 ml.
2 tsp.	ground cinnamon	10 ml.
½ tsp.	ground allspice	2 ml.

Mix the carrots with the beaten eggs, milk, brown sugar, salt, ginger, cinnamon and allspice. Beat all for two minutes. Turn the filling into a pie plate lined with dough. Bake in a preheated 400° F. [200° C.] oven for 15 minutes, then reduce the heat to 350° F. [180° C.] and bake for 45 minutes longer.

CLAIRE SUGDEN
THE ROMANTIC AND PRACTICAL SIDE OF COOKERY

Country-Style Herb Tart

Torta Rustica di Erbe

The techniques of shaping lattices appear on pages 26-29.

	To make one 10-inch [25-cm.] tart	
¾ lb.	short-crust dough (recipe, page 162)	⅓ kg.
2 lb.	beet greens or Swiss chard, stems removed, parboiled for 5 minutes, drained, squeezed dry and very finely chopped	1 kg.
2 tbsp.	sugar	30 ml.
1 tbsp.	unsweetened cocoa	15 ml.
½ cup	chopped blanched almonds	125 ml.
2	eggs, lightly beaten	2
2 tbsp.	kirsch (optional)	30 ml.

Mix the chopped greens with the sugar, cocoa, almonds, eggs and, if desired, a little of the kirsch. Line a tart pan with half of the rolled dough, put in the filling and top with a lattice made from the remaining rolled dough. Bake in a preheated 350° F. [180° C.] oven for about 45 minutes, or until the pastry is golden brown.

MARIÙ SALVATORI DE ZULIANI
LA CUCINA DI VERSILIA E GARFAGNANA

Bishop Auckland Cheese Cakes

These were named cheese cakes because the potato-based filling resembled one made with farmer or pot cheese.

	To make 8 tartlets	
½ lb.	short-crust dough (recipe, page 162)	¼ kg.
2	medium-sized potatoes, boiled, peeled and mashed (about 1½ cups [375 ml.])	2
4 tbsp.	butter, melted	60 ml.
½ cup	superfine sugar	125 ml.
1	egg, lightly beaten	1
2 tbsp.	grated lemon peel	30 ml.
¼ tsp.	lemon extract	1 ml.
1 cup	dried currants, soaked in warm water for 15 minutes and drained	¼ liter
	rum	

Put the mashed potatoes in a bowl and beat in the butter, sugar, egg, lemon peel and extract. Fold in the currants. Line eight tartlet pans with the rolled dough, then fill them with the potato mixture and bake in a preheated 350° F.

[180° C.] oven for 30 minutes, or until the filling is lightly browned. When cooked, sprinkle a few drops of rum onto each tartlet. Serve hot or cold.

PEGGY HUTCHINSON
OLD ENGLISH COOKERY

Pumpkin Pie

Some cooks vary the ordinary taste of pumpkin pie by adding a little hard cider, brandy or sherry to the custard.

	To make one 9-inch [23-cm.] pie	
½ lb.	short-crust dough (recipe, page 162)	¼ kg.
2 cups	sieved cooked pumpkin	½ liter
4	eggs, the yolks separated from the whites, the yolks beaten until lemon-colored, and the whites stiffly beaten	4
1 cup	brown sugar	¼ liter
½ tsp.	ground cinnamon	2 ml.
½ tsp.	grated nutmeg	2 ml.
½ tsp.	ground allspice	2 ml.
⅓ cup	heavy cream	75 ml.
4 tbsp.	butter, melted	60 ml.
1 tbsp.	cornstarch	15 ml.
¼ cup	honey (optional)	50 ml.
½ cup	finely chopped pecans (optional)	125 ml.

Line a pie plate with the rolled dough. Then set the pastry shell aside in a cool place. Combine the beaten egg yolks with the sugar, cinnamon, nutmeg and allspice, and blend until the sugar is thoroughly dissolved.

Mix the pumpkin with the cream and melted butter until thoroughly blended, and then stir into the yolk mixture. Beat the cornstarch into the beaten egg whites, then fold the whites into the pumpkin mixture.

Pour the pumpkin filling into the prepared pastry shell and bake for 10 minutes in a preheated 450° F. [230° C.] oven to set the crust, then reduce the heat to 350° F. [180° C.] and continue baking for a further 20 to 25 minutes, or until a knife blade comes out clean when inserted into the filling.

To give added flavor, mix the honey with the chopped pecans and pour the mixture over the surface of the tart when it is thoroughly cold.

LOUIS P. DE GOUY
THE GOLD COOK BOOK

Pumpkin Custards

To make six 4-inch [10-cm.] tartlets

½ lb.	short-crust dough (recipe, page 162)	¼ kg.
1¼ lb.	cooked pumpkin, sieved	600 g.
2	eggs, lightly beaten	2
1¼ cups	milk	300 ml.
3 tbsp.	sugar	45 ml.
2 tbsp.	strained fresh lime juice	30 ml.
2 tsp.	grated nutmeg	10 ml.
1 tbsp.	brandy	15 ml.

Mix together the pumpkin, eggs, milk, sugar, lime juice, 1 teaspoon [5 ml.] of the nutmeg, and the brandy. Stir well.

Roll out the dough and line deep tartlet pans with it; pour the pumpkin-filling mixture into the pastry-lined pans. Sprinkle the remaining nutmeg over the tops.

Bake in a preheated 350° F. [180° C.] oven for 45 minutes, or until the filling has set. These are best served cold.

MRS. W. E. KINSEY
THE "NEXT MEAL" COOKERY BOOK

Pumpkin Macadamia Chiffon Pie

To make one 9-inch [23-cm.] pie

2 cups	cooked pumpkin	½ liter
1¼ cups	finely chopped macadamia nuts	300 ml.
1 cup	finely crumbled brown-sugar cookies	¼ liter
2 tbsp.	finely chopped crystallized ginger	30 ml.
¾ tsp.	salt	4 ml.
8 tbsp.	butter, melted	120 ml.
4	eggs, the yolks separated from the whites	4
1 cup	sugar	¼ liter
½ cup	milk	125 ml.
½ tsp.	ground cinnamon	2 ml.
½ tsp.	grated nutmeg	2 ml.
1 tbsp.	unflavored powdered gelatin	15 ml.
¼ cup	cool water	50 ml.
	whipped cream (optional)	

In a mixing bowl, combine the cookie crumbs, ¾ cup [175 ml.] of the macadamia nuts, 1 tablespoon [15 ml.] of the ginger, and ¼ teaspoon [1 ml.] of the salt, then stir in the melted butter until the mixture is smooth. Press the mixture

evenly into a piepan and bake it in a preheated 375° F. [190° C.] oven for 15 minutes, or until the pie shell is firm and lightly browned. Remove the pan from the oven and let the pie shell cool.

In the top pan of a double boiler, beat the egg yolks with ½ cup [125 ml.] of the sugar and the remaining salt until the mixture is very thick. Blend in the pumpkin, milk, cinnamon, nutmeg and the remaining ginger. Set the pan over simmering water and cook the mixture until it begins to clear the sides of the pan. Soften the gelatin in the water and add it to the pumpkin mixture, stirring until it dissolves. Let the mixture cool completely and stir in the remaining nuts.

Beat the egg whites to the soft-peak stage. Add the remaining sugar, a little at a time, continuing to beat until the whites are stiff. Fold them into the cooled pumpkin mixture. Spread the filling in the pie shell and chill it until it is set. Serve the pie with whipped cream if desired.

CHARLOTTE ADAMS & DORIS MC FERRAN
THE FAMILY COOKBOOK: DESSERT

Sweet Pumpkin Tart

La Tarte de Courge Sucrée

The techniques of shaping lattices are shown on pages 26-29.

To make one 9-inch [23-cm.] tart

1 lb.	short-crust dough (recipe, page 162)	½ kg.
2 lb.	pumpkin, quartered, seeded, flesh scooped out and diced	1 kg.
4 tbsp.	butter	60 ml.
2 tbsp.	flour	30 ml.
1 tsp.	orange-flower water	5 ml.
2 tbsp.	grated orange peel	30 ml.
1 tsp.	grated lemon peel	5 ml.
½ cup	superfine sugar	125 ml.
2 or 3	eggs, lightly beaten	2 or 3
¼ cup	rum	50 ml.
	confectioners' sugar	

Cook the pumpkin in the butter over low heat, in a covered pan, until soft enough to be puréed with a potato masher or put through a food mill. Sprinkle the puréed pumpkin with the flour, then stir in the orange-flower water, grated orange and lemon peels, sugar, eggs and rum.

Line a tart pan with rolled dough and fill this shell with the pumpkin mixture. Cover with a lattice of dough strips, cut with a serrated pastry wheel. Bake in a preheated 375° F. [190° C.] oven for 40 to 45 minutes.

Immediately on removing the tart from the oven, sprinkle it with confectioners' sugar. Serve warm or cold.

JOSÉPHINE BESSON
LA MÈRE BESSON "MA CUISINE PROVENÇALE"

Shaker Pieplant Pie

Pieplant is an old-fashioned term for rhubarb.

To make one 8-inch [20-cm.] pie

1 lb.	rich short-crust dough (recipe, page 162)	½ kg.
½ lb.	rhubarb, cut into 1-inch [2½-cm.] lengths (about 2 cups [½ liter])	¼ kg.
1 tbsp.	flour	15 ml.
1½ cups	brown sugar	375 ml.
3 tbsp.	butter, cut into small pieces	45 ml.
1	egg, beaten	1

Roll about half of the dough to a thickness of ⅛ inch [3 mm.]. Line the piepan with as much of the dough as required. Roll out to the same thickness enough of the remaining dough to provide a top crust for the pie. In a mixing bowl, combine the flour and sugar. Coat the pieces of rhubarb with the mixture and spread the rhubarb in the prepared pie shell. Dot the rhubarb with bits of butter. Brush the edge of the shell with beaten egg and fit on the dough top. Trim off the excess and press the edges together to seal them. Brush the top with the remaining beaten egg and pierce it in several places to allow steam to escape during baking. Bake in a preheated 450° F. [230° C.] oven for 15 minutes. Reduce the heat to 350° F. [180° C.] and continue baking for 25 minutes longer, or until the pastry is golden brown. Cool the pie before serving.

CHARLOTTE ADAMS & DORIS MC FERRAN
THE FAMILY COOKBOOK: DESSERT

Sorrel Tart

Tourte de Jus d'Oseille

To make one 8-inch [20-cm.] tart

1	partially baked pie shell, made from ½ lb. [¼ kg.] short-crust dough (recipe, page 162)	1
½ lb.	sorrel leaves (about 2 cups [½ liter])	¼ kg.
½ cup	granulated sugar	125 ml.
½ tsp.	ground cinnamon	2 ml.
3	almond macaroons, crumbled	3
2 tbsp.	butter	30 ml.
3	egg yolks	3
1 tbsp.	finely chopped candied lemon peel	15 ml.
1 tsp.	orange-flower water	5 ml.
	superfine sugar	

Pound the sorrel leaves in a mortar. Wrap the pounded leaves in cheesecloth and twist the cheesecloth tightly over a

bowl to extract the juice. Mix the sorrel juice with the sugar, cinnamon, macaroons, butter, egg yolks, candied lemon peel and orange-flower water. Stirring constantly, cook this mixture over low heat until it thickens.

Fill the pastry shell with the sorrel mixture and bake in a preheated 350° F. [180° C.] oven for 30 minutes, or until the top of the filling is lightly browned. Serve sprinkled with superfine sugar.

PIERRE DE LUNE
LE NOUVEAU CUISINIER

Spinach Tart

A handful of raisins macerated in brandy, as well as a few pine nuts, may be added to the filling. The techniques of shaping lattices are demonstrated on pages 26-29.

To make one 9-inch [23-cm.] tart

1 lb.	short-crust dough (recipe, page 162)	½ kg.
2 lb.	spinach, stemmed and washed	1 kg.
2 tbsp.	butter	30 ml.
3 or 4	eggs	3 or 4
1½ cups	heavy cream	375 ml.
½ cup	sugar	125 ml.
	grated nutmeg	
	ground allspice	
1 tsp.	grated lemon peel	5 ml.
1	egg yolk, beaten with 1 tbsp. [15 ml.] water	1

Plunge the spinach into a large pot of boiling water, parboil it for one minute, then drain it in a colander and run cold water over it. Squeeze out the excess moisture with your hands. Chop the spinach and sauté it for about two minutes in the butter. Beat the eggs, cream and sugar together. Stir in pinches of nutmeg and allspice, and the lemon peel. Combine this mixture thoroughly with the spinach.

Line a tart pan with the rolled dough. Fill the pastry shell with the spinach mixture and cover with a lattice made from strips of the remaining dough. Brush the lattice top and tart rim with the egg-yolk mixture.

Bake in a preheated 350° F. [180° C.] oven for 35 minutes, or until the pastry is lightly browned. The tart is best when eaten neither hot nor cold, but a bit warmer than tepid—about 30 minutes out of the oven.

PETITS PROPOS CULINAIRES

Sweet Spinach Pie

Tarte aux Épinards Provençale

The techniques of shaping lattices are demonstrated on pages 26-29. This pie can also be made without a lattice crust as shown on pages 38-39, but the amount of dough should be reduced to ½ pound [¼ kg.]. If desired, the open pie may be garnished with ½ cup [125 ml.] of pine nuts.

To make one 9-inch [23-cm.] pie

1 lb.	short-crust dough *(recipe, page 162)*	½ kg.
1 cup	pastry cream *(recipe, page 166)*	¼ liter
1 lb.	spinach, trimmed, parboiled for 5 minutes, drained, squeezed dry, finely chopped and seasoned lightly with grated nutmeg	½ kg.
1 tsp.	grated lemon peel	5 ml.
½ tsp.	vanilla extract	2 ml.
	salt	
	preserved tangerine or melon slices (optional)	
	egg yolk	

Line a piepan with half of the dough. Prick the dough all over with a sharp-tined fork. Line this pan with another pan of the same size and weight this down with dried beans. Bake for 10 minutes in a preheated 400° F. [200° C.] oven. Remove the bean-filled pan from the shell. The pie shell will then be half-cooked and dry on the surface. This dryness prevents the filling from soaking into the pastry and spoiling the texture of the finished pie.

When the pastry has cooled, combine the pastry cream, spinach, lemon peel, vanilla extract and a pinch of salt. Spread this mixture evenly over the pastry in the pie plate. Cover with the slices of preserved melon or tangerine, if using. Cut the remaining dough into narrow strips and braid these across the top of the pie in a latticework design. Brush with egg yolk and bake in a preheated 375° F. [190° C.] oven for about 25 minutes. Serve hot or cold.

JEAN NOEL ESCUDIER AND PETA J. FULLER
THE WONDERFUL FOOD OF PROVENCE

Squash Pie

Any winter squash such as acorn, butternut, buttercup or Hubbard may be used for this recipe. To produce the quantity of flesh required, you will need about 1½ pounds [¾ kg.] of squash. To prepare it, halve the squash, remove the seeds and fibers, scoop out the flesh and boil it in a little water over low heat until soft —about 15 to 20 minutes.

To make one 9-inch [23-cm.] pie

1	unbaked pie shell, made from ½ lb. [¼ kg.] short-crust dough *(recipe, page 162)*	1
2 cups	boiled squash	½ liter
1 cup	brown sugar	¼ liter
3	eggs, beaten	3
2 tbsp.	molasses	30 ml.
1 tbsp.	butter, melted	15 ml.
1 tbsp.	ground ginger	15 ml.
1 tsp.	ground cinnamon	5 ml.
	salt	
2 cups	milk	½ liter

Combine the cooked squash, sugar, eggs, molasses, melted butter, ground ginger, ground cinnamon, a pinch of salt and the milk. Pour the mixture into the unbaked pie shell. Bake in a preheated 425° F. [220° C.] oven for 40 to 45 minutes, or until a knife inserted in the center comes out clean.

MRS. GRACE TOWNSEND
IMPERIAL COOK BOOK

Dolly's Sweet-Potato Pie

To make one 9-inch [23-cm.] pie

1	unbaked pie shell, made from ½ lb. [¼ kg.] short-crust dough *(recipe, page 162)*	1
2 cups	mashed, boiled sweet potatoes	½ liter
4 tbsp.	butter, melted	60 ml.
1	egg	1
1 to 1⅓ cups	sugar	250 to 325 ml.
2 tbsp.	milk or cream	30 ml.
2 tbsp.	flour	30 ml.
1 tsp.	lemon extract	5 ml.
¼ tsp.	salt	1 ml.

Mix the filling ingredients until smooth. Place in the pie shell. Bake in a preheated 425° F. [220° C.] oven for 15 minutes. Reduce the oven temperature to 350° F. [180° C.] and bake for about 25 minutes more, or until the filling is firm.

THE JUNIOR LEAGUE OF GAINESVILLE, FLORIDA
GATOR COUNTRY COOKS

Swiss Chard Pie

Tourte de Blettes

To make one 10-inch [25-cm.] pie

3½ cups	flour, sifted	875 ml.
5 tbsp.	butter	75 ml.
1	egg	1
⅓ cup	granulated sugar	75 ml.
¾ cup	milk	175 ml.
2 tsp.	baking powder	10 ml.
	salt	

Swiss chard and apple filling

3 lb.	Swiss chard, ribs removed	1½ kg.
3	apples, peeled, cored and thinly sliced	3
	salt	
1 cup	raisins, soaked in ½ cup [125 ml.] milk for 15 minutes	¼ liter
½ cup	pine nuts	125 ml.
2 tbsp.	currant jelly	30 ml.
½ cup	light brown or superfine sugar	125 ml.
½ cup	finely shredded Edam or Gruyère cheese	125 ml.
2	eggs, lightly beaten	2
1 tsp.	grated lemon peel	5 ml.
3 tbsp.	rum	45 ml.

Work all of the dough ingredients together until they are thoroughly blended. Refrigerate the dough.

Drop the chard leaves into boiling salted water and cook for 15 minutes. Drain the chard, squeeze it dry and chop it fine. Simmer the raisins in the milk for about 10 minutes, or until plump; drain and rinse them.

Combine the chard, apples, raisins, pine nuts, jelly, sugar, cheese, eggs, lemon peel and rum.

Oil a fairly deep tart pan. Roll out two thirds of the dough and use it to line the pan. Spread the filling mixture in the pastry shell and cover it with the remaining rolled dough.

Bake in a preheated 425° F. [220° C.] oven for 30 minutes, or until the pastry is golden brown. The pie may be dusted with superfine sugar when it comes out of the oven. Serve hot.

RAYMOND ARMISEN AND ANDRÉ MARTIN
LES RECETTES DE LA TABLE NIÇOISE

Green-Tomato Pie

The techniques of shaping lattices are shown on pages 26-29.

To make one 9-inch [23-cm.] pie

1 lb.	short-crust dough (recipe, page 162)	½ kg.
4 cups	sliced green tomatoes	1 liter
½ cup	water	125 ml.
½ cup	seedless raisins, soaked in warm water for 15 minutes and drained	125 ml.
1 cup	sugar, mixed with 2 tbsp. [30 ml.] flour	¼ liter
¾ tsp.	ground cinnamon	4 ml.
½ tsp.	ground ginger	2 ml.
¼ tsp.	grated nutmeg	1 ml.
2 tbsp.	butter, cut into small pieces	30 ml.
1 tsp.	grated lemon peel	5 ml.
1½ tbsp.	fresh lemon juice	22 ml.
¼ cup	brandy or whiskey	50 ml.

Roll out half of the dough and line a piepan with it.

Pour the water over the tomatoes and let them simmer for five minutes, or until the tomatoes have absorbed most of the water and seem tender. Add the raisins and cook a little longer. Drain off any remaining liquor, saving it, and dump the tomatoes and raisins into the dough-lined piepan. Sprinkle the tomatoes with the sugar-flour mixture and the cinnamon, ginger and nutmeg. Dot the surface with the butter. Add the grated lemon peel and lemon juice. Now pour over the whole, the brandy or whiskey. If the pie will hold it, add a few tablespoonfuls of the tomato liquor to moisten the tomatoes well. Roll out the remaining dough and top the pie with a slashed solid crust or use strips across the top, as you prefer. Set the pan in a preheated 450° F. [230° C.] oven for 15 minutes. Reduce the heat to 375° F. [190° C.] and leave one half hour longer, or until the crust is brown.

MARION FLEXNER
OUT OF KENTUCKY HOMES

Beef-Marrow Pie

Tarte à la Moelle

Raw marrow may be extracted from cross-cut slices of beef foreshank or hindshank bone (the hindshank contains more marrow) with the help of a small fork or spoon.

To make one 8-inch [20-cm.] pie

1 lb.	short-crust or rich short-crust dough (recipes, page 162)	½ kg.
1 cup	diced beef marrow	¼ liter
1	dinner roll, soaked in water and squeezed dry	1
2	eggs, beaten	2
½ cup	sugar	125 ml.
¼ cup	rum or kirsch	50 ml.
1 tsp.	ground cinnamon	5 ml.
¼ cup	finely chopped blanched almonds	50 ml.
1	egg yolk, lightly beaten	1

Mix together the marrow, soaked dinner roll, eggs, sugar, rum, cinnamon and almonds to form a smooth mixture.

Roll out the dough and use two thirds of it to line a tart pan. Fill with the marrow mixture and cover with the remaining dough. Seal the edges, brush the top with the egg yolk and make three slits in the top. Bake in a preheated 400° F. [200° C.] oven for 25 minutes, until the top is brown and a knife inserted in a slit comes out clean. Serve hot.

HUGUETTE COUFFIGNAL
LA CUISINE RUSTIQUE

Salt-Pork and Rose-Water Tart

Tourte au Lard

To make one 8-inch [20-cm.] tart

½ lb.	short-crust dough (recipe, page 162)	¼ kg.
1½ oz.	salt pork with the rind removed, blanched in boiling water for 5 minutes, drained and finely chopped (about ⅓ cup [75 ml.])	40 g.
	rose water	
12	blanched almonds, coarsely chopped	12
2 or 3	egg yolks, lightly beaten	2 or 3
½ tsp.	ground cinnamon	2 ml.
½ cup	sugar	125 ml.

Pound the salt pork in a mortar with a few drops of rose water until a perfectly smooth paste is formed. Pound the almonds separately, then add them to the pork and pound the mixture together, adding a few more drops of rose water if necessary for a creamy consistency. Add to this mixture the egg yolks, cinnamon and sugar. Mix all together well.

Roll out the dough and line a tart pan. Spread the pork-filling mixture in the tart shell and bake in a preheated 350° F. [180° C.] oven for 45 minutes, or until the pastry is golden and the filling is set.

JOSEPH DU CHESNE
LE POURTRAICT DE LA SANTÉ

Sweet Lamb Pie from Westmorland

To make one 10-inch [25-cm.] pie

1 lb.	short-crust dough (recipe, page 162)	½ kg.
6 oz.	boneless lean lamb	175 g.
3 oz.	lamb fat	90 g.
2	medium-sized apples, peeled, cored and chopped	2
1 cup	dried currants, soaked in warm water for 15 minutes and drained	¼ liter
1 cup	raisins, soaked in warm water for 15 minutes and drained	¼ liter
1 cup	seedless white raisins, soaked in warm water for 15 minutes and drained	¼ liter
½ cup	chopped, candied mixed fruit peel	125 ml.
3 tbsp.	strained fresh orange juice	45 ml.
1 tbsp.	strained fresh lemon juice	15 ml.
½ cup	chopped blanched almonds	125 ml.
¼ cup	rum	50 ml.
	salt and freshly ground pepper	
½ tsp.	ground mace	2 ml.
½ tsp.	grated nutmeg	2 ml.
1	egg, beaten, or heavy cream	1

Chop the lamb fine, both the lean and the fat. Put it into a bowl and mix in the remaining filling ingredients except for the beaten egg or heavy cream, making sure that everything is well distributed. Add a little more spice if you like.

Roll out half of the dough and line a piepan. Turn enough of the filling into the pastry to mound up over the level of the rim. Roll out the remaining dough and cover the pie, brushing the rim of the bottom crust first with some of the beaten egg or the cream. Press down and crimp the edge. Make a central hole in the lid, and brush it all over with the remaining egg or cream. Bake for 30 minutes in a preheated 400° F. [200° C.] oven. The pie is done when the top is golden brown. Serve hot or cold.

JANE GRIGSON
ENGLISH FOOD

Puff Pastries

Puff-Pastry Twists

Sacristains

To make about 80 twists

1 lb.	chilled puff-pastry dough *(recipe, page 164)*	½ kg.
1	egg, beaten	1
1 cup	coarsely broken rock candy	¼ liter
1 cup	chopped blanched almonds	¼ liter

Working quickly on a lightly floured table, roll out the cold dough into a 5½-by-15-inch [14-by-38-cm.] rectangle about ¹⁄₁₆ inch [1½ mm.] thick. Cut the dough lengthwise into two equal strips. Fold one of the strips in half and refrigerate it. Brush the other strip with a little beaten egg. Sprinkle it with ¼ cup [50 ml.] of the rock candy and ¼ cup of the chopped almonds. Lightly press the candy and almonds into the dough with the rolling pin. Turn the strip upside down, and brush the other side with a little beaten egg, then sprinkle it with candy and chopped almonds.

Cut this strip of dough crosswise into slices ¾ inch [2 cm.] wide; twist each slice slightly to form a cookie. Place the twists on baking sheets. Bake in a preheated 400° F. [200° C.] oven for 10 minutes, then reduce the heat to 325° F. [160° C.] and bake for 20 minutes. The twists will puff up and become shorter. Meanwhile, remove the second strip of dough from the refrigerator and repeat the procedure. Bake the second batch of twists while the first batch cools.

GASTON LENÔTRE
LENÔTRE'S DESSERTS AND PASTRIES

Glazed Matchsticks

Allumettes Glacées

To make 36 sticks

½ lb.	puff-pastry dough *(recipe, page 164)*	¼ kg.
1 cup	confectioners' sugar	¼ liter
1	egg white	1
	fresh lemon juice	

Using a spoon, make an icing by beating the confectioners' sugar with the egg white for about two minutes, until the mixture is light and homogeneous. Stir in the lemon juice.

On a lightly floured table, roll out the dough into a 16-by-8-inch [40-by-20-cm.] rectangle. Using a ruler and a knife, cut the dough into three pieces 16 inches long. Fold two of these pieces and refrigerate them. Place the third piece of dough on a slightly damp baking sheet. Cover the dough

with the icing, spreading it evenly about ¹⁄₁₆ inch [1½ mm.] thick. Using a damp knife, cut the dough into 12 strips of equal width. Ice and cut the two remaining refrigerated pieces of dough the same way. Place all of the sticks on the same baking sheet. Before baking, place a ¾-inch-high [2-cm.] tartlet ring at each corner of the baking sheet. Place a wire cake rack on top of the tartlet rings so that the dough will rise evenly and each pastry will be the same height.

Bake in a preheated 400° F. [200° C.] oven for 10 minutes, keeping the oven door slightly ajar. Bake until golden brown. During the baking, the sticks will shrink a little in width and will separate. If you used too much icing and the pastries stick together, cut them apart while they bake.

GASTON LENÔTRE
LENÔTRE'S DESSERTS AND PASTRIES

Caramelized Puff-Pastry Spirals

Opus Incertum

The arrangement of the pieces of dough accounts for the Latin name of this pastry: Opus incertum means irregular stonework or brickwork, and the dough pieces are laid on the baking sheet like bricks. Their pattern is irregular in the sense that there are spaces between bricks.

	To make one 6-by-12-inch [15-by-30-cm.] pastry	
½ lb.	puff-pastry dough *(recipe, page 164)*, turned 6 times	¼ kg.
6 tbsp.	superfine sugar	90 ml.
2 tbsp.	confectioners' sugar	30 ml.

Spread 2 tablespoons [30 ml.] of the superfine sugar over your work surface and give the dough a seventh turn, incorporating the sugar as if it were flour. Then sprinkle the dough with 2 more tablespoons of superfine sugar and give it an eighth, and final, turn. The sugar should be completely incorporated into the dough. Refrigerate for 30 minutes.

After 30 minutes, roll the dough out into a rectangle approximately 8 inches [20 cm.] long, simultaneously sprinkling it with the remaining 2 tablespoons of superfine sugar.

Cut the dough crosswise into three equal pieces, each about 2½ inches [6 cm.] wide. Using a pastry brush, moisten the bands of dough with a little water, then stack them one on top of the other. Tap the stack lightly with the rolling pin to make sure the three layers adhere, then place the block of dough in the freezer for 15 to 20 minutes. This will make it easier to slice the dough one more time.

Cover a lightly oiled baking sheet with parchment paper, then dust it with confectioners' sugar, sifting it through a fine sieve. With your fingers, sprinkle on a little water.

Remove the dough from the freezer and cut it crosswise into five equal strips; these "bricks" should now be about ½ inch [1 cm.] thick. Turn them cut side up and arrange two pieces on the baking sheet, parallel to each other on their long sides and about 1 inch [2½ cm.] apart. Set the third brick directly under the 1-inch space and just touching the first two bricks. Now align the last two pieces below and touching the bottom of the third piece, with the same 1-inch space between them that the first pair has. The effect is of a tall, narrow letter H.

Bake the pastry in a preheated 450° F. [230° C.] oven for 15 minutes. The five bricks will have expanded and rounded out somewhat and should have merged together around the center piece. Turn all five over together, maneuvering them with two large spatulas. Then reduce the oven temperature to 400° F. [200° C.] and bake the pastry for five minutes longer. Turn off the oven and let the pastry remain inside five more minutes; check to be sure that it does not scorch.

When the baking is completed, the pastry should have expanded into five connected pieces, each with a visible, caramelized spiral pattern. Let the pastry cool on the baking sheet for 30 minutes. Cover a silver platter with a white napkin and place the pastry on the napkin in one piece. Set the platter in the center of the table for guests to help themselves, breaking off pieces of the spirals with their fingers.

JEAN & PIERRE TROISGROS
THE NOUVELLE CUISINE OF JEAN & PIERRE TROISGROS

Puff-Pastry Slices with Whipped Cream

Millefeuille à la Crème Légère

Puff pastry tends to shrink in the oven. To avoid this, cut out the rectangles the day before you bake them and let them rest overnight in the refrigerator, protected by plastic wrap.

When strawberries and raspberries are in season, you can add 2 cups [½ liter] of one—or a mixture of both—to the whipped cream when you fold the two creams together. Keep a few berries to one side for decorating the top. You can also make a crisscross, or *quadrillage*, pattern of caramel in the confectioners'-sugar coating by laying a thin steel skewer, heated to white hot in a fire or gas flame, on the sugar at intervals across the top.

To make one 6-by-8-inch [15-by-20-cm.] pastry

¾ lb.	puff-pastry dough *(recipe, page 164)*	⅓ kg.
1 cup	pastry cream *(recipe, page 166, but use one half of the quantities called for)*	¼ liter
⅓ cup	heavy cream, chilled	75 ml.
2 tsp.	confectioners' sugar	10 ml.

Lightly flour a work surface and roll out the dough into an 8-by-18-inch [20-by-45-cm.] rectangle ½ inch [1 cm.] thick. Using a heavy knife, cut the dough cleanly into three 6-by-8-inch [15-by-20-cm.] strips.

Brush a large baking sheet with water, lay the three strips of dough on it and prick the surfaces all over with a fork to stop the dough from puffing too much during cooking.

Bake the pastry in a preheated 425° F. [220° C.] oven for 20 minutes, or until puffed and browned. Remove the pastry from the baking sheet and let it cool on a wire rack; the pastry should be a beautiful hazelnut brown.

While the pastry is baking, make the pastry cream and cool it rapidly, stirring and aerating it well with a whisk.

Combine the light cream and 1 tablespoon [15 ml.] of the confectioners' sugar in a chilled bowl, and beat with a small wire whisk for one minute, then beat more rapidly for a further five minutes until the cream is the consistency of egg whites whipped until they form soft peaks. Add the pastry cream to the whipped cream and fold the two together carefully, using a wooden spatula and an upward motion to aerate the mixture and retain its light texture.

With a metal spatula, spread half of the cream mixture on one of the strips of pastry. Place the second strip on top, spread with the rest of the cream and cover it with the last strip, smooth side up. Sprinkle the pastry with the remaining confectioners' sugar to give it an even white coating. Place it on a serving dish and slice it carefully with a serrated knife in front of your guests.

MICHEL GUÉRARD
MICHEL GUÉRARD'S CUISINE GOURMANDE

Cream Horns

If desired, you may substitute ½ cup [125 ml.] of pistachios for the candied cherries.

To make 8 cream horns

½ lb.	puff-pastry dough *(recipe, page 164)*	¼ kg.
½ cup	heavy cream, whipped, sweetened and flavored	125 ml.
1	egg white, lightly beaten	1
2 tbsp.	superfine sugar	30 ml.
2 tbsp.	jam	30 ml.
8	candied cherries	8

Roll out the dough into a rectangle at least 4 inches [10 cm.] wide, 24 inches [60 cm.] long and 1/16 inch [1½ mm.] thick. Cut the dough into eight long strips ½ inch [1 cm.] wide. Dampen the tops with water. Carefully wrap each strip around a cream-horn mold—starting at the point of the mold and working toward the open end; each turn should overlap the top half of the preceding one. Brush each horn with egg white and dip it into the superfine sugar.

Place the horns on a baking sheet covered with parchment paper and refrigerate them for an hour.

Bake in a preheated 425° F. [220° C.] oven for about 20 minutes, or until golden brown. While the horns are still warm, remove the molds by first giving them a slight twist, then let them cool. Pipe a little jam into each horn. Using a pastry bag with a star tube, fill each horn with suitably flavored, sweetened whipped cream. Finish neatly with a little rosette and decorate with a cherry.

L. J. HANNEMAN
PATISSERIE

Apricot Tart

Tourte d'Abricots

To make one 8-inch [20-cm.] tart

½ lb.	puff-pastry dough *(recipe, page 164)*	¼ kg.
1 lb.	fresh apricots	½ kg.
4 tbsp.	superfine sugar	60 ml.
½ cup	finely chopped candied lemon peel	125 ml.

Halve the apricots. Then remove the pits, crack the pits with a mallet; remove and halve their kernels. (If the apricots are not quite ripe, plunge them into boiling water, return the water to a boil, and drain them before halving them.)

Line a tart pan with rolled dough, sprinkle 2 tablespoons [30 ml.] of the superfine sugar over the base, then sprinkle on the candied lemon peel. Arrange the apricot halves cut side up in concentric circles in the pastry shell, topping each half of fruit with half a kernel from a pit. Dust with the remaining superfine sugar and bake for 15 minutes in a preheated 425° F. [220° C.] oven. Reduce the heat to 375° F. [190° C.] and continue baking for 20 to 30 minutes, or until the pastry is puffed and golden brown.

MENON
LES SOUPERS DE LA COUR

Apple Turnover

Chausson aux Pommes

To make 1 large turnover

¾ lb.	puff-pastry dough *(recipe, page 164)*	⅓ kg.
9	apples, peeled, cored and thinly sliced	9
5 tbsp.	sugar	75 ml.
½ tsp.	ground cinnamon	2 ml.
2 tbsp.	Calvados	30 ml.
2 tbsp.	butter	30 ml.
1	egg, beaten	1

In a bowl, combine the sugar, cinnamon and Calvados. Add the apples and turn them with a spoon to coat them evenly. Roll the puff-pastry dough into an oval ⅛ inch [3 mm.] thick. Place the coated apple slices on one half of the oval and fold the other half over them. Lightly moisten the edges of the pastry and press them together firmly to seal in the apples.

Place the turnover on a buttered baking sheet and brush the top with the beaten egg. Bake in a preheated 425° F. [220° C.] oven for 45 minutes, or until the top is golden.

MARIE BISSON
LA CUISINE NORMANDE

Apple Cream Turnover

Feuilleté aux Pommes

To make one 8-by-6-inch [20-by-15-cm.] turnover

1 lb.	puff-pastry dough *(recipe, page 164)*	½ kg.
6	Golden Delicious apples, peeled, quartered, cored and sprinkled with fresh lemon juice	6
2 tbsp.	granulated sugar	30 ml.
6 tbsp.	butter	90 ml.
1¼ cups	pastry cream *(recipe, page 166)*	300 ml.
1	egg, beaten	1
	confectioners' sugar	
1 cup	heavy cream, lightly sweetened	¼ liter

Place the apple quarters in a pie dish and toss them with the granulated sugar and the butter. Bake in a preheated 425° F. [220° C.] oven for 15 minutes. (The sugar should caramelize slightly.) Let the apples cool.

Roll out the dough into a 16-by-12-inch [40-by-30-cm.] rectangle. Transfer it to a large baking sheet. Spread the pastry cream over half of the dough and arrange the apple quarters in rows on top of the cream. Fold over the other half of the dough and seal the edges. Decorate the top with scraps of dough, if you like, and glaze it with the beaten egg. Bake for 20 minutes, or until puffed and golden brown, sprinkling the top with confectioners' sugar toward the end of the baking time. Serve very hot, accompanied by cold, thick cream.

LA REYNIÈRE
200 RECETTES DES MEILLEURES CUISINIÈRES DE FRANCE

Apple and Lemon Pie

Tarte aux Pommes Citronnee

To make one 9-inch [23-cm.] pie

1	unbaked pie shell, made from ½ lb. [¼ kg.] flaky-pastry dough *(recipe, page 164)*	1
5 to 7	apples	5 to 7
1 tsp.	grated lemon peel	5 ml.
1 cup	lemon or lime marmalade	¼ liter
3 tbsp.	fresh lemon juice	45 ml.
2 to 4 tbsp.	dark or light rum	30 to 60 ml.
2 tbsp.	unsalted butter	30 ml.
	salt	

Peel and core the apples, and cut them into eight slices each. As soon as the apples are peeled and sliced, marinate them in the rum. Toss well to make sure that all the apples are in contact with the rum. Add the lemon peel and toss again.

Empty the marmalade into a small pot. Melt it over low heat. Add the lemon juice, butter and salt. Arrange the apples in the pie shell in one layer of concentric circles. Strain half of the marmalade over this. Arrange the remainder of the apples in a second layer of concentric circles, but this time reverse the direction of the apple slices. Mix the remainder of the marmalade, peels and all, and without straining, spoon it over the apples.

Bake the pie on the bottom shelf of a preheated 375° F. [190° C.] oven for 20 minutes. Then, raise it to the top shelf and continue baking for at least another 25 to 30 minutes, or until the marmalade starts to caramelize lightly. Cool and serve in the pie plate.

MADELEINE M. KAMMAN
WHEN FRENCH WOMEN COOK

Upside-Down Apple Pie

To make one 10-inch [25-cm.] pie

¾ lb.	puff-pastry dough (recipe, page 164)	⅔ kg.
9	medium-sized McIntosh apples, peeled, cored and thinly sliced	9
6 tbsp.	unsalted butter	90 ml.
¾ cup	sugar	175 ml.
⅓ cup	apricot preserves	75 ml.
	whipped cream (optional)	

With 4 tablespoons [60 ml.] of the butter, coat the bottom and sides of a 10-inch [25-cm.] iron skillet. Sprinkle the buttered bottom and sides with ½ cup [125 ml.] of the sugar. Arrange the apple slices in the pan in layers, mounding them slightly at the center and leaving about ¼ inch [6 mm.] of the inside rim of the pan exposed. Dot each layer with bits of the remaining butter. Top each buttered layer with a sprinkle of the remaining sugar. Set the skillet aside.

Remove the chilled dough from the refrigerator, unwrap and place it on a lightly floured surface. Lightly dust the top of the pastry with flour, and roll it out into an 11- or 12-inch [28- or 30-cm.] square, approximately ¼ inch thick. Set an inverted 10-inch dinner plate on the dough and, with a small, sharp knife, cut around the plate to make a 10-inch disk. Lay the disk loosely on the mounded apples, letting the edge of the dough touch the exposed inner rim of the skillet. Using a knife, cut a vent in the center of the dough, then place the skillet in the refrigerator and allow the dough to chill for 20 minutes.

Preheat the oven to 425° F. [220° C.] and set a cookie sheet on the middle shelf of the oven. Remove the skillet from the refrigerator and place it on the cookie sheet in the oven. Reduce the oven heat to 350° F. [180° C.] and bake the pie for 40 minutes, or until the pastry is deep gold.

Take the skillet from the oven. If you can see the butter-sugar mixture bubbling around the edge of the pastry, set the skillet over medium heat and let the juices cook away until the mixture no longer bubbles. Let the pie cool for 30 minutes. Place an inverted cake plate over the top of the skillet. With both hands, tightly hold together the plate and skillet, then turn them over. Lift the skillet.

Spoon the apricot preserves into a small saucepan and melt over low heat. Push the melted preserves through a fine sieve onto the surface of the apples, spreading the glaze evenly with a metal spatula. Serve warm immediately or at room temperature. If you like, serve with whipped cream.

JOHN CLANCY & FRANCES FIELD
CLANCY'S OVEN COOKERY

Open-faced Apple Slices

Peaches, plums or cherries can be substituted for apples, and they need not be soaked in lemon juice. For darker-colored fruits, omit the dried currants and use currant glaze made by substituting currant jelly for the apricot jam.

To make about twelve 3½-by-2-inch [9-by-5-cm.] slices

1 lb.	puff-pastry dough (recipe, page 164)	½ kg.
2	large apples, peeled, cored and thinly sliced	2
2 tbsp.	strained fresh lemon juice	30 ml.
1 tsp.	vanilla extract	5 ml.
1	egg, beaten with 1 tbsp. [15 ml.] milk	1
½ cup	dried currants, soaked in warm water for 15 minutes and drained	125 ml.
½ cup	sliced blanched almonds	125 ml.
1 tsp.	grated lemon peel	5 ml.
¼ cup	sugar, mixed with a pinch of ground cinnamon	50 ml.
1 cup	apricot jam, sieved	¼ liter
2 to 4 tbsp.	Cognac, kirsch, applejack or Calvados (optional)	30 to 60 ml.

Roll out the dough ¼ inch [6 mm.] thick. Trim the edges. Cut the dough into 12 strips, each 3½ by 2 inches [9 by 5 cm.], and arrange the strips on an ungreased baking sheet. Refrigerate, uncovered.

While the pastry is chilling, soak the sliced apples in the lemon juice mixed with the vanilla. Brush the pastry strips with the egg-and-milk mixture. Drain the apples and arrange the slices down the center of each pastry strip, overlapping the slices slightly. Sprinkle with a mixture of the currants, almonds, lemon peel and cinnamon sugar. Bake in a preheated 350° F. [180° C.] oven for about 35 minutes, or until the strips are golden brown. Meanwhile, bring the sieved jam to a boil and stir in the brandy of your choice. Brush the apples with the jam while both are still hot.

PAULA PECK
THE ART OF FINE BAKING

Eleanor's Apple Tart

Tarte Eleonore

To make three 7-inch [18-cm.] tarts

½ lb.	flaky-pastry dough *(recipe, page 164)*	200 g.
6 tbsp.	applesauce	90 ml.
5	cooking apples, peeled, cored and quartered	5
	confectioners' sugar	
4 tbsp.	butter, cut into small pieces	60 ml.
3 tbsp.	tart cream *(recipe, page 166)* or heavy cream (optional)	45 ml.

Roll out the flaky-pastry dough until it is ⅛ inch [3 mm.] thick. Cut the dough into three equal-sized circles; place about a third of the excess dough in the center of each circle. Roll out each circle until it is 7 inches [18 cm.] wide, then place the three circles on baking sheets.

In the center of each circle of dough, spread a thin layer of applesauce, leaving an uncovered border 1½ inches [4 cm.] wide around the edge. Cut the quartered apples into halves and arrange these pieces of apple in a circle over the applesauce on top of each tart. Sprinkle each tart generously with confectioners' sugar and scatter the small pieces of butter on top of the sugar.

Bake the tarts in a preheated 450° F. [230° C.] oven for about 20 minutes. Five minutes before the end of baking, sprinkle each tart again with confectioners' sugar to glaze the fruit. Serve while warm—either as is, or with a tablespoon [15 ml.] of *crème fraîche* or heavy cream on each tart.

GASTON LENÔTRE
LENÔTRE'S DESSERTS AND PASTRIES

Irish Baked Apples

Apple Niamh Chinn Oir

To make 6 pastries

1 lb.	puff-pastry dough *(recipe, page 164)*	½ kg.
6	apples, peeled and cored	6
8 tbsp.	butter	120 ml.
¼ cup	Irish whiskey liqueur	50 ml.
1 tbsp.	honey	15 ml.
1 tsp.	grated lemon peel	5 ml.
1 tbsp.	sugar	15 ml.

Mash together the butter with the liqueur, honey, lemon peel and sugar. Fill the cored apples with this mixture. Roll

out the dough and cut it into six pieces. Place an apple on each piece of dough and wrap the dough around the apple. Place the wrapped apples on a baking sheet and bake them in a preheated 350° F. [180° C.] oven for 20 to 25 minutes, or until the pastry is golden brown. Serve hot.

IRISH RECIPES TRADITIONAL AND MODERN

Normandy Apple Tart

Tarte le Deun

To make one 10-inch [25-cm.] tart

¾ lb.	puff-pastry dough *(recipe, page 164)*	⅓ kg.
5	apples, peeled, cored and thinly sliced	5
1 cup	blanched almonds, coarsely chopped	¼ liter
1 cup	flour	¼ liter
7 tbsp.	butter, cut into small pieces	100 ml.
1 cup	superfine sugar	¼ liter
2 tbsp.	vanilla sugar	30 ml.
½ tsp.	ground cinnamon	2 ml.
	heavy cream (optional)	

In a bowl, combine the chopped almonds, flour, butter, the sugars and cinnamon. Mix these briskly with your finger tips until the mixture resembles fine crumbs.

Roll out the dough and line a buttered pie dish with it. Fill the pastry case with the apples and cover them with the almond mixture. Bake in a preheated 400° F. [200° C.] oven for 40 minutes, or until the topping is golden brown. Serve hot, with heavy cream if desired.

MARIE BISSON
LA CUISINE NORMANDE

Deep-Dish Pear Pie

To make one 8-inch [20-cm.] pie

½ lb.	puff-pastry dough *(recipe, page 164)*	¼ kg.
6	large pears, peeled, cored and sliced thin	6
½ cup	sugar	125 ml.
1	egg yolk, beaten	1
2 cups	wine custard *(recipe, page 167)*, made with port	½ liter

In a deep pie plate, pile the pear slices in the shape of a pyramid and sprinkle them with the sugar. Roll out a 9-inch [23-cm.] round of puff-pastry dough to the thickness of ¼ inch [6 mm.] and cover the pears with it, taking care not to pull the dough. Wet the edge of the pie plate and the underside of the edge of the dough, and press the dough against the pie plate. Paint the top of the dough with the egg yolk. Make a few slashes in the dough with the point of a knife. Bake in a preheated 425° F. [220° C.] oven for about 25 minutes. Serve the port wine custard separately in a sauceboat.

RAYMOND OLIVER
LA CUISINE

Caramelized Pears on Puff Paste

Feuilleté de Poires au Caramel

To serve 6

1 lb.	puff-pastry dough *(recipe, page 164)*	½ kg.
3	ripe, medium-sized pears	3
1½ cups	sugar	375 ml.
¼ cup	water	50 ml.
1 cup	heavy cream	¼ liter

Spread 1 cup [¼ liter] of the sugar on the table. Using the sugar as if it were flour to prevent the dough from sticking, roll the dough ¼ inch [6 mm.] thick. Sprinkle with sugar and fold into thirds like a letter.

Roll out the dough again into a rectangle about ⅜ inch [1 cm.] thick. Using a large oval cookie cutter (about 5½ inches [14 cm.] long by 3 inches [8 cm.] wide), cut six pastries. Place them on a baking sheet lined with parchment paper and set them in the refrigerator for one hour or in the freezer for 30 minutes.

Bake the pastries in a preheated 400° F. [200° C.] oven for 25 minutes, until nice and brown. Remove the pastries from the parchment paper as soon as possible, lest the sugar that has melted around them hardens and sticks to the paper. Cool them on a wire rack.

Peel the pears, cut them in half, then core them. In a large saucepan mix together the remaining ½ cup [125 ml.] of sugar and the water, and place over high heat. Cook this syrup until it turns into a caramel, about six to eight minutes. Add the halved pears to the caramel, cover, and cook over low heat for no more than five minutes, depending on the ripeness of the fruit. (Do not let the pears fall apart; they will render some juice and thin the caramel.) As soon as the pears feel tender when poked with the point of a knife, add the cream, bring the mixture to a boil and simmer, uncovered, for about three minutes.

Remove the pan from the heat and cool the pears until lukewarm. Remove the pears from the caramel, slice each half and arrange the slices in a slightly overlapping row down the center of a pastry. Pour some of the caramel sauce on top of and around the pastries and serve immediately.

JACQUES PÉPIN
LA MÉTHODE

Pineapple Tart

This 1827 recipe suggests grating loaf sugar—the form in which white sugar was commonly available then—over the tarts. Today, a sprinkling of superfine sugar is a substitute.

To make two 9-inch [23-cm.] tarts

2	fully baked tart shells, made from 1 lb. [½ kg.] flaky- or puff-pastry dough *(recipe, page 164)*	2
1	large or 2 small pineapples, peeled, eyes removed, quartered, cored and cut into small pieces	1
2 cups	superfine sugar	½ liter
1 cup	heavy cream	¼ liter

Mix the pineapple with the sugar, and set it away in a covered dish until sufficient juice is drawn out to stew the fruit. Stew the pineapple in the sugar and juice until quite soft; then mash it to a marmalade with the back of a spoon and set it away to cool.

When the shells are baked and cool, mix the pineapple with the cream, and fill the shells with the mixture. Grate loaf sugar over the top.

MISS LESLIE OF PHILADELPHIA
SEVENTY-FIVE RECEIPTS FOR PASTRY, CAKES, AND SWEETMEATS

Rhubarb Pie

Tart à la Rhubarbe

To make one 8-inch [20-cm.] pie

½ lb.	puff-pastry dough *(recipe, page 164)* or short-crust dough *(recipe, page 162)*	¼ kg.
1 lb.	rhubarb, peeled if necessary, and cut into pieces	½ kg.
2 tbsp.	sugar	30 ml.
2 tbsp.	light brown sugar	30 ml.
	ground cinnamon	
3 tbsp.	cold water	45 ml.
1	egg, lightly beaten	1

Arrange the rhubarb in a deep pie dish. Sprinkle the rhubarb with both kinds of sugar and with a pinch of cinnamon. Moisten with the water.

Roll out the dough to the shape of the dish. Cover the pie dish with the pastry, sealing the edges well. Trim off excess pastry with a knife. Using a pastry brush, paint the top with the beaten egg. Prick the top all over with a fork. Bake in a preheated 375° F. [190° C.] oven for about 45 minutes, or until the top is golden brown.

PHILEAS GILBERT
LA CUISINE DE TOUS LES MOIS

Strawberry Strip

Bande aux Fraises

To make one 8-by-12-inch [20-by-30-cm.] pastry

1 lb.	puff-pastry dough *(recipe, page 164)*	½ kg.
5 cups	fresh strawberries or raspberries	1¼ liters
1	egg plus 1 egg yolk, lightly beaten	1
2 tbsp.	confectioners' sugar	30 ml.
¾ cup	raspberry preserves or currant jelly, warmed, strained, and mixed with 1 tbsp. [15 ml.] raspberry brandy, kirsch or Cognac	175 ml.

Roll the dough into a rectangle approximately 15 inches long [38 cm.] by 10 inches [25 cm.] wide and not more than ⅛ inch [3 mm.] thick. Line a large baking sheet with parchment paper. Roll the dough onto the rolling pin and unroll it onto the parchment paper. Trim the edges of the dough to make them straight; the dough should be about 9 inches [23 cm.] wide after trimming. Brush the long edges with water, then fold them toward the center. Cut a small strip from the long outer edges so that, instead of being folded, the border is in two layers.

Brush the borders with the beaten egg. Prick the center of the dough with a fork to prevent it from puffing too much, and score the border with the point of a knife to form a design. To set the dough before cooking, place the dough in the freezer for 10 to 15 minutes, or in the refrigerator for one hour. Then bake in a preheated 375° F. [190° C.] oven for 25 minutes. If the center puffs too much, push it down with a towel; the strip should be browned and well cooked.

Clean the berries and set aside 2 cups [½ liter] of the nicest berries. Arrange the remaining fruit on the baked, cooled strip. Sprinkle with confectioners' sugar and press the berries to crush them slightly so that they release a little of their juice. Arrange the nicer berries on top and, using a brush or teaspoon, coat the top with the glaze. Serve the pastry as soon as possible.

JACQUES PÉPIN
LA MÉTHODE

Maids of Honor Cakes

These cakes are said to derive their name from Queen Elizabeth I of England's maids of honor. The recipe is taken from a 16th Century cooking manuscript.

To make about 12 tarts

½ lb.	puff-pastry dough *(recipe, page 164)*	¼ kg.
1¼ cups	milk	300 ml.
2 tbsp.	fresh white bread crumbs	30 ml.
8 tbsp.	butter, cut into small pieces	120 ml.
2 tbsp.	sugar	30 ml.
½ cup	blanched almonds, ground in a nut grinder, or in a food processor operated at short spurts	125 ml.
1 tsp.	grated lemon peel	5 ml.
3	eggs	3

Boil the milk with the bread crumbs and let the mixture stand for a few minutes, then add the butter, sugar, almonds and lemon peel. Beat in the eggs, one at a time. Line tartlet pans with the dough and spoon the mixture into them. Bake in a preheated 425° F. [220° C.] oven for 20 minutes, or until the tartlets are golden brown.

BERNARD DARWIN
RECEIPTS AND RELISHES

Almond Cream Turnovers

Chaussons à la Crème d'Amandes

The author suggests that the dough may be cut into six rounds that can be filled in the same way as the large turnover, then baked at the same temperature, but for only 15 to 18 minutes. The almonds and sugar for the filling may be ground in a food processor; the result, however, will be grainier than if the almonds and sugar cubes were pounded in a mortar. One cup [¼ liter] of granulated sugar may replace the cubes.

To make 1 large or 6 individual turnovers

1 lb.	puff-pastry dough *(recipe, page 164)*	½ kg.
1⅔ cups	blanched almonds	400 ml.
¼ tsp.	almond extract	1 ml.
½ lb.	sugar cubes	¼ kg.
6	eggs	6
10 tbsp.	butter, softened	150 ml.
1 tbsp.	orange-flower water	15 ml.
1	egg, beaten with ¼ cup [50 ml.] water	1
	superfine sugar	

To make the filling, pound the almonds, almond extract and sugar cubes in a large mortar and pass the pounded mixture through a fine sieve; return to the mortar for more pounding whatever will not go through the sieve. Return all of the sieved mixture to the mortar and incorporate the eggs, one by one, then the butter and orange-flower water.

Roll out the dough into a rectangle 8 by 10 inches [20 by 25 cm.]. Place the cream mixture on one half of the dough and fold over the other half to enclose the cream completely. Brush the edges of the dough with a little water and pinch them to seal in the filling.

Place the turnover on a baking sheet and brush with the beaten egg. Bake in a preheated 450° F. [230° C.] oven for 25 to 30 minutes, or until the pastry is well puffed and golden brown. A minute before removing from the oven, sprinkle the top with the superfine sugar to make a shiny glaze.

J. B. REBOUL
LA CUISINIÈRE PROVENÇALE

Chou Pastries

Cream Puffs

Profiteroles au Chocolat

Alternatively, these puffs may be filled with ice cream. To make the pastries known as "religieuses," demonstrated on pages 68-69, the baked puffs are filled with flavored pastry cream or whipped cream, stacked together in pairs and decorated with fondant icing (recipe, page 167), then garnished with butter cream.

To make 12 cream puffs

¼ lb.	chou paste *(recipe, page 163)*	125 g.
1½ cups	pastry cream *(recipe, page 166)* or sweetened whipped cream	375 ml.
	Hot chocolate sauce	
5 oz.	semisweet chocolate	150 g.
7 tbsp.	water	100 ml.
1 tsp.	cornstarch, dissolved in 1 tsp. water	5 ml.
2 tbsp.	butter	30 ml.

On a baking sheet, form 12 small balls of the chou paste. Bake in a preheated 400° F. [200° C.] oven for 20 minutes, or until well puffed and browned. Remove the puffs from the baking sheet and let them cool. Slit each of them close to the base and, with a spoon or a pastry bag, fill them with the pastry cream or whipped cream.

In a bowl over hot water, melt the chocolate with the water. When the chocolate is melted and syrupy, stir in the dissolved cornstarch and let the sauce thicken for a minute or two. Add the butter and stir until it melts.

Arrange the filled puffs on a serving platter or on individual plates. Cover them with the hot chocolate sauce and serve immediately.

HENRI PAUL PELLAPRAT
LE NOUVEAU GUIDE CULINAIRE

Mocha Cream Puffs

To make 12 to 16 cream puffs

1 lb.	chou paste *(recipe, page 163)*	½ kg.
2½ to 3 tbsp.	instant coffee	37 to 45 ml.
2 cups	heavy cream	½ liter
1	egg, the yolk separated from the white, and the yolk lightly beaten	1
4 to 6 tbsp.	superfine sugar	60 to 90 ml.
3 to 4 tbsp.	confectioners' sugar	45 to 60 ml.

With a pastry bag, press the dough onto a baking sheet in portions the size of walnuts or, if desired, the size of small eggs. With a fine pastry brush, coat the top of each puff with the egg yolk. Bake the puffs in a preheated 425° F. [220° C.] oven for 25 minutes. Reduce the heat to 350° F. [180° C.] and bake for an additional 20 to 25 minutes, or until a thin skewer, when inserted, comes out almost dry. Cool the puffs and split them in half.

Whip the heavy cream slowly until it forms stiff peaks, adding all but 1 tablespoon [15 ml.] of the superfine sugar. Combine the remaining sugar with 1½ tbsp. [22 ml.] of the instant coffee. Sprinkle this sugar-coffee mixture over the top of the whipped cream, distributing it as evenly as possible. Gently fold together. Using a pastry bag fitted with a star tube, divide the whipped cream among the puffs. Refrigerate the filled bottoms.

In a small bowl or a round-bottomed coffee cup, mix the egg white, confectioners' sugar and the remaining instant coffee until the mixture turns into a light brown, shiny "royal" icing. Dribble the icing over the tops of the puffs. Let it dry at room temperature. Place the tops on the refrigerated cream-filled bottoms. Serve.

LOUIS SZATHMÁRY
THE CHEF'S SECRET COOK BOOK

Fresh Banana Eclairs

The techniques of baking éclairs are demonstrated on pages 66-67. To toast almonds, place them on a baking sheet in a preheated 300° F. [150° C.] oven for a few minutes, turning them once or twice.

This pastry is good only when it is made from bananas so ripe that the skins are thin, soft and almost brown (or at least more than half-brown). Do not try to make it from lemon-colored, firm-skinned bananas. It will not have any taste at all. If you cannot get ripe bananas, store unripened ones in a brown paper bag for two to three days to let them ripen before trying to use them. Do not run the bananas through a food mill; they will turn into a liquid. If gently pressed with a fork, they will retain their pulpy consistency.

To make two 12-inch [30-cm.] éclairs

1 lb.	chou paste *(recipe, page 163)*	½ kg.
4	ripe bananas	4
½ cup	water	125 ml.
2 tbsp.	unflavored powdered gelatin, softened in 3 tbsp. [45 ml.] cold water	30 ml.
2 cups	heavy cream	½ liter
6 to 8 tbsp.	sugar	90 to 120 ml.
2 to 3 tbsp.	rum	30 to 45 ml.
3 oz.	semisweet baking chocolate	90 g.
2 tbsp.	sliced toasted almonds	30 ml.

Chocolate sauce

½ cup	unsweetened cocoa	125 ml.
1 oz.	semisweet baking chocolate	30 g.
4 tbsp.	unsalted butter	60 ml.
1 cup plus 2 tbsp.	sugar	¼ liter plus 30 ml.
1 cup	milk	¼ liter
1 tbsp.	cornstarch, diluted with ¼ cup [50 ml.] cold water	15 ml.
⅓ cup	water	75 ml.
¼ cup	brandy	50 ml.

For the chocolate sauce, melt the butter in a very heavy saucepan with 1 cup [¼ liter] of the sugar and the cocoa until the mixture starts to caramelize. Immediately add the milk, stirring constantly; the hard lumps will dissolve as the liquid comes to a boil. Stirring constantly, pour the diluted cornstarch in a slow stream into the boiling syrup. Remove from the heat and allow to cool to room temperature. In a separate saucepan, combine the semisweet baking chocolate, the water and the remaining 2 tablespoons [30 ml.] of the sugar. Cook over low heat until a smooth syrup is formed. Stir the chocolate syrup and brandy into the cocoa mixture. Refrigerate the sauce.

For the éclairs, spoon the dough into two strips, each as long as the baking sheet (approximately 12 inches [30 cm.]). Bake the éclairs in a preheated 425° F. [220° C.] oven for 20 to 25 minutes without opening the oven door. Reduce the heat to 350° F. [180° C.] and bake for 20 minutes more. Reduce the heat again to 325° F. [160° C.] and bake for an additional 10 minutes.

Meanwhile, bring the water to a boil and stir in the softened gelatin. Cool the mixture in an ice-water bath until it starts to jell. Whip the heavy cream with half of the sugar until the cream forms stiff peaks. Gently fold the rum into the cooled gelatin. Pour the gelatin all over the surface of the whipped cream and, using a spatula, fold it in.

Press the bananas with a fork until they turn into a pulp. Stir in the remaining sugar. Fold this banana-sugar mixture into the whipped cream. Chill.

When the éclairs have cooled, split them in half lengthwise, parallel with the bottoms. Remove and discard the soft inside parts. With a pastry bag fitted with a star tube, fill the bottom of each éclair with the banana-cream mixture. Chill the filled éclair bottoms in the freezer for one hour.

Melt the chocolate in a small saucepan and brush the top parts of the éclairs with the melted chocolate. Sprinkle the almonds over the chocolate while it is still warm. Allow the chocolate to dry.

With a sharp knife, cut the top of each éclair into serving-sized pieces. Place the top pieces on the chilled, banana-cream-filled éclair bottom and finish cutting through the éclairs. Serve with the chocolate sauce.

LOUIS SZATHMÁRY
THE CHEF'S SECRET COOK BOOK

Eclairs

Éclairs au Café ou au Chocolat

To make 18 éclairs

½ lb.	chou paste *(recipe, page 163)*	¼ kg.
1½ cups	pastry cream *(recipe, page 166)* flavored with coffee or chocolate	375 ml.
⅔ cup	fondant icing *(recipe, page 167)* flavored with coffee or chocolate	150 ml.

With a pastry bag, pipe onto a baking sheet 18 strips of chou paste about 3½ inches [9 cm.] long and as thick as your little finger. Bake in a preheated 400° F. [200° C.] oven for 20 minutes, or until puffed and golden brown. Allow to cool.

Slit each éclair along one side and fill it with pastry cream. Glaze the éclairs with an icing of the same flavor as the cream filling.

HENRI PAUL PELLAPRAT
LE NOUVEAU GUIDE CULINAIRE

Chou Cake with Toasted-Almond Cream

*To make one 9- to 10-inch
[23- to 25-cm.] cake*

1 cup	unbleached flour	¼ liter
1 cup	water	¼ liter
6 tbsp.	unsalted butter, cut into small pieces	90 ml.
	salt	
4 to 5 tbsp.	granulated sugar	60 to 75 ml.
1 tsp.	grated lemon peel	5 ml.
5	large eggs	5

Toasted-almond cream filling

3 oz.	almonds, toasted in a 350° F. [180° C.] oven for 5 minutes and ground in a nut grinder, or in a food processor operated at short spurts	90 g.
1 cup	milk	¼ liter
1½ tbsp.	cornstarch	22 ml.
½ cup	light brown sugar	125 ml.
1	egg, plus 1 egg yolk, lightly beaten	1
1 tsp.	vanilla extract	5 ml.
1 cup	heavy cream	¼ liter
1 tbsp.	almond liqueur (optional)	15 ml.
3 cups	sliced strawberries	¾ liter

To make the chou paste, combine the water, butter, a pinch of salt, 1 tablespoon [15 ml.] of the granulated sugar and the lemon peel in a heavy saucepan. Bring to a rolling boil over medium heat, then pour in all of the flour at once. Keeping the pan over the heat, stir vigorously with a large wooden spoon until the ingredients merge into a smooth, pasty ball. Keep spreading and stirring the mixture until it firms and dries. (A covering film of paste on the bottom of the pan is a good indication that the dough is dry enough.)

Remove from the heat, let cool a moment, then stir in the five eggs, one at a time; each egg added will cause the mass to break apart, but vigorous stirring will return it to cohesion.

Oil or butter a soufflé dish or metal tin with straight sides. Spoon in the paste and bake in a preheated 400° F. [200° C.] oven for 50 minutes. Remove from the oven and turn out the pastry. Carefully slice off the top and remove all of the soft, undercooked dough from both the top and the base. Place the cut-out lid on a baking sheet and return both sections of the cake to the oven for 10 minutes. Brush the top of the cake lid with a little water and sprinkle the remaining granulated sugar over it. Place the lid under the broiler briefly to caramelize the sugar. Let the cake cool to room temperature before filling it.

To make the toasted-almond cream filling, combine the cornstarch and brown sugar; scald the milk and pour it over the brown sugar mixture. Whisk the milk mixture into the beaten egg, then return this custard to a gentle heat and continue whisking, without boiling, until it thickens. Add the vanilla extract and the ground almonds. Chill.

When the custard is cool, whip the cream and fold it into the custard along with the liqueur, if you are using it. Fill the bottom of the cake with the almond cream, heap on the sliced strawberries and replace the cake lid.

JUDITH OLNEY
SUMMER FOOD

Croquembouche

Pièce-Montée ou Croquembouche

The technique of assembling a croquembouche is on page 70.

To make one large pyramidal pastry		
1 lb.	chou paste *(recipe, page 163)*	½ kg.
2 cups	pastry cream *(recipe, page 166),* flavored with 2 tbsp. [30 ml.] rum	½ liter
1 cup	sugar	¼ liter
2 tbsp.	water	30 ml.

On an ungreased baking sheet, shape chou paste into small balls with a spoon. Bake them in a preheated 400° F. [200° C.] oven for 20 minutes, or until they are puffed and golden brown. Let them cool completely.

When the chou balls are cold, fill them with the pastry cream, using a pastry bag or spooning in the cream through a slit cut close to the base of each ball.

Over medium heat, dissolve the sugar in the water and boil until this syrup is a light golden, caramel color. Remove from the heat.

Dip the top of each filled chou ball in turn into the hot caramel and arrange the balls on a serving dish, forming tiers of decreasing size. The caramel will harden and hold the pyramid together.

NICOLE VIELFAURE AND A. CHRISTINE BEAUVIALA
FÊTES, COUTUMES ET GÂTEAUX

Cream-Puff Tart

Gâteau St. Honoré

The techniques for preparing this tart are demonstrated on pages 68-69.

	To make one 10-inch [25-cm.] tart	
½ lb.	rich short-crust dough *(recipe, page 162)*	¼ kg.
1 lb.	chou paste *(recipe, page 163)*	½ kg.
1	egg, beaten with 2 tbsp. [30 ml.] milk	1
1 cup	heavy cream, whipped	¼ liter
1¼ cups	sugar	300 ml.
½ cup	water	125 ml.
3 cups	pastry cream *(recipe, page 166)*	¾ liter
1 tbsp.	unflavored powdered gelatin	15 ml.
6	egg whites	6
	candied cherries (optional)	

Roll out the rich short-crust dough ¼ inch [6 mm.] thick and cut it in a circle, using a 10-inch [25-cm.] plate as a guide. Set the circle on a buttered baking sheet. Form an edge of chou paste about the thickness of a thumb all around the circle. Brush the top of the chou-paste ring with some of the egg-and-milk mixture.

Bake this in a preheated 400° F. [200° C.] oven for 25 to 30 minutes, or until the chou circle has puffed up and the whole tart is brown.

Next make some small cream puffs. Drop walnut-sized balls of the chou paste onto a dampened baking sheet, leaving a space of about 2 inches [5 cm.] between them. Brush the tops with the remaining egg-and-milk mixture and bake in a preheated 400° F. oven for 25 minutes, or until the pastry balls are puffed, brown and crisp. Take the puffs from the oven, slide them onto a wire rack and prick the sides of the puffs to release the steam. When the cream puffs are cold, fill them with pastry cream or with the whipped cream.

Make some caramel by mixing in a heavy saucepan 1 cup [¼ liter] of the sugar with ½ cup [125 ml.] of water. Let the sugar dissolve over medium heat and boil the syrup over high heat until it thickens and turns golden. Dip the filled cream puffs into the caramel and arrange them on the pastry edge, attaching them with the caramel.

Make the pastry cream. Soften the gelatin in 2 tablespoons [30 ml.] of cold water and add it to the pastry cream while it is still hot. Beat the egg whites until stiff, adding the remaining sugar during the last few minutes of beating. Fold them into the pastry cream.

Fill the center of the tart with the pastry-cream mixture, putting a small amount into a pastry bag fitted with a fancy tube to decorate the top. Candied cherries can be used to decorate the tops of the small puffs if wished.

LOUIS DIAT
HOME COOK BOOK—FRENCH COOKING FOR AMERICANS

Strudel and Phyllo Pastries

Apple Strudel

Apfelstrudel

The techniques of filling and rolling strudel are demonstrated on pages 76-77.

	To make three 16-inch [40-cm.] strudels	
1½ lb.	strudel dough *(recipe, page 165)*	¾ kg.
12	medium-sized apples (about 4 lb. [2 kg.]), peeled, cored and thinly sliced	12
14 tbsp.	butter, melted	200 ml.
1½ cups	dry bread crumbs, browned in 4 tbsp. [60 ml.] butter	375 ml.
1 cup	chopped walnuts	¼ liter
½ cup	raisins, soaked in warm water for 15 minutes and drained	125 ml.
⅔ cup	sugar	150 ml.
¼ tsp.	ground cinnamon	1 ml.
¼ tsp.	ground cloves	1 ml.
1½ tbsp.	strained fresh lemon juice	22 ml.
1 tbsp.	rum	15 ml.
½ cup	heavy cream, whipped	125 ml.
	confectioners' sugar	

On a large, floured board or cloth, roll out the strudel dough and stretch it with your hands until it is almost transparent. Sprinkle the dough with half of the melted butter. Then, leaving a 1-inch [2½-cm.] border, cover half of the dough with the apples, mixed with the browned bread crumbs, walnuts, raisins, sugar, cinnamon, cloves, lemon juice and rum. Pour a little melted butter over the apple filling, then spread the top with the whipped cream.

Roll up the strudel so that the filling is completely enclosed in the pastry. Brush off any excess flour. Cut the strudel into three 16-inch [40-cm.] sections and place them on buttered baking sheets. Bake in a preheated 350° F. [180° C.] oven for 30 to 40 minutes, basting occasionally with the remaining melted butter. The strudel is done when it is golden brown. Sprinkle generously with confectioners' sugar before serving the pastry either hot or cold.

HANS KARL ADAM
DAS KOCHBUCH AUS SCHWABEN

Vienna Apple Strudel

The techniques of filling and rolling a strudel are demonstrated on pages 76-77.

To make one 4-foot [120-cm.] strudel

1½ lb.	strudel dough *(recipe, page 165)*	¾ kg.
18	apples, peeled, cored and sliced (about 6 lb. [3 kg.])	18
2½ cups	fresh bread crumbs	625 ml.
12 tbsp.	butter, 6 tbsp. [90 ml.] melted	180 ml.
1 cup	chopped almonds	¼ liter
½ cup	raisins, soaked in warm water for 15 minutes and drained	125 ml.
1 cup	sugar	¼ liter
1 tsp.	ground cinnamon	5 ml.
1 tsp.	grated lemon peel	5 ml.
1 tbsp.	grated orange peel	15 ml.

Brown the bread crumbs in the butter and let them cool slightly. Sprinkle them onto the pulled strudel dough. Distribute the apples, almonds and raisins evenly over the crumb-coated dough. Sprinkle the apple mixture with the sugar and cinnamon, and the grated lemon and orange peels. Roll up the strudel and place it on a baking sheet. If the strudel is too long to fit the sheet, curve it into a horseshoe shape. Brush the top with the melted butter. Bake in a preheated 325° F. [160° C.] oven for about one hour, or until the pastry is golden brown and crisp. Serve hot or cold.

BERT J. PHILLIPS
THE PASTRY CHEF

Cherry Strudel

Tresnovy Zavin

The techniques of filling and rolling a strudel are demonstrated on pages 76-77. The filled strudel may be curved into a horseshoe shape, if desired.

To make one 3-foot [90-cm.] strudel

1 lb.	strudel dough *(recipe, page 165)*	½ kg.
2 lb.	cherries, pitted	1 kg.
8 tbsp.	butter, melted	120 ml.
1 cup	fresh bread crumbs, browned in 3 tbsp. [45 ml.] butter	¼ liter
½ to 1 cup	confectioners' sugar	125 to 250 ml.

Brush the dough generously with part of the melted butter and sprinkle it with the browned bread crumbs. Spread the cherries evenly over the dough; sprinkle them with confec-

tioners' sugar. With both hands, grasp one side of the cloth holding the strudel dough. Lift the cloth slowly and start rolling up the dough, brushing the underside with butter as you roll. Roll the strudel from the cloth onto a greased baking sheet. Brush the top with butter and bake in a preheated 350° F. [180° C.] oven for about 30 minutes, or until golden brown. Dust with confectioners' sugar. Serve sliced.

JOZA BŘÍZOVÁ
THE CZECHOSLOVAK COOKBOOK

Cottage Cheese Strudel

Túrós Töltelék

The techniques of preparing strudel dough and filling a strudel are demonstrated on pages 74-77. The filled strudel may be curved into a horseshoe shape, if desired.

To make one 3-foot [90-cm.] strudel

1 lb.	strudel dough *(recipe, page 165)*	½ kg.
1 lb.	cottage cheese, sieved	½ kg.
3	eggs, the yolks separated from the whites, and the whites stiffly beaten	3
4 tbsp.	butter, softened	60 ml.
¾ cup	vanilla sugar	175 ml.
½ cup	sour cream	125 ml.
1 tbsp.	flour	15 ml.
¼ cup	raisins, soaked in warm water for 15 minutes and drained	50 ml.
½ tsp.	grated lemon peel	2 ml.
	salt	
4 tbsp.	melted butter or lard	60 ml.
1 tbsp.	semolina	15 ml.

Beat the egg yolks with the butter and the sugar until the mixture is foamy. Slowly beat in the sour cream, flour, raisins, lemon peel and a pinch of salt. Let the mixture stand for 15 minutes. Fold the cottage cheese into the stiffly beaten egg whites. Mix this with the egg-yolk mixture.

Sprinkle melted butter or lard over the prepared sheet of strudel dough. Sprinkle the semolina on one third of the dough. Spread the cottage-cheese filling on top of the semolina. Roll up the strudel, place it on a buttered baking pan and spread the top with the remaining melted butter or lard. Bake in a preheated 375° F. [190° C.] oven for about 40 minutes, or until the strudel is crisp and brown. Serve while still warm, cut into short lengths.

GEORGE LANG
THE CUISINE OF HUNGARY

Poppy-seed Strudel

Mákos Töltelék

The techniques of filling and rolling strudel are demonstrated on pages 76-77. If necessary, this strudel may be curved into a horseshoe shape, to fit the pan.

Although many traditional recipes mix the poppyseeds with apricot jam, you will find substituting grated apple, as in this recipe, a wonderful taste alternative. For yet another variation, reduce the quantity of poppyseeds to ¼ pound [125 g.] and, instead of the apple, use 1 pound [½ kg.] of pumpkin flesh, diced and cooked.

To make one 3-foot [90-cm.] strudel

1 lb.	strudel dough *(recipe, page 165)*	½ kg.
½ lb.	poppy seeds, ground in a mortar and pestle	¼ kg.
¾ cup	vanilla sugar	175 ml.
2	eggs, the yolks separated from the whites, and the whites stiffly beaten	2
1 tbsp.	flour	15 ml.
½ tsp.	grated lemon peel	2 ml.
6 tbsp.	unsalted butter, softened	90 ml.
1 cup	milk, heated	¼ liter
¼ cup	raisins, soaked in warm water for 15 minutes and drained	50 ml.
1	apple, peeled, cored and grated	1
4 tbsp.	butter or lard	60 ml.

In a bowl, beat the vanilla sugar with the egg yolks until the mixture is smooth and light-colored. Beat the flour, lemon peel, butter and—finally—hot milk into the egg-and-sugar mixture. Put the mixture into a saucepan. Bring it gently to a simmer and mix in the poppy seeds. When the mixture returns to a simmer, turn off the heat. Let the mixture cool.

When the mixture is cooled, mix in the raisins and grated apple, then fold in the stiffly beaten egg whites; if this filling is too thick to spread, add a little cold water.

Sprinkle melted butter or lard over the prepared sheet of strudel dough. Spread the filling on one third of the dough and roll up the strudel. Bake in a preheated 375° F. [195° C.] oven for about 40 minutes, or until the strudel is crisp and brown. Serve while still warm, cut into short lengths.

GEORGE LANG
THE CUISINE OF HUNGARY

Turkish Strudel

Türkenstrudel

The techniques of filling and rolling strudel are demonstrated on pages 76-77.

To make one 18-inch [45-cm.] strudel

½ lb.	strudel dough *(recipe, page 165)*	¼ kg.
9 tbsp.	unsalted butter	135 ml.
½ cup	superfine sugar	125 ml.
5	eggs, the yolks separated from the whites, and the whites stiffly beaten	5
1 tsp.	finely grated lemon peel	5 ml.
½ cup	finely chopped candied lemon peel	125 ml.
1 tsp.	ground ginger	5 ml.
½ cup	seedless raisins, soaked in water for 15 minutes, drained and chopped	125 ml.
½ cup	chopped dried figs	125 ml.
½ cup	chopped, pitted dates	125 ml.
1¼ cups	walnuts, chopped	300 ml.
	melted butter	
	confectioners' sugar	

Cream together the unsalted butter, superfine sugar and egg yolks until the mixture is light and fluffy. Add the lemon peel, candied lemon peel, ginger, raisins, figs, dates and walnuts. Mix them together, then fold in the egg whites.

Roll out the strudel dough to make a large, thin sheet, pulling it out until it is virtually transparent. Spread the filling evenly over the sheet, leaving a wide border. Fold three sides of the border over the filling and roll up the dough, enclosing the filling completely.

Place the strudel on a buttered baking sheet, curving the strudel if necessary to fit, and brush the top with melted butter. Bake in a preheated 375° F. [190° C.] oven for about 40 minutes, or until golden brown and crisp. Serve warm or cold, sprinkled with confectioners' sugar.

EVA BAKOS
MEHLSPEISEN AUS ÖSTERREICH

The Snake

M'hanncha

To make one 9-inch [23-cm.] pastry

8	phyllo sheets, each about 12 by 18 inches [30 by 45 cm.], made from 1 lb. [½ kg.] phyllo dough *(recipe, page 164)*	8
9 tbsp.	unsalted butter, melted and cooled (or more)	135 ml.
½ lb.	blanched almonds, finely ground in a nut grinder, or in a food processor operated at short spurts	¼ kg.
½ tsp.	almond extract	2 ml.
⅛ tsp.	gum arabic (optional)	½ ml.
¾ to 1 cup	confectioners' sugar	175 to 250 ml.
¼ cup	rose water or orange-flower water	50 ml.
1	egg, beaten	1
	ground cinnamon	
	confectioners' sugar	

For the filling, mix 4 tablespoons [60 ml.] of the cooled melted butter with the ground blanched almonds and almond extract. Pound the gum arabic—if you are using it—in a mortar until it is finely ground and add it to the almond mixture. Add ¾ cup [175 ml.] of the sugar and the rose water or orange-flower water to the mixture, then mix well and knead to a solid, well-blended mass. Chill.

Separate the chilled almond paste into 20 balls of equal size and roll each ball into a 2½-inch [8-cm.] cylinder. Chill.

Spread out two phyllo sheets lengthwise, overlapping one end by 4 or 5 inches [10 or 13 cm.]. Brush the sheets with some of the remaining melted butter. Cover with a second layer of two sheets and brush with butter again. Place 10 cylinders of almond paste along the lower edge of the second layer of sheets, 2 inches [5 cm.] from the bottom. Tuck in the two ends and roll up the pastry tight. Shape this roll into a loose coil of concentric rings. Brush a 9-inch [23-cm.] round cake pan lightly with butter and place the coil in the center. Repeat the stacking, buttering and rolling process with the remaining phyllo sheets and paste cylinders, and coil this roll around the first one to fill the pan.

Beat the egg and add ½ teaspoon [2 ml.] of ground cinnamon. Brush the pastry top with the cinnamon-egg mixture and bake in a preheated 350° F. [180° C.] oven for 30 minutes, or until golden brown. Invert the pastry onto a baking sheet and return it to the oven for 10 minutes. Invert the pastry onto a serving plate and dust the top with confectioners' sugar. Dribble cinnamon in straight lines to form a lattice pattern. Serve warm.

PAULA WOLFERT
COUSCOUS AND OTHER GOOD FOOD FROM MOROCCO

Custard Swirls

Galatoboureko Roulo

Shaping custard swirls is demonstrated on pages 78-79.

To make twenty-four 4-inch [10-cm.] swirls

24	phyllo sheets, each about 12 by 18 inches [30 by 45 cm.], made from 2 lb. [1 kg.] phyllo dough *(recipe, page 164)*	24
6	egg yolks	6
1 cup	sugar	¼ liter
1 cup	farina	¼ liter
6 cups	milk, scalded	1½ liters
2 tbsp.	vanilla extract	30 ml.
1 lb.	unsalted butter, melted	½ kg.
Lemon-sugar syrup		
3 tbsp.	strained fresh lemon juice	45 ml.
2 cups	sugar	½ liter
2 cups	water	½ liter

Prepare the syrup by combining the fresh lemon juice, sugar and water. Bring to a boil. Continue to boil for 15 minutes, until the syrup thickens. Set the syrup aside to cool.

Prepare the custard filling in a heavy saucepan or the top of a double boiler by first beating the egg yolks and sugar until the mixture is thick and smooth. Add the farina and mix well. Slowly stir in the scalded milk. Add the vanilla extract. Stirring constantly, cook over medium heat for about five minutes, or until the custard thickens enough to coat the spoon. Cool the custard.

For each swirl, brush one sheet of phyllo dough with butter, then fold the sheet in half to make a 16-by-6-inch [40-by-15-cm.] strip. Brush the top of the strip with butter, and spoon or pipe the filling along one long edge, leaving a narrow margin exposed at the edge and the sides of the strip. Fold in the sides; roll up the filling in the phyllo to form a long cylinder. Brush the ends of the cylinder with butter. Carefully take one end of the cylinder and turn it inward to make a circle. Then coil the cylinder into a swirl.

Place all the swirls on ungreased baking sheets. Brush the top of each swirl with additional butter. Bake the swirls in a preheated 350° F. [180° C.] oven for approximately 45 minutes or until golden. Remove from the oven and cool for about five minutes. Carefully ladle a spoonful of the cooled lemon-sugar syrup over each swirl.

WOMEN OF ST. PAUL'S GREEK ORTHODOX CHURCH
THE REGIONAL COOKING OF GREECE

Honey-dipped Pastry Stuffed with Figs

Klandt bil Karmouss

To make 28 small pastries, approximately 2 by 1 ¼ inches [5 by 1 cm.]

14	phyllo sheets cut into 16-by-12-inch [40-by-30-cm.] sheets, made from 1 lb. [½ kg.] phyllo dough (recipe, page 164)	14
¾ lb.	dried figs, pitted and chopped	⅓ kg.
⅓ cup	apricot preserves	75 ml.
½ cup	chopped blanched almonds	125 ml.
	ground cinnamon	
8 tbsp.	unsalted butter, melted and cooled	120 ml.
⅔ cup	sugar	150 ml.
⅔ cup	water	150 ml.
⅔ cup	dark, heavy honey	150 ml.
3 tbsp.	orange-flower water (optional)	45 ml.
	oil for frying (optional)	

Push the figs with a little water through a food grinder. Combine the figs with the apricot preserves and the almonds. Add cinnamon to taste. Knead until well blended. Separate the mixture into 28 equal-sized balls.

Keeping the stack of phyllo under a damp towel, brush one sheet sparingly with melted butter. Cut the sheet lengthwise into two equal parts, fold each in half and place some of the fig mixture at the bottom of each half. Fold the sides lengthwise over the filling. Then fold the bottom over and roll up the phyllo like a rug. If necessary, seal the last inch of phyllo with a flour-and-water paste.

To make the syrup, first combine the sugar and the water in a heavy saucepan. Bring the mixture to a boil and cook for five minutes at a simmer. Off the heat, stir in the honey, orange-flower water and a pinch of ground cinnamon. Return the pan to the stove and keep the syrup at a low simmer.

Bake the stuffed pastries in a preheated 350° F. [180° C.] oven for 30 minutes, or until puffed and golden on both sides; or fry them in not-too-hot oil until golden—turning once.

Transfer the pastries, five or six at a time, to the simmering honey syrup; let the syrup penetrate each batch for two or three minutes. Remove the pastries to a flat dish to dry.

PAULA WOLFERT
MEDITERRANEAN COOKING

Nut-filled Pastry Bathed in Fragrant Syrup

Baklava

The baklava recipe that follows is made with walnuts and a syrup flavored with cloves and lemon. If you wish to substi-

tute chopped almonds or pecans for the walnuts, flavor the syrup with 2 teaspoons [10 ml.] of rose water and 2 tablespoons [30 ml.] of brandy or with two cinnamon sticks and two pieces of orange peel.

To make 30 to 36 small pastries

20 to 30	phyllo sheets, each about 12 by 18 inches [30 by 45 cm.], made from 2 lb. [1 kg.] phyllo dough (recipe, page 164)	20 to 30
4 lb.	walnuts, finely chopped, or coarsely ground in a nut grinder, or in a food processor operated at short spurts	2 kg.
1 tsp.	ground cinnamon	5 ml.
¼ tsp.	ground cloves	1 ml.
1 cup	sugar	¼ liter
1 lb.	unsalted butter, melted and kept warm	½ kg.
Honey syrup		
½ cup	honey	125 ml.
2 cups	sugar	½ liter
2 cups	cold water	½ liter
1	thin lemon slice with peel	1
2 tbsp.	fresh lemon juice	30 ml.
2	whole cloves	2

To make the filling, place the chopped or ground walnuts in a large mixing bowl. Add the cinnamon, ground cloves and sugar. Mix well with your hands and set aside.

Brush melted butter over the sides, corners and bottom of a large rectangular baking pan—about 18 by 12 by 2 inches [45 by 30 by 5 cm.].

Lay one sheet of phyllo dough flat on the bottom of the pan. Brush with melted butter. When you have stacked 10 sheets of buttered phyllo on top of one another, you have the bottom crust for the baklava.

Sprinkle the 10th sheet lightly with some of the nut mixture. Continue adding buttered phyllo sheets; sprinkle every second sheet with the nut mixture until all of it is used.

Preheat the oven to 325° F. [160° C.]. Make the top crust of the baklava with the remaining sheets of individually buttered phyllo. When you finish, roll down any buttered edges and tuck them inside the pan.

Brush the top of the baklava liberally with warm melted butter and sprinkle with about 10 drops of cold water—to prevent the phyllo from curling up when baking. Using a sharp-pointed knife, cut only the top layers of phyllo into small diamonds or triangular pieces. Bake for one and a half hours, or until golden brown.

Make the syrup while the baklava is baking. In a saucepan, combine the sugar with the water, lemon slice, lemon juice and whole cloves, and bring to a fast boil. Reduce the heat and boil gently for 20 minutes. Remove the saucepan from the heat and discard the lemon slice and cloves. Stir in the honey and set the syrup aside to cool.

When the baklava is done, remove it from the oven and pour half of the syrup slowly all over it. Twenty minutes later, slowly dribble the rest of the syrup over the pastry. Let the pastry rest in the pan for at least four hours, preferably overnight, before cutting and serving. Do not refrigerate.

When you are ready to remove the pieces from the pan, remember that you have cut through only the top layers of the pastry before baking; you must now cut through the entire pastry, including the bottom crust. Using a sharp knife, cut deeply and at least twice, so each piece will come out cleanly and easily.

ANNE THEOHAROUS
COOKING THE GREEK WAY

Layered Walnut and Honey Pastry

Baklava

To make 25 small cakes

20	phyllo sheets, each about 12 by 18 inches [30 by 45 cm.], made from 2 lb. [1 kg.] phyllo dough *(recipe, page 164)*	20
1 lb.	butter, melted	½ kg.
2 cups	finely chopped walnuts	½ liter
1 cup	honey	¼ liter
1 cup	water	¼ liter

Spread out five sheets of phyllo dough, one on top of the other. Place a large square pan in the center of these and cut around it, through all of the sheets. Place the sheets in the pan, one at a time, brushing each generously with melted butter. Scatter the dough trimmings over the top sheet and brush the trimmings with butter. Repeat with five more sheets of phyllo.

Spread the walnuts evenly in the pan and continue adding layers of phyllo until all of the sheets have been used, adding the last trimmings beneath the last sheet.

With a sharp knife, score the top of the pastry diagonally into five sections in each direction, making 25 diamond-shaped cakes. Let rest for two hours.

Preheat the oven to 450° F. [230° C.], then reduce the temperature to 350° F. [180° C.]. Pour one half of the remaining butter over the pastry and bake for seven minutes. Pour over the rest of the butter, reduce the oven temperature to 325° F. [170° C.] and bake for 20 minutes longer. Remove the baklava from the oven. Use a bulb baster to drain off excess butter. Return the pastry to the oven for five minutes. Again drain off any excess butter and bake for five minutes longer.

In a saucepan, combine the honey and water, and boil to a thick syrup. Pour the hot syrup around the edge of the pan and over the pastry. Let cool and cut into diamonds along the scored markings so that the pieces can absorb the syrup.

ANN SERANNE
THE COMPLETE BOOK OF DESSERTS

Fried Pastries

Polish Bow Ties

Chrusciki

To make about 80 bow ties, each 5 by 1 ½ inches [13 by 4 cm.]

4 cups	flour, sifted	1 liter
5	large egg yolks	5
1	whole egg	1
1 tsp.	vanilla extract	5 ml.
2 tbsp.	sugar	30 ml.
1 tbsp.	butter, melted	15 ml.
2 tbsp.	sour cream	30 ml.
½ cup	milk	125 ml.
2 tbsp.	bourbon whiskey (optional)	30 ml.
	confectioners' sugar	
	vegetable shortening	

Mix together the egg yolks, whole egg, vanilla extract, sugar, melted butter, sour cream, milk and the whiskey, if desired. Add 2 cups [½ liter] of the flour to the liquid mixture. Form the dough into a ball. Pile the remaining flour on a table, place the ball of dough on top of the flour and knead the mixture for 15 to 20 minutes, or until it no longer sticks to the table or your hands.

Cut the dough into four pieces for easy handling. Working each piece separately, roll out the dough into strips about 5 inches [13 cm.] long and 1½ inches [4 cm.] wide. Make a slit down the middle of each strip and pull one end of the strip through the slit to make a bow. Melt a 2½-inch [6-cm.] layer of vegetable shortening in a heavy skillet. Heat the shortening to 375° F. [190° C.] on a deep-frying thermometer and test it by dropping in one bow tie; it should rise to the top almost instantly. Fry the bow ties five to seven at a time (depending on the size of the skillet) for 30 to 60 seconds on each side, or until evenly browned. Remove the pastries with a long-handled slotted spoon and drain them on paper towels. When all of the bow ties are fried, sprinkle each with confectioners' sugar. Serve at once or store, stacked lightly, in a tightly closed can.

ELINOR SEIDEL (EDITOR)
CHEFS, SCHOLARS & MOVABLE FEASTS

Spanish Fritters

Churros

To make about 6 fritters

1¼ cups	flour, sifted	300 ml.
1¼ cups	water	300 ml.
4 tbsp.	butter, cut into small pieces	60 ml.
	salt	
3	large eggs, or 4 small ones, lightly beaten	3
½ tsp.	vanilla extract or 2 tsp. [10 ml.] fresh lemon juice, rum, or orange-flower water	2 ml.
	oil for deep frying	
	sugar	

Put the water and the butter in a small saucepan with a pinch of salt. Stir until the butter melts. As soon as the liquid boils, remove the saucepan from the heat, add the flour and stir vigorously with a wooden spoon, until the mixture is a perfectly smooth paste. Now place the pan over low heat and stir until the paste no longer clings to the pan or to the spoon.

Remove the pan from the heat; then add the eggs, one at a time, mixing thoroughly so that the paste absorbs them. Add the flavoring and, when the paste is firm, put a little of it into a pastry bag fitted with a tube about ½ inch [1 cm.] wide. Pipe the paste into a deep pan of hot oil in lengths of 12 inches [30 cm.] each and fry until golden. The *churros* will curl and swell to about 1 inch [2½ cm.] in thickness. Drain them on a cloth in the oven. Serve hot, sprinkled with sugar.

COUNTESS MORPHY
RECIPES OF ALL NATIONS

Fried Pies

Fruits suitable for this recipe include pitted prunes, dried apricots and peaches, or applesauce. To prepare the dried fruit, simmer 1 cup [¼ liter] of it in ½ cup [125 ml.] of water until it is plump and tender but not soft—five to 10 minutes. Drain, and sweeten the fruit to taste.

To make twelve 4-inch [10-cm.] pies

2 cups	sifted flour	½ liter
1 tsp.	salt	5 ml.
8 tbsp.	shortening	120 ml.
about ⅓ cup	cold water	about 75 ml.
	chopped stewed fruit	
	fat for deep frying	

Sift together the flour and salt, and cut in the shortening with two knives or a pastry blender. Gradually add water, about a tablespoonful [15 ml.] at a time, until the dough coheres. Roll out the dough on a floured board to a thickness of ⅛ inch [3 mm.]. With a cookie cutter about 4 inches [10 cm.] in diameter, cut the dough into rounds. On the center of each round, place 1½ tablespoons [22 ml.] of fruit. Moisten the edges of the round with cold water, fold over the dough to make a semicircle and press the edges together with a fork. In deep fat preheated to 370° F. [190° C.] on a deep-frying thermometer, fry for three to four minutes, or until golden brown. Drain on paper towels. Or, these pies can be sautéed in a small amount of fat and then browned in a preheated 425° F. [220° C.] oven.

RUTH BEROLZHEIMER (EDITOR)
THE UNITED STATES REGIONAL COOK BOOK

Puffed Fritters with Apricot Sauce

Beignets Soufflés

To make about sixty 1-inch [2½-cm.] fritters

1 cup	sifted flour	¼ liter
1 cup	water	¼ liter
8 tbsp.	butter	120 ml.
1 tsp.	sugar	5 ml.
	salt	
4	eggs	4
1 tsp.	vanilla extract	5 ml.
	fat for deep frying	
Apricot sauce		
1½ cups	apricot preserves	375 ml.
2 tbsp.	apricot brandy	30 ml.
½ cup	water	125 ml.
2 tbsp.	sugar	30 ml.

Mix the apricot preserves, water and sugar in a heavy saucepan. Heat to boiling and simmer for five minutes, stirring often. Sieve the apricot sauce and add the brandy.

Combine the water, butter, sugar and salt in a heavy saucepan. Heat to boiling. When the butter melts, add the flour. Beat with a wooden spoon over medium heat just until the mixture pulls away from the side of the pan. Remove the saucepan from the heat and beat in the eggs, one at a time, until the batter is smooth. Beat in the vanilla extract.

Heat the fat in a heavy skillet to 375° F. [190° C.]. Drop the batter by teaspoonfuls into the hot fat. Deep fry until brown on both sides—about five minutes. Remove with a slotted spoon and drain on paper towels. Keep warm. Serve with warm or cooled apricot sauce.

EVE BROWN
THE PLAZA COOKBOOK

Sweet Ribbons

Galani Dolci

To make 40 to 50 pastries

5 to 6 cups	sifted flour	1 ¼ to 1 ½ liters
½ cup	sugar	125 ml.
1 ½ tsp.	salt	7 ml.
8 tbsp.	butter, cut into small pieces and softened	120 ml.
3	large eggs	3
	cooking oil	
	confectioners' sugar	

Place 4 cups [1 liter] of the flour, the sugar and the salt in a bowl. Mix thoroughly. Add the softened butter pieces to the dry ingredients and knead together until a mealy texture is attained. Beat the eggs with a fork while gradually piling in a little flour from the sides of the well. When the ingredients are well mixed, add sufficient flour to produce a dough that can be kneaded without sticking to your hands.

Turn the dough onto a flour-dusted pastry board and knead until uniform—for at least five minutes; and better, 10 minutes or more.

Fill a deep fryer or large, deep saucepan halfway with cooking oil. Heat the oil to 400° F. [200° C.] as measured on a deep-frying thermometer.

Take a piece of dough slightly larger than a golf ball and roll it out into a very thin sheet—much thinner than for a pie crust. Using a rotary cutting wheel, preferably with a serrated edge, cut the dough into squares, triangles or any interesting shapes you may wish; but the greatest dimension should be 4 to 5 inches [10 to 13 cm.] since the *galani* will expand when cooking.

A good idea at this point is to cut only one *galano* and cook it in order to check the thickness of the dough and the oil temperature. When added to the oil, the *galano* should start bubbling immediately but not violently. After 45 seconds or a few seconds longer, turn the *galano* with a fork; it should be a medium golden brown color. After half a minute, the *galano* should be ready to remove from the oil. Place it on paper towels to cool. Break it open to see if the dough is completely cooked; the *galano* should be crisp but not burnt. If the outside is golden but the inside soggy, roll the dough thinner and try again. If the *galano* is pale, increase the oil temperature a little.

Once the dough thickness and the oil temperature have been set, all the *galani* may be cooked fairly quickly, two or three at a time. Continue rolling out, cutting and cooking the *galani* until all of the dough is used up. When the *galani* have cooled, dust them with confectioners' sugar.

H. F. BRUNING JR. AND CAV. UMBERTO BULLO
VENETIAN COOKING

Sweet Walnut Fritters

Samsa

To make 72 fritters approximately 1-inch [2 ½-cm.] square

1 ½ cups	flour, sifted	375 ml.
⅔ cup	lukewarm water	150 ml.
½ tsp.	salt	2 ml.
4 tbsp.	unsalted butter, softened	60 ml.
	vegetable oil	
	confectioners' sugar	

Sweet walnut filling

6 oz.	walnuts, ground in a nut grinder, or in a food processor, operated in short spurts	180 g.
1 ½ tbsp.	unsalted butter, softened	22 ml.
1 ½ tbsp.	granulated sugar	22 ml.

To make the filling, toss the walnuts, butter and sugar together in a large mixing bowl. Set the mixture aside at room temperature.

To make the dough, first place the flour in a deep mixing bowl and make a well in the center. Pour in the water, salt and 2 tablespoons [30 ml.] of the butter; slowly stir the flour into the other ingredients until well absorbed. Then beat vigorously with a large spoon until a firm dough is formed. Gather the dough into a ball. On a lightly floured surface, roll it into a rectangle approximately 16 inches [40 cm.] wide by 18 inches [46 cm.] long. Brush the dough with the additional 2 tablespoons of butter and fold it into quarters. Roll it out again as thin as possible and, with a pastry wheel or knife, trim the dough into a rectangle 16 inches wide by 18 inches long. Cut the rectangle into 2-inch [5-cm.] squares.

Heap 1 teaspoon [5 ml.] of the filling in the center of a square of dough and draw up the four corners to meet in the middle, thus enclosing the filling. Dip your fingers in water and pinch the corners firmly together to seal them. Fill and seal the remaining squares similarly.

Fill a deep-fat fryer or deep, heavy pot with enough oil to come 4 inches [10 cm.] up the sides of the pot, and heat until the oil reaches 375° F. [190° C.] on a deep-frying thermometer. Drop in 10 to 12 fritters, turning them occasionally with a slotted spoon. Fry them for about three minutes, or until they are golden brown and crisp. Then drain them on paper towels while you fry the remaining fritters similarly. Arrange the fritters on a serving platter, sprinkle them with confectioners' sugar and serve.

FOODS OF THE WORLD/RUSSIAN COOKING

Ricotta-filled Pastry Tubes

Cannoli

The author suggests that the fried pastry tubes can safely be stored —unfilled —for several weeks if kept well covered in a cool, dry place. For additional color and flavor, ¼ to ½ cup [50 to 125 ml.] of chopped candied cherries may be added to the filling.

To make about 24 filled tubes

3 cups	sifted flour	¾ liter
3 tbsp.	butter, melted	45 ml.
1 tbsp.	sugar	15 ml.
⅛ tsp.	salt	½ ml.
about ¾ cup	sweet red wine	about 175 ml.
1	egg white, slightly beaten	1
	fat for deep frying	
	Ricotta filling	
3 lb.	ricotta cheese	1½ kg.
¾ cup	confectioners' sugar	175 ml.
¼ cup	crème de cacao or other sweet liqueur	50 ml.
3 tbsp.	grated semisweet baking chocolate	45 ml.
2 tbsp.	finely chopped candied orange peel	30 ml.
½ cup	chopped pistachios	125 ml.

Mix together the flour, butter, sugar and salt. Add enough wine to make a stiff but manageable dough. Knead for about 15 minutes, or until the dough is smooth and soft; if necessary, add a bit more flour to prevent sticking. Roll the dough into a ball, cover, and place it in the refrigerator for one hour.

Divide the dough into two parts and on a lightly floured board roll it into paper-thin sheets. Cut the sheets into 4-inch [10-cm.] circles or squares. Place a metal *cannoli* tube from corner to corner, diagonally across each square or circle. Fold the opposite corners together around the tube. Brush the corners with beaten egg white to seal them and then press them together.

Heat 3 inches [8 cm.] of fat to 390° F. [195° C.]. Fry the *cannoli,* two or three at a time, turning if necessary, until deep golden brown on all sides. Remove them with tongs or a slotted spatula and drain them on absorbent paper. When cool to the touch, remove the pastries from the metal tubes, being careful not to break the pastry. Cool completely before filling. Fill the pastries just before serving so that they are crisp. If you do not intend to use the fried pastries immediately, store them in a cool dry place; they will keep unfilled for several weeks.

Beat the ricotta vigorously for two minutes. Add the confectioners' sugar and liqueur, and continue beating for five minutes longer, or until the mixture is smooth. Mix in the chocolate and orange peel, and refrigerate the filling until you are ready to serve the *cannoli.*

Use a small spoon to stuff the filling into the tubes. Dip the ends in the chopped pistachios. Serve at once.

ALFRED LEPORE
FERRARA'S LITTLE ITALIAN COOKBOOK

Stuffed Pastry Tubes

Cannoli alla Siciliana

For the technique of deep frying cannoli, see pages 80-81.

To make 12 to 15 cannoli

2 cups	flour, sifted	½ liter
¼ cup	Marsala	50 ml.
1 tbsp.	sugar	15 ml.
	salt	
	oil for deep frying	
	Ricotta-nut-fruit filling	
½ lb.	ricotta cheese	¼ kg.
1 tbsp.	pistachios, sliced lengthwise	15 ml.
2 tbsp.	finely chopped candied fruit	30 ml.
½ cup	confectioners' sugar	125 ml.
	salt	
	chopped pine nuts	

Make a mound of the flour on the tabletop; scoop out the center and mix in the Marsala wine, sugar and a pinch of salt. Knead until a firm dough is obtained. Roll it into a ball, wrap it in a slightly damp cloth and let it rest for two hours.

Then roll out the dough into sheets about ⅟₁₆ inch [1½ mm.] thick; cut it into 5-inch [13-cm.] squares and roll diagonally around metal *cannoli* tubes.

When all of the *cannoli* have been prepared, heat plenty of oil to 390° F. [195° C.] for deep frying. Put the *cannoli* in the oil a few at a time and remove them when golden brown (about five minutes). Drain, cool and reserve the *cannoli*. As they get cold, the metal tubes can—with care—be removed.

To prepare the filling, put the ricotta, confectioners' sugar and a pinch of salt in a mixing bowl (or blender). Mix well until smooth and pass through a fine sieve. Then combine with the pistachios and candied fruit. Using a pastry bag, fill the tubes with the filling; sprinkle chopped pine nuts over the filling at the extremities of the *cannoli*.

LUIGI CARNACINA
LUIGI CARNACINA PRESENTS ITALIAN HOME COOKING

Thousand-Leaf Pastries

Pastelitos de Mil Hojas

The techniques of shaping pastry flowers are demonstrated on pages 82-83. Quince paste, which is produced in Spain and many Latin American countries, is obtainable in cans where Latin American foods are sold.

To make 18 pastries

4½ cups	flour, sifted	1,125 ml.
19 tbsp.	unsalted butter, chilled and cut into small pieces	285 ml.
¼ tsp.	salt	1 ml.
2 tsp.	fresh lemon juice	10 ml.
2	egg yolks, beaten	2
1 cup	cold water	¼ liter
1½ cups	quince paste, combined with ⅔ cup [150 ml.] muscatel	375 ml.
	vegetable shortening for deep frying	

Vanilla sugar syrup

½ tsp.	vanilla extract	2 ml.
1 cup	sugar	¼ liter
¼ cup	water	50 ml.

In a large mixing bowl, combine 4 cups [1 liter] of the flour, 11 tablespoons [165 ml.] of the butter and the salt. Using your finger tips, rub together the flour and butter until they blend and look like flakes of coarse meal. Make a well in the center, add the lemon juice and egg yolks, and, stirring the dough, add the water, ¼ cup [50 ml.] at a time. When all of the water has been absorbed and the dough is quite smooth, place it on a lightly floured surface. Knead the dough for about 10 minutes, or until it is smooth and elastic. Cover the dough with a dry towel and chill it for two or three hours.

Melt the remaining butter and let it cool. With a lightly floured rolling pin, roll the dough into a 32-inch [80-cm.] square. Brush it evenly with a little melted butter and sprinkle it lightly with flour. With the palms of your hands, smooth the flour over the dough until the flour absorbs the butter and the surface looks dry. Fold the dough in half to form a 32-by-16-inch [80-by-40-cm.] rectangle. Repeat the buttering, flouring and folding process twice again, producing finally an 8-inch [20-cm.] square. Roll the dough into a 16-inch square, using the remaining flour to prevent it from sticking to the board.

With a small knife or pastry wheel and a ruler, trim the dough to a perfect 15-inch [38-cm.] square, and cut it into thirty-six 2½-inch [6-cm.] squares.

In the center of each of 18 of the squares, place about 1 teaspoon [5 ml.] of the quince-paste mixture. Lightly moisten the dough around the filling with cold water. Set the remaining squares on top at an angle that forms individual eight-pointed stars, pressing the dough around the filling to secure it firmly. Pinch the stars into flower-like shapes.

To make the syrup, first combine the sugar and water in a small saucepan. Stirring constantly, bring the syrup to a boil over high heat. Immediately stop stirring, then boil steadily until the syrup reaches a temperature of 230° F. [110° C.] on a candy thermometer, or until a bit dropped into cold water forms a coarse thread. Remove the pan from the heat and stir in the vanilla extract. Cover the syrup and keep it warm while you fry the pastries.

In a deep fryer or heavy saucepan, melt enough shortening to form a layer 3 inches [8 cm.] deep. Heat the shortening until it reaches 175° F. [80° C.] on a deep-frying thermometer. Drop in two pastries at a time, and deep fry them for three to four minutes, basting the pastries once or twice with the fat, until the petals of dough begin to separate and open somewhat. (Do not let the pastries brown.) Drain them on paper towels.

Increase the temperature of the shortening to 375° F. [190° C.] and fry the pastries again on each side for one minute, or until golden brown. With tongs, remove the pastries from the fat and drain them again on paper towels. Then dip them in the warm syrup and place them on a serving plate. Serve at room temperature.

FOODS OF THE WORLD/LATIN AMERICAN COOKING

Fillings

Almond Paste

To make 1 ½ pounds [¾ kg.] almond paste

3 cups	blanched almonds, ground in a nut grinder, or in a food processor operated at short spurts	¾ liter
1 ½ cups	confectioners' sugar	375 ml.
¾ cup	superfine sugar	175 ml.
1 tbsp.	strained fresh lemon juice	15 ml.
¾ tsp.	orange-flower water	4 ml.
¾ tsp.	vanilla extract	4 ml.
2	egg yolks, lightly beaten	2

Sift the confectioners' sugar into a bowl and mix with the ground almonds and superfine sugar. Add the lemon juice, orange-flower water, vanilla extract and enough egg yolk to bind the ingredients into a pliable but dry paste. Knead thoroughly with your hands until smooth.

MRS. BEETON'S EVERYDAY COOKERY

Butter Cream

La Crème au Beurre

The technique of making sugar syrup is demonstrated on pages 8-9. It is preferable to use the butter cream immediately, but it may be covered and kept in the refrigerator overnight. For variation in flavor, 3 ounces [90 g.] of semisweet baking chocolate melted over hot water, or 1 tablespoon [15 ml.] of rum, kirsch or fruit-flavored liqueur may be substituted for the coffee or vanilla extract.

To make 1 pound [½ kg.] butter cream

16 tbsp.	butter (½ lb. [¼ kg.])	240 ml.
⅔ cup	sugar	150 ml.
½ cup	water	100 ml.
5	egg yolks	5
1 tbsp.	coffee extract or vanilla extract	15 ml.

Cook the sugar and water together until they form a syrup that spins a thin thread when the spoon is lifted. Remove from the heat. Place the egg yolks in a bowl and, whisking vigorously, gradually pour in the hot syrup. Continue to whisk until the mixture is cool; it will be light and fluffy. Work the butter until it is creamy. Add the yolk mixture, stirring with a spatula until the cream is firm and shiny. Stir in the flavoring of your choice, and the cream is ready to use.

JEAN KELLER
LES PÂTISSERIES ET LES BONBONS

Lemon Curd

Lemon curd may be used as a filling for tarts and pies.

To make about 1 cup [¼ liter] filling

½ cup	strained fresh lemon juice	125 ml.
1 tbsp.	grated lemon peel	15 ml.
4 tbsp.	unsalted butter	60 ml.
½ cup	sugar	125 ml.
4	egg yolks	4

In a heavy 1½- to 2-quart [1½- to 2-liter] saucepan, combine the fresh lemon juice, butter, sugar and egg yolks. Stirring constantly, cook over the lowest possible heat, until the mixture thickens enough to coat heavily the back of a spoon. (Do not let the mixture boil or the egg yolks will curdle.) Pour the mixture into a small bowl and stir in the grated lemon peel. Refrigerate until ready to use.

FOODS OF THE WORLD/THE COOKING OF THE BRITISH ISLES

Strawberry Vanilla Cream

To make about 6 cups [1 ½ liters] filling

4 cups	strawberries, hulled	1 liter
2 cups	heavy cream, whipped	½ liter
1 tbsp.	fresh lemon juice	15 ml.
¾ cup	sugar	175 ml.
2 tbsp.	unflavored powdered gelatin, softened in ¼ cup [50 ml.] cold water	30 ml.

Mash the strawberries and strain them through a fine sieve. Add the fresh lemon juice and sugar, and stir until the sugar is completely dissolved. Place the softened gelatin in a pan over hot water and stir until the gelatin is dissolved. Add the dissolved gelatin to the strawberry mixture and stir over cracked ice until the mixture begins to thicken. Then fold in the whipped cream.

ANN SERANNE
THE COMPLETE BOOK OF HOME BAKING

Mincemeat

In 1870, when this recipe was written, cooks could store the mincemeat in a cool well house or root cellar. Today the mincemeat must be kept refrigerated.

To bake this mincemeat, take some out of a jar; if not moist enough, add a little hot water and strew a few whole raisins over each pie. Instead of boiled stew meat, a braised beef heart or leftover roast beef may be used.

To make 7 quarts [7 liters] mincemeat

5 lb.	boneless beef stew meat	2½ kg.
1 tbsp.	salt	15 ml.
3 lb.	beef suet	1½ kg.
4 lb.	seedless raisins, soaked in warm water for 15 minutes, drained and coarsely chopped	2 kg.
4 lb.	dried currants, soaked in warm water for 15 minutes and drained	2 kg.
1 lb.	candied citron, thinly sliced	½ kg.
9 lb.	tart apples, cored, peeled and finely chopped	4½ kg.
4 tbsp.	ground cinnamon	60 ml.
2 tbsp.	ground cloves	30 ml.
2 tbsp.	ground ginger	30 ml.
4	whole nutmegs, grated	4
⅓ cup	fresh lemon juice	90 ml.
2 tsp.	grated lemon peel	10 ml.
1 tsp.	pepper	5 ml.
2 lb.	sugar	1 kg.
1 quart	apple juice, boiled until reduced by half, or red-currant juice or grape juice	1 liter
1 quart	molasses or maple syrup	1 liter
2 to 3 tbsp.	syrup from sweet pickles (optional)	30 to 45 ml.
8 tbsp.	butter	120 ml.

Put the stew beef to boil in enough water to cover it; take off the scum that rises when it reaches the boiling point, then simmer, adding hot water from time to time until the meat is tender. Remove the lid from the pot, salt the meat, let it boil until almost dry, occasionally turning over the meat in the liquor. Take the pot from the heat and let it chill overnight to get thoroughly cold. Pick any gristle or stringy bits from the meat, chop it very fine, chopping the suet fine at the same time. Put the mixture in a pan with the raisins, currants, candied citron, apples, spices, lemon juice and peel, salt, pepper and the sugar.

Put the juice—apple, currant or grape—molasses or maple syrup, sweet-pickle syrup (if desired) and butter in an enameled saucepan. Let this mixture come to a boil, then pour it over the meat and fruits, mixing thoroughly.

Pack the mincemeat in jars and put them in a cool place; when cold, pour over the top a layer of molasses ⅛ inch [3 mm.] thick and cover tightly. This will keep two months.

THE BUCKEYE COOKBOOK: TRADITIONAL AMERICAN RECIPES

Chocolate Bavarian Cream

To make about 1 ½ cups [375 ml.] custard

2 oz.	unsweetened baking chocolate	60 g.
2-inch	piece vanilla bean	5-cm.
1 cup	milk	¼ liter
3	large egg yolks	3
½ cup	sugar	125 ml.
	salt	
1 tbsp.	unflavored powdered gelatin, softened in ¼ cup [50 ml.] cold water	15 ml.
1 cup	heavy cream, whipped	¼ liter

Combine the vanilla bean and the milk in a saucepan, and gently heat the milk until bubbles form around the edges of the pan—stirring to prevent a skin from forming on the surface. Remove the pan from the heat.

Beat the egg yolks lightly in the top part of a double boiler set over simmering water, or in a heavy 1-quart [1-liter] saucepan over low heat. Gradually beat in the sugar. Add a dash of salt. Then gradually add the hot milk, including the vanilla bean. Stir, and cook the custard until it coats a metal spoon. Remove the custard from the heat. Remove the vanilla bean. (Rinse it and save it for use in another dessert.) Strain the custard into a bowl, and stir in the softened gelatin and the chocolate. Cool the cream over ice, beating to prevent a skin from forming on the surface. Fold in the whipped cream.

HENRI PAUL PELLAPRAT
THE GREAT BOOK OF FRENCH CUISINE

Standard Preparations

Short-Crust Dough

This basic short-crust dough is suitable for any two-crust, deep-dish or lattice pie; turnover; or open-faced tart.

To make 2 pounds [1 kg.] dough

4 cups	flour	1 liter
1 tsp.	salt	5 ml.
20 tbsp.	unsalted butter, cut into pieces	300 ml.
6 to 8 tbsp.	ice water	90 to 120 ml.

Into a large mixing bowl, sift together the flour and salt. Add all of the butter. Rub together the butter and flour, using the tips of your fingers; or cut the butter into the flour with two knives or a pastry blender, until the mixture has a coarse, mealy texture.

Stirring lightly with a knife or using the pastry blender, sprinkle the water over the mixture a spoonful at a time until the dough begins to cohere. Gather the dough into a ball, pressing it together with your hands. Cover the dough with plastic wrap, wax paper or foil, and refrigerate it for one or two hours before using it. The dough can safely be kept in the refrigerator for two days, in the freezer for one month. If frozen, let the dough defrost in the refrigerator for one day before using it.

To roll out dough: Unwrap the dough and put it on a cool, floured surface (a marble slab is ideal). Divide the ball, if necessary; rewrap the excess portion and return it to the refrigerator. Partially press out the dough with your hand, then give it a few gentle smacks with the rolling pin to flatten it and render it more supple. Roll out the dough from the center, turning it 90 degrees clockwise after each roll, until it forms a round, an oblong or a rectangle—depending on the shape called for in the recipe—about ⅛ inch [3 mm.] thick.

To line a pan or flan form: Roll the dough onto the rolling pin, lift it up, and unroll it over a piepan, tart pan or a flan form set on a baking sheet. Press the dough firmly against the bottom and sides of the pan or flan form. For a piepan, use a small knife to trim off the excess dough around the rim, leaving a margin ½ inch [1 cm.] wide. Fold this margin toward the center of the pan to create a double thickness, then crimp the edge. For a tart pan or flan form, roll the pin across the top to cut off the excess dough around the rim.

To prebake or "blind bake" a pastry shell: Cut a piece of parchment paper, wax paper or foil slightly larger than the piepan, tart pan or flan form. Press the paper into the dough-lined pan or form, and fill the center with dried peas, beans or rice. Bake in a preheated 400° F. [200° C.] oven for about 10 minutes, or until the dough is set. Remove the filled paper or foil and, with a fork, lightly prick the bottom of the dough lining. For a partially baked pastry shell, return the pan or form to the oven for five minutes. For a fully baked shell, return the pan or form to the oven for 10 to 15 minutes, or until the pastry is crisp and golden brown. Cool the pastry shell in the pan or form for about five minutes. Then remove the fully baked shell and cool it on a wire rack before using it.

Rich Short-Crust Dough

Rich short-crust dough can be used interchangeably with basic short-crust dough in any recipe calling for a one-crust pie or tart shell—unbaked, partially baked or fully baked. Roll out rich short-crust dough, and use it to line a pan or a flan form as described for basic short crust *(left)*. The partial prebaking procedure is also identical, but for a fully baked shell allow 10 minutes at 400° F. [200° C.] with the lining in place—then remove the lining, reduce the temperature to 375° F. [190° C.] and let the shell crisp for 10 to 12 minutes.

To make 2 pounds [1 kg.] dough

4 cups	flour	1 liter
2 tbsp.	superfine or confectioners' sugar	30 ml.
2 tsp.	salt	10 ml.
¾ lb.	unsalted butter, softened	⅓ kg.
2	eggs	2
	water (optional)	

Sift the dry ingredients together onto a marble slab or pastry board. Make a well in the center of the dry ingredients, and put in the butter and eggs. Using the fingers of one hand, pinch the butter and eggs together until they are lightly blended. With a spatula, gradually cut the dry ingredients into the butter-egg mixture, chopping and blending until the dough is crumbly. If necessary, add a little water, drop by drop, to make the dough cling together. Form the dough into a ball, pressing it together with your hands, and wrap it in plastic wrap or foil. Chill the dough in the refrigerator for at least two hours before rolling it out. Tightly covered, the dough can be safely kept in the refrigerator for two to three days, in the freezer for two to three months. If frozen, the dough should be defrosted overnight in the refrigerator before it is used.

Refrigerator Dough

Like nut dough *(right)*, refrigerator dough is rolled ¼ inch [6 mm.] thick, so allow about 1 pound [½ kg.] to line a 9-inch

[23-cm.] piepan or flan form. You can fully prebake the blind, or unfilled, shell as described for nut dough.

To make 3 ½ pounds [1 ¾ kg.] dough

7 cups	sifted cake flour	1 ¾ liters
4 cups	confectioners' sugar, sifted	1 liter
1 lb.	unsalted butter, softened	½ kg.
1	egg	1
	salt	
	vanilla extract (optional)	
	grated lemon peel (optional)	

In a large mixing bowl, cream the sugar with the butter by beating them against the sides of the bowl with a wooden spoon until the mixture is pale and fluffy. Continuing to beat, add the egg, a pinch of salt and vanilla extract or grated lemon peel to taste. Fold in the sifted flour. Spoon the mixture onto a strip of foil or parchment paper, pat it into a thick cake and wrap the foil or paper around it. Chill the dough in the refrigerator for at least four hours before using it. Tightly wrapped, it can be kept refrigerated for up to four days.

Nut Dough

Nut dough is too fragile to be rolled much thinner than ¼ inch [6 mm.], so you will need 1 pound [½ kg.] of it to line a 9-inch [23-cm.] piepan or flan form. A blind, or unfilled, nut-dough shell may be fully prebaked by lining it with parchment paper or foil, filling it with dried peas, beans or rice, baking it for 10 minutes in a preheated 375° F. [190° C.] oven, then removing the lining with the beans, and baking it for an additional 10 to 15 minutes until it crisps and browns.

To make 3 pounds [1 ½ kg.] dough

4 ¾ cups	sifted cake flour	1,175 ml.
6 oz.	blanched hazelnuts, almonds or a mixture of the two, ground in a nut grinder, or in a food processor operated at short spurts	175 g.
1 ½ tsp.	ground cinnamon (optional)	7 ml.
½ tsp.	baking powder	2 ml.
	salt	
¾ lb.	unsalted butter, softened	⅓ kg.
1 ¼ cups	sugar	300 ml.
1	egg, plus 1 yolk	1
½ tsp.	vanilla extract	2 ml.
2 tsp.	grated lemon peel	10 ml.
½ cup	dry bread or cake crumbs	125 ml.

Sift the flour, cinnamon, if using, baking powder and a pinch of salt into a bowl. In a separate bowl, cream the butter with the sugar by beating them against the sides of the bowl with a wooden spoon until the mixture is soft and pale yellow. Beat in the whole egg and then the egg yolk. The mixture should now be fluffy. Add the vanilla extract and the grated lemon peel. Beat in the ground hazelnuts and almonds, and the crumbs. Finally fold in the flour mixture.

Pat the dough into a flat cake, cover it with plastic wrap or foil, and refrigerate it for at least four hours before using it. Tightly wrapped, the dough can be safely stored in the refrigerator for four days, in the freezer for one month. If frozen, the dough should be defrosted overnight in the refrigerator before it is used.

Chou Paste

To make 1 pound [½ kg.] paste

1 cup	flour	¼ liter
1 cup	water	¼ liter
8 tbsp.	unsalted butter, cut into pieces	120 ml.
1 tsp.	salt	5 ml.
4	eggs	4

Put the water in a heavy saucepan over low heat. Add the butter. Sift the flour and salt onto parchment or wax paper.

When the butter has melted, increase the heat to bring the water to a boil. Turn off the heat and slide all of the flour off the paper into the water. Stir the mixture until thoroughly combined, then stir over medium heat until the mixture forms a solid mass that comes away cleanly from the sides of the pan. Reduce the heat to low and stir constantly for three minutes to dry the dough slightly. Remove the pan from the heat and cool the mixture for a few minutes.

Break one egg into a bowl and add it to the contents of the pan, beating with a spoon to incorporate the egg thoroughly. Repeat with the remaining eggs. Continue beating until the ingredients are smoothly blended.

To make cream puffs: Cover a buttered baking sheet with parchment paper. Fill a pastry bag with the chou paste and pipe mounds of it about 1½ inches [4 cm.] in diameter onto the paper, spacing the mounds about 1½ inches apart. (Alternatively, you may use a teaspoon to form the mounds of paste.) Bake in a preheated 400° F. [200° C.] oven for 20 minutes, or until the cream puffs have more than doubled in size and are lightly browned and firm to the touch. Pierce them and return them to the oven for a few minutes to dry them out. Cool on a rack. One pound of chou paste makes about fifteen 3-inch [7½-cm.] puffs.

To make éclairs: Cover a buttered baking sheet with parchment paper. Fill a pastry bag with the chou paste and pipe 4-inch [10-cm.] strips, about 1½ inches [4 cm.] apart, onto the paper. Bake in a preheated 400° F. oven for 20 minutes, or until the éclairs are puffed and light brown, and firm to the touch. Cool on a rack. One pound of chou paste makes about twelve 5-inch [13-cm.] éclairs.

Flaky-Pastry Dough

To make 2 pounds [1 kg.] dough

3½ cups	flour	875 ml.
½ cup	cake flour	125 ml.
1 tsp.	salt	5 ml.
24 tbsp.	unsalted butter (¾ lb. [⅓ kg.]), cut into small pieces	360 ml.
about ¾ cup	cold water	about 175 ml.

Sift the two flours and the salt into a mixing bowl. Add a quarter of the butter pieces, and rub them into the flour with your finger tips—or cut in the butter with two knives or a pastry blender—for about a minute, or until the mixture looks like bread crumbs. Add just enough cold water, a few spoonfuls at a time, to make the crumbs cohere in a mass. Work the dough with your hands until it is smooth and comes cleanly away from the sides of the bowl. Shape the dough into a ball, wrap it in plastic wrap or foil, and refrigerate it for about 15 minutes to allow the dough to relax and the butter to become firm.

On a floured board, roll the dough into a rectangle about ½ inch [1 cm.] thick and three times as long as it is wide. Dot two thirds of the length of the rectangle with about a third of the butter, pressing the pieces lightly into place. Fold the unbuttered third of the rectangle over the center, then fold over the remaining buttered third. Wrap and chill the dough for 15 minutes. Repeat the rolling, buttering, folding and chilling twice more, then roll the dough to make the final folds cohere. Chill for two or three hours before using. The wrapped dough can be kept in the refrigerator for two to three days, in the freezer for one month. If frozen, let the dough defrost in the refrigerator overnight.

Puff-Pastry Dough

To make 2 pounds [1 kg.] dough

3 cups	all-purpose flour	¾ liter
1 cup	cake flour	¼ liter
2 tsp.	salt	10 ml.
1 lb.	unsalted butter	½ kg.
10 to 12 tbsp.	cold water	150 to 200 ml.

Sift the flours and salt into a bowl. Cut a quarter of the butter into small pieces and add them to the bowl. Using your finger tips, rub the butter into the flour. Add just enough cold water—a few tablespoonfuls at a time—to bind the ingredients and work the dough into a ball. Wrap the dough in floured plastic wrap and chill it in the refrigerator for about 30 minutes.

Meanwhile, place the remaining butter between two sheets of parchment or wax paper and, with a rolling pin, flatten the butter into a slab about 6 inches [15 cm.] square and ½ inch [1 cm.] thick. Chill the butter in the refrigerator for about 30 minutes.

Place the dough on a lightly floured board and roll it into a 12-inch [30-cm.] square. Place the square of butter diagonally in the center of the dough and fold the corners of the dough over the butter so that they meet in the center. Roll the dough into a rectangle 12 by 18 inches [30 by 45 cm.].

Fold the dough into thirds and give it a quarter turn. Roll the dough again into a rectangle and fold it again into thirds. Wrap, and chill the dough for at least one hour. Roll and turn the dough twice more, refrigerate for two hours, and repeat, giving it six turns in all. After a final turn, refrigerate for four hours before using it. Tightly wrapped, the dough can safely be kept in the refrigerator for two or three days, in the freezer for two or three months. If frozen, defrost it in the refrigerator overnight.

Phyllo Dough

Any excess dough can be restretched. With practice in stretching the dough, you may be able to make a 6-foot [180-cm.] square out of just 1 pound [½ kg.] of it.

To make 2 pounds [1 kg.] dough or about twenty-four 12-by-18-inch [30-by-45-cm.] sheets

4 cups	bread flour	1 liter
1½ tsp.	salt	7 ml.
1½ cups	tepid water	375 ml.
4 tbsp.	olive oil	60 ml.
	cornstarch	

Sift the flour and salt into a deep bowl. Beating constantly with a large spoon, gradually add the water. Continue to beat until the flour and water are well blended. Then knead the dough in the bowl for five to 10 minutes, or until it can be gathered into a soft, somewhat sticky ball.

In the bowl, or on a board lightly sprinkled with flour, add the olive oil—1 tablespoon [15 ml.] at a time—kneading the dough well after each addition. Continue kneading for about 25 minutes longer, or until the dough is smooth and satiny. Cover the bowl with plastic wrap and let the dough rest at room temperature for at least two hours.

Cover a large table completely with a cloth that has been sprinkled lightly with cornstarch. Place the dough in the center of the table, dust it with cornstarch and flatten it as thin as possible with a rolling pin or with your palms. Then stretch the dough across the backs of your hands by lifting an edge and pulling your hands apart. Work from each side of the table in turn to stretch the dough evenly until it is paper-thin and measures at least 6 feet [180 cm.] square. Cut off the thick edges all around.

Let the dough dry for about 30 minutes. Then, using a pastry wheel or small knife and ruler, cut a 12-inch [30-cm.] strip from along one side of the stretched dough. Divide the strip into 16-inch [40-cm.] sheets, stacking them on a baking sheet and dusting each one with cornstarch as you proceed. Repeat the process until all of the dough is cut into sheets and stacked. The sheets can be used immediately, or the stack can be wrapped tightly in foil or plastic wrap and kept refrigerated for up to two weeks.

Strudel Dough

The 2 pounds [1 kg.] of dough produced by this recipe can be stretched into a sheet about 6 feet [180 cm.] square—enough for two 3-foot [90-cm.] strudels. Any excess dough can be restretched. With practice in stretching the dough, you may be able to make a 6-foot square out of 1 pound [½ kg.] of dough.

To make 2 pounds [1 kg.] dough		
4 cups	flour, preferably bread flour	1 liter
2 tsp.	salt	10 ml.
2	eggs	2
2½ cups	water	625 ml.
8 tbsp.	unsalted butter, melted	120 ml.
1 tsp.	white vinegar or strained fresh lemon juice (optional)	5 ml.

Sift the flour and salt onto a board or into a large bowl. Make a well in the center. Lightly beat the eggs with a fork, then beat in the water and half of the melted butter. Add the vinegar or lemon juice, if desired. Pour the egg mixture into the well in the flour. Stir until all of the flour is incorporated into the egg mixture and the dough is smooth. On a flour-sprinkled board, knead the dough for at least 10 minutes, or until it is smooth, shiny and blistered on the surface. Brush

the dough generously with melted butter, place it in a bowl, cover it with plastic wrap and let it rest for 30 minutes.

Cover a large table completely with a floured cloth. Place the dough in the center of the cloth and, working in all directions, roll out the dough as thin as possible. Spread a little melted butter over the dough, and stretch it with your hands—working carefully all around the table to avoid tearing the dough—until it is very thin and almost transparent. As you stretch, brush the dough with more butter as necessary. Cut off any thick edges, then let the dough rest for about 15 minutes before using it.

Crumb Crust

Among the suitable bases for this crust are graham crackers, gingersnaps, vanilla or chocolate wafers, zwieback, and stale or fresh cake or bread—including pumpernickel bread. To produce crumbs, break or tear the crackers, cookies, cake or bread into small pieces and pulverize them, a small batch at a time, in a blender or food processor. The amount and kind of sugar and spices can be adjusted to taste. To make a chocolate-flavored crust, melt 1 to 3 ounces [30 to 90 g.] of semisweet baking chocolate with the butter.

To make a 9-inch [23-cm.] pie or tart shell		
2 cups	fine crumbs	½ liter
8 tbsp.	unsalted butter, melted	120 ml.
3 tbsp.	granulated or brown sugar	45 ml.
	salt	
	ground cinnamon or grated nutmeg (optional)	

In a mixing bowl, combine the butter and sugar with a pinch of salt and a little cinnamon or nutmeg, if using. Stir in the crumbs. When the mixture is well blended, spoon it into a heavily buttered piepan. With a rubber spatula, spread the crust evenly over the bottom and sides of the pan. Chill the pie shell for 15 minutes to firm it. Bake the crust in a preheated 325° F. [160° C.] oven for about 10 minutes, or until it is crisp and dry to the touch. Cool the crust in the pan before adding the filling.

Almond Cream Filling

To make 2 ¼ cups [300 ml.] filling

1 cup	blanched almonds, ground in a nut grinder, or in a food processor operated at short spurts	¼ liter
8 tbsp.	unsalted butter, softened	120 ml.
½ cup	superfine sugar	125 ml.
2	eggs	2
¼ cup	flour, sifted	50 ml.
½ tsp.	almond extract	2 ml.
	kirsch or rum (optional)	

In a bowl, cream together the butter and sugar by beating them with a wooden spoon until light and fluffy. Beat in the eggs, one at a time, then stir in the almonds. Add the almond extract and, if desired, kirsch or rum to taste. Sift in the flour, then fold it into the mixture. Cover the bowl with plastic wrap or foil and refrigerate the almond cream until you are ready to use it. The cream will keep in the refrigerator for two days, in the freezer for one month.

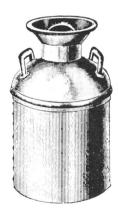

Tart Cream

For this recipe, an American version of France's *crème fraîche*, pasteurized—not ultrapasteurized—heavy cream should be used.

To make about 2 cups [½ liter] tart cream

2 cups	heavy cream	½ liter
1 tbsp.	buttermilk	15 ml.

In a small, heavy enameled saucepan, stir the cream and buttermilk together until well blended. Set the pan over low heat and insert a meat-and-yeast thermometer into the cream mixture. Stirring gently but constantly, warm the mixture until the thermometer registers 85° F. [30° C.].

Immediately remove the pan from the heat and pour the cream mixture into a 1-quart [1-liter] jar. Cover the jar loosely with foil or wax paper. Set the cream mixture aside at a room temperature of 60° to 85° F. [15° to 30° C.] for eight to 24 hours, or until it reaches the consistency of lightly beaten cream. The heavy cream has now become *crème fraîche.*

Cover the jar tightly and refrigerate the cream until you are ready to use it. It will keep refrigerated for about a week.

Pastry Cream

Crème Pâtissière

This cream may be lightened by the addition of stiffly beaten egg whites or whipped cream.

To make about 2 ½ cups [625 ml.] pastry cream

½ cup	sugar	125 ml.
5 or 6	egg yolks	5 or 6
¼ cup	flour	50 ml.
	salt	
2 cups	milk	½ liter
2-inch	piece vanilla bean	5-cm.

With a whisk, mix together the sugar and egg yolks, beating until the mixture is thick and cream colored. Gradually work in the flour and season with a pinch of salt.

In a heavy saucepan, combine the milk with the vanilla bean, and bring the milk to a boil. Remove the vanilla bean. Stirring constantly, pour the hot milk into the egg mixture in a thin stream. Strain the egg-milk mixture into the saucepan and, beating vigorously, cook over medium heat until the pastry cream comes to a boil. Boil for about two minutes. Remove the pan from the heat and let the pastry cream cool, stirring it occasionally to prevent a skin from forming. The pastry cream may safely be kept refrigerated in a covered bowl for two days.

Chocolate pastry cream. Add ¼ pound [125 g.] of unsweetened baking chocolate to the finished pastry cream and stir until the chocolate melts.

Coffee pastry cream. Combine 2 tablespoons [30 ml.] of crushed coffee beans with the milk before heating it, and strain the milk after bringing it to a boil.

Praline pastry cream. Combine ¼ cup [50 ml.] of sugar and ¼ cup of blanched almonds in a small, heavy pan, and cook over low heat, stirring constantly, until the sugar is caramelized and is a light amber color. Pour this praline mixture onto an oiled baking sheet. Let it cool completely, then break the praline into pieces, and crush them to a coarse powder with a mortar and pestle or in a blender or food processor. Stir about ¼ cup of the praline powder into the pastry cream while it is being cooled.

Wine Custard

Sabayon

To make about 6 cups [1 ½ liters] custard

5	egg yolks	5
1 cup	superfine sugar	¼ liter
1¼ cups	dry white wine, port, Sauternes, Champagne, Marsala or sherry	300 ml.
6	strips lemon peel, cut into tiny julienne (optional)	6

In a sabayon pan or a broad 2-quart [2-liter] saucepan, beat together the egg yolks and sugar until the mixture is thick and creamy, and forms a slowly dissolving "ribbon" when it is dribbled back into the pan from the lifted whisk. This will take about seven to 10 minutes.

Set the pan over a larger pan partly filled with water heated to just below the boiling point. Whisking constantly, slowly pour in the wine of your choice and, if desired, add the lemon peel julienne. Continue to whisk until the mixture froths to almost triple its original volume and is pale yellow in color. Remove the pan from the water bath and continue whisking for a minute or so.

The wine custard may be used hot or cold. For a cold sauce, chill the custard quickly by setting the pan in a bowl of ice cubes and whisking the custard until it is cold. Whipped cream may be added to the cold sauce, if desired.

Fondant

Making fondant is demonstrated on pages 10-11.

To make 2 cups [½ liter] fondant

2 cups	sugar	½ liter
½ cup	water	125 ml.
2 tbsp.	light corn syrup or ⅛ tsp. [½ ml.] cream of tartar	30 ml.

Combine the sugar, water, and corn syrup or cream of tartar in a small, heavy saucepan. Let the sugar soak for 10 minutes, then stir over low heat to dissolve it. With a brush dipped in hot water, wash down any grains of sugar that have collected on the side of the pan. Increase the heat to bring the syrup to a boil, and place a candy thermometer in the pan. Without stirring, boil the syrup for about five minutes, or until it reaches a temperature of 238° F. [115° C.]. Lacking a thermometer, test the syrup by dropping a little into a bowl of ice water; it should form a lump that you can roll into a soft ball between your fingers.

At once pour the syrup on a cool work surface—a marble slab or large baking pan is ideal—that has been lightly moistened with cold water. Leave the syrup for about three minutes, or until it feels warm, not hot, to the touch. Scrape the syrup from the edges of the mass toward the center with a palette knife, sugar scraper or pastry scraper. Then spread the syrup into a flat sheet about ¼ inch [6 mm.] thick and immediately gather it toward the center again. Continue to work the syrup with the knife or scraper for about 15 minutes, until it becomes thick and opaque. Then knead the cooled syrup with your hands for about 10 minutes, until it is white and firm. The fondant can be used at once. Or, it can be formed into a smooth ball, packed in an airtight container and stored in a cool place for up to four months.

Fondant Icing

To make about 1 cup [¼ liter] icing

⅔ cup	fondant (recipe, left)	150 ml.
½ cup	sugar	125 ml.
¼ cup	water	50 ml.

Combine the sugar and water in a small, heavy saucepan. Let the sugar soak for 10 minutes, then stir over low heat to dissolve it. With a brush dipped in hot water, wash down any grains of sugar that have collected on the sides of the pan. Stop stirring, increase the heat and bring the sugar syrup to a boil. Remove the syrup from the heat.

Place the fondant in a heatproof bowl set over a pan of hot water, stirring constantly until the fondant begins to melt. Then stir in the syrup—a few spoonfuls at a time—adding only enough to make the icing thin enough to pour easily from the spoon. Use the icing at once.

Chocolate icing. Cut up or coarsely chop 1 ounce [30 g.] of semisweet baking chocolate. Add the chocolate to the fondant before adding the sugar syrup, and stir until the chocolate dissolves.

Coffee icing. Boil 1 cup [¼ liter] of strong, black liquid coffee for about 10 minutes, or until it is reduced to 2 tablespoons [30 ml.] of coffee essence. Add the coffee to the fondant before adding the syrup.

Lemon icing. Stir 1 tablespoon [15 ml.] of strained fresh lemon juice into the fondant before adding the sugar syrup.

Recipe Index

All recipes in the index that follows are listed by English titles except in cases where a dish of foreign origin, such as baklava or croquembouche, is universally recognized by its source name. Entries are organized in separate categories by major ingredients specified in the recipe titles. Foreign recipes are listed under the country or region of origin. Recipe credits appear on pages 174-176.

General Index/ Glossary

Included in this index to the cooking demonstrations are definitions, in italics, of special culinary terms not explained elsewhere in this volume. The Recipe Index begins on page 168.

glazing, 66; icing, 66, 67; piping strips with pastry bag, 66

Eggs: adding to phyllo, 78; beating whites for meringue, 13, 44; beating yolks to ribbon for pastry cream, 12; in chou paste, 63, 64; egg wash, 53, 55; glaze made with egg and milk, 68; glaze made with egg and water, 24, 25, 35, 53, 55; glaze made with egg whites, 26; glaze made with egg yolk and milk, 66; mixing into rich short-crust dough, 18; reaction between copper and egg whites, 13; in strudel dough, 74

Fat: in pastry dough, 7; in short-crust dough, 15; substitutions, 7; using unsalted butter, 7, 15. *See also* Butter; Lard; Oil

Filling: almond cream, 28, 30, 31; for baked and fried turnovers, 34; *cannoli*, 80; cheesecake, 40; for chou puffs, 68; cream horns, 58; for a crumb crust, 84; for deep-dish pies, 24; éclairs, 66; fully baked tart shells, 42; for *gâteau Saint-Honoré*, 68; for *jalousie*, 54; for large, free-form tarts, 36; for lattice pie, 26; mass-produced tartlets, 30; for meringue shells, 86; in napoleons, 56; for partially prebaked tart shells, 38; pastry cream, 12; phyllo, 78; for *Pithiviers*, 54; puff-pastry tart, 52; puff-pastry turnovers, 58; refrigerator dough, 28; strudel, 72, 76; for tart baked upside down, 32; thousand-leaf pastries, 82; for two-crust pies, 22

Flaky puff-pastry dough: buttering, 50, 51; molding and filling cream horns, 58-59; rolling and folding, 50-51; shaping and baking turnovers, 58-59

Flan form: blind-baking tart shell in, 38-39; shaping *Linzertorte*, 28-29

Flour: adding acid to promote gluten development, 74; all-purpose, 7, 16, 48, 74; in chou paste, 7, 64; gluten content, 7, 15, 48; in phyllo, 7, 78; in puff pastry, 7, 48; in refrigerator dough, 20; in short crust, 7, 15, 16; in strudel, 7, 73, 74. *See also* Bread flour; Cake flour; Gluten

Fondant icing, 10-11; adding flavorings, 10; chocolate, 11, 66, 67; coffee, 69; cooking sugar syrup, 10; diluting with syrup to make icing, 11; kneading, 11; preventing crystallization, 10; storing, 10

Food processor: grinding nuts, 20; making bread crumbs, 21, 84; mixing basic short-crust dough, 16; mixing rich short-crust dough, 18

Framboise: *a colorless, raspberry-flavored French liqueur.*

Frangipane. *See* Almond cream

Fruits: ascorbic acid in, 36; choosing a wine to accompany, 7; in deep-dish pies, 24; filling free-form tart, 36; filling turnovers with dried fruits, 34-35; in lattice-pie fillings, 26; poaching in sugar syrup to prepare a glaze, 8-9, 42, 43; poaching in wine,

32-33; preventing discoloration, 36-37; sweating fresh fruits, 26, 27, 52, 53; thickening agents, 22; in two-crust pies, 22-23; uncooked, filling puff-pastry tart, 52-53

Gâteau Saint-Honoré, 68-69; base of rich short crust, 68; filling case with pastry cream, 69; filling chou puffs, 68, 69; piping ring of chou paste, 68

Glaze: amount of sugar in fruit glazes, 8; apricot jam, 9, 30, 31, 36, 37; of beaten egg whites, 26; of confectioners' sugar, 24; egg and milk, 68; egg and water, 24, 25, 35, 53, 55; egg wash, 53, 55; egg yolk and milk, 66; fruit, 8-9; made with jam, 8, 9, 30, 31, 36, 37, 59; melting jelly, 8; from poaching liquid, 42; of sugar syrup, 8, 82, 83

Gluten: in all-purpose flour, 7; in bread flour, 7, 74, 78; in cake flour, 7, 15, 20, 48; developing in *cannoli* dough, 80; developing in strudel dough, 74; preventing development in short-crust dough, 15, 16; promoting development with acids added to dough, 74; in puff-pastry dough, 48; in refrigerator dough, 15, 20; in rich short crust, 15; in wheat flour, 7

Grapes: filling tartlets, 43

Hazelnuts: peeling, 20; in refrigerator dough, 20, 21

Icing. *See* Fondant icing

Jalousie, 54-55; constructing free-form shell from puff pastry, 54-55; filling with strawberry jam, 54; glazing with egg wash, 55

Jam: filling *jalousie*, 54, 55; filling for mass-produced tartlets, 30; filling tarts made with refrigerator dough, 28, 29; glaze, 8, 9, 30, 31, 36, 37, 59

Jelly: glazing tart, 36; making glaze with, 8

Julienne: *a French term for food cut into strips.*

Kirsch: *a colorless German, French or Swiss brandy made from the Morello cherry —a type of small black cherry widely grown in Europe. The use of crushed cherry stones in the brandy gives it a distinctively bitter-almond flavor;* 31, 34

Kneading: butter, 48, 49, *cannoli* dough, 80, 81; dough for thousand-leaf pastries, 82; fondant, 11; phyllo dough, 78; strudel dough, 74, 75

Lard: using in pastry dough, 7

Lattice: cutting lattice strips from short crust, 26; fresh-fruit pie fillings, 26; glazing, 26; laying lattice on pie, 26; making lattice-top *Linzertorte,* 28-29; strawberry and rhubarb pie, 26-27; weaving strips, 26-27

Lemon: filling for lemon meringue tart, 44-45; flavoring fondant, 10; flavoring sugar syrup, 8, 79

Linzertorte, 28-29; making lattice for, 28; molding refrigerator dough, 28-29

Marble slab: rolling out short-crust

dough, 22; working fondant on, 10; working surface for rich short-crust dough, 18

Marsala: *a sweet, brown, fortified wine. Named for the region of Sicily where it originated, but now made in America as well.*

Meringue: adding sugar in stages, 13; baking a topping, 44; baking shells, 86; beating egg whites, 13; cutting meringue, 44; filling shells, 86; molding meringue for shells and pie shells, 86; piping a border of molding meringue, 44, 45; piping shells, 86; preventing weeping, 13, 44; proportion of eggs and sugar in, 13, 86; spreading meringue, 13, 44-45; topping, 44-45

Mille-feuille, 46

Napoleons, 46, 56-57; blind-baking layers of dough, 56-57; frosting with fondant icing, 57; piping chocolate lines, 56, 57; spreading filling of pastry cream, 56

Nut dough. *See* Refrigerator dough

Nuts: adding to refrigerator dough, 20; grinding in food processor, 20. *See also* Almonds; Hazelnuts; Pine nuts; Pistachios; Walnuts

Oil: deep frying *cannoli* in, 80; deep frying chou paste strips in, 67; deep frying thousand-leaf pastries in, 83; frying turnovers in, 34; regulating frying temperature, 34

Orange-flower water: *a flavoring made by distilling orange-flower oil. Produced in the Middle East; available at pharmacies and specialty shops.*

Oranges: filling prebaked short-crust tart, 42-43; flavoring fondant, 10; poaching in sugar syrup, 43

Parboil: *to cook food briefly in boiling liquid in order to soften the food or to shorten its final cooking;* 20, 38

Pastries: baklava, 78-79; *cannoli,* 80-81; cheese strudel, 76-77; dessert wines with, 7; phyllo, 78-79; phyllo coil, 78-79; small poppy-seed strudels, 76-77; strudel, 72, 74-77; thousand-leaf, 82-83. *See also* Chou pastries; Puff pastries; Refrigerator dough; Rich short-crust; Short-crust; Tarts

Pastry: in ancient Greece, 5; early cookbooks, 6; in Egyptian times, 5; European, 6; history and evolution of, 5-6; ingredients, 5, 7; in Persia, 5; regulating oven temperature, 7; serving wine with, 7

Pastry bag, 44; choosing tubes for, 44; filling bag with chou paste, 65; filling *cannoli*, 81; filling chou puffs, 68, 69; filling coiled phyllo pastry, 78; how to fill, 45; making chou puffs, 68; piping a border of whipped cream, 59, 85; piping chou paste for deep frying, 67; piping éclair shells, 66; piping filling into thousand-leaf pastries, 82; piping meringue shell, 86; piping molding meringue, 44, 45; piping ring of chou paste, 68; piping

whipped cream into cream horns, 59; shaping chou-paste swans, 62, 71

Pastry cream: cooking, 12; filling chou puffs, 68, 69; filling éclairs, 66; filling meringue shells, 86; filling napoleons, 56-57; flavorings, 12; flavoring with puréed spinach for tart, 38-39; mixing with gelatin and beaten egg whites, 12, 68, 69; in napoleons, 56-57; orange-liqueur flavored, 43; with poached fruit in a tart, 42-43; in short-crust tartlets, 43; vanilla-flavored, 43

Pastry pin: rolling pie dough with, 22, 23; transferring dough around, 23

Peaches: filling puff-pastry turnovers, 58, 59; preventing discoloration, 59

Pears: poaching in red wine, 32-33; poaching in sugar syrup, 8-9

Phyllo: adding eggs to, 78; bread flour in, 7, 78; defrosting frozen leaves, 78; dough, 73, 78-79; filling and coiling a single leaf, 78-79; layering leaves to make baklava, 78-79; preparing honey-flavored syrup, 79; stretching and resting dough, 78

Pies: blind-baking a crumb crust, 84; blind-baking a crust, 38-39; brushing pie lid with glaze of egg and water, 24, 25; chocolate Bavarian cream, 84-85; cooking a Bavarian cream filling, 84, 85; cutting butter into flour with two knives, 17; cutting lattice strips from short crust, 26; cutting steam vents, 24, 25; decorating edge of two-crust pie, 23; deep-dish, 24-25; fancy pies of times past, 6; fashioning a collar of dough to anchor lid of deep-dish pie, 25; filling a deep-dish pie, 24-25; fillings for crumb crusts, 84; fillings for deep-dish pies, 24; fillings for lattice pies, 26; fillings for two-crust pies, 22; flavoring crumb crust with chocolate, 84-85; handling short-crust dough, 16, 22; lattice pie, 26-27; laying lattice on pie, 26; making chocolate scrolls to decorate a pie, 85; making a lid for deep-dish pie, 24-25; making meringue topping, 13, 44-45; making a pie shell of meringue, 86; mixing basic short-crust dough, 16-17; pan for baking crumb crust, 84; preparing apple filling for two-crust pie, 22-23; rolling out short-crust dough, 22-23, 24; shaping a crumb crust, 84-85; strawberry and rhubarb filling for a lattice pie, 26-27; sweating rhubarb, 26; thickening agents for fruit fillings, 22; thickening blueberries for deep-dish pie filling, 24; two-crust pie, 22-23; using unsalted butter in short-crust dough, 7, 15; weaving a lattice of short-crust strips, 26-27

Pine nuts: sautéed on a spinach tart, 14, 39

Pistachios: blanched and peeled, 31; decorating cream horns, 59; parboiling, 20; on tartlets, 30

Pithiviers, 46, 54-55; almond

Recipe Credits

The sources for the recipes in this volume are shown below. Page references in parentheses indicate where the recipes appear in the anthology.

Ackart, Robert, *Fruits in Cooking.* Copyright © 1974 by Robert Ackart. Published by Macmillan Publishing Co., Inc. By permission of the publisher(111, 113, 133).

Adam, Hans Karl, *Das Kochbuch aus Schwaben.* © Copyright 1976 by Verlagsteam Hölker. Published by Verlagsteam Hölker, Münster. Translated by permission of the publisher(150).

Adams, Charlotte and Doris Townsend, *The Family Cookbook: Desserts.* Copyright 1972 by The Ridge Press. Published by The Ridge Press. By permission of the publisher(115, 135, 136).

American Heritage, the editors of, *The American Heritage Cookbook.* © 1964 by American Heritage Publishing Co., Inc., New York. Published by American Heritage Publishing Co., Inc. By permission of the publisher(93).

Amish Dutch Cookbook. © 1980 by Ben Herman Dutch Books, Inc. Published by Ben Herman Dutch Books, Inc. By permission of the publisher(117).

Anderson, Jean, *The Grass Roots Cookbook.* Copyright 1977 by Jean Anderson. Published by Times Books, a division of Quadrangle/The New York Times Book Co., Inc. By permission of the publisher(98, 109, 117).

Armisen, Raymond and André Martin, *Les Recettes de la Table Niçoise.* © Librairie Istra 1972. Published by Librairie Istra, Strasbourg. Translated by permission of the publisher(138).

The Art of Greek Cookery. The Women of St. Paul's Greek Orthodox Church. Copyright © 1961, 1963 by St. Paul's Greek Orthodox Church. Published by Doubleday & Company, Inc. By permission of the publisher(122).

Ayrton, Elisabeth, *The Cookery of England.* © Copyright Elisabeth Ayrton, 1974. Published by Penguin Books Ltd., London. By permission of the publisher(131).

Bakos, Eva, *Mehlspeisen aus Österreich.* © 1975 by Carl Ueberreuter Verlag, Wien-Heidelberg. Published by Carl Ueberreuter Verlag. Translated by permission of the publisher(152).

Bartley, Mrs. J., *Indian Cookery General for Young Housekeepers.* Seventh Edition, 1935. Eighth Edition, 1946. Published by C. Murphy for Thacker & Co., Ltd. Bombay(128).

Beeton, Mrs. Isabella, *Mrs. Beeton's Everyday Cookery.* © Ward Lock Limited 1963. Published by Ward Lock Limited, London. By permission of the publisher(160).

Benoit, Felix and Henry Clos Jouve, *La Cuisine Lyonnaise.* © Solar, 1975. Published by Solar, Paris. Translated by permission of the publisher(88).

Berolzheimer, Ruth (Editor), *The United States Regional Cook Book.* Copyright © 1947 by Delair Publishing Company, Inc., New York. By permission of the publisher(156).

Besson, Josephine, *La Mère Besson "Ma Cuisine Provençale."* © Éditions Albin Michel, 1977, Paris. Published by Éditions Albin Michel, Paris. Translated by permission of the publisher(99, 135).

Bisson, Marie, *La Cuisine Normande.* © Solar, 1978. Published by Solar, Paris. Translated by permission of the publisher(142).

Boni, Ada, *Italian Regional Cooking.* Copyright © 1969 by Arnaldo Mondadori Editore. Published by Arnaldo Mondadori Editore, Spa Milan. Translated by permission of the publisher(110).

Booth, Letha (Editor), *The Williamsburg Cookbook.* (With commentary by Joan Parry Dutton.) © 1971, 1975 by The Colonial Williamsburg Foundation. Published by The Colonial Williamsburg Foundation, Virginia. By permission of the publisher and Holt, Rinehart and Winston, Inc.(89).

Boulestin, X. Marcel, *The Finer Cooking.* Published by Cassel and Company Limited, London, 1937. By permission of A. D. Peters and Co., Ltd., Writers' Agents(127).

Břízová, Joza, *The Czechoslovak Cookbook.* © Copyright 1965 by Crown Publishers, Inc. Translated and adapted by Adrienne Vahala. Published by Crown Publishers. By permission of the publisher(151).

Brown, Eva, *The Plaza Cookbook.* © 1972 by Eva Brown. Published by Prentice Hall, Inc. By permission of the publisher(117, 156).

Bruning, H. F., Jr. and Cav. Umberto Bullo, *Venetian Cooking.* Copyright © 1973 by H. F. Bruning Jr. Published by Macmillan Publishing Co., Inc. By permission of the publisher(157).

The Buckeye Cookbook: Traditional American Recipes. As published by the Buckeye Publishing Co., 1883. Published by Dover Publications, 1975(161).

Byron, May, *Puddings, Pastries and Sweet Dishes.* Published by Hodder and Stoughton Ltd., London, 1929. By permission of the publisher(96).

Carnacina, Luigi, *Luigi Carnacina Presents: Italian Home Cooking.* Copyright © 1972 by Luigi Carnacina. Published by Doubleday & Company, Inc. By permission of the publisher(124, 158).

Cavazzuti, Giorgio (Editor), *Il Mangiarfuori: Almanacco della Cucina Modenese.* Published by Camera di Commercio di Modena, 1965. Translated by permission of Camera di Commercio Industria Artigianato e Agricolture Modena(129).

Chantiles, Vilma Liacouytas, *The Food of Greece.* Copyright © 1975 by Vilma Liacourtas Chantiles. Published by Atheneum Publishers Inc. By permission of the author(130).

Clancy, John and Francis Field, *Clancy's Oven Cookery.* © 1976 by John Clancy and Francis Field. Published by Delacourte Press. By permission of the publisher(122, 143).

Couffignal, Huguette, *La Cuisine Rustique.* © 1970 Robert Morel Éditeur. Published by Robert Morel Editeur, 84400 Apt., France. Translated by permission of the publisher(139).

Curnonsky, *Recettes des Provinces de France.* Published by Les Productions de Paris, Paris(88).

Cutler, Carol, *Woman's Day Low Calorie Dessert Cookbook.* Copyright © 1980 by CBS Consumer Publications, a division of CBS, Inc. Published by Houghton-Mifflin. By permission of the publisher(123).

Dall'Ara, Renzo and Emilio Fanin, *Mangiar Mantovano.* © Copyright by Renzo Dall'Ara ed Emilio Fanin, 1976. Published by Litografica Cannestese di Attilio e Giorgio Mussini, Mantova. Translated by permission of Renzo Dall'Ara, Milan(127).

Darwin, Bernard, *Receipts and Relishes.* Published by Whitbread & Co., Ltd., London, 1950(146).

David, Elizabeth, *Spices, Salt and Aromatics in the English Kitchen.* © Copyright Elizabeth David, 1970. Published by Penguin Books Ltd., London. By permission of the publisher(121).

de Bonnefons, Nicholas, *Les Delices de la Campagne.* 1655(107).

de Fuliani, Mariu Salvatori, *La Cucina di Versilia e Garfagnana.* © Copyright by Franco Angeli, Editore, Milano. Published 1969 by Franco Angeli, Editore, Milan. Translated by permission of the publisher(134).

de Gouy, Jean, *La Cuisine et La Patisserie Bourgeoise.* Published by S. Lebeque-C.i.e. Libraires Éditeurs, Paris, 1896(103).

de Gouy, Louis P., *The Gold Cook Book* (revised edition). Copyright 1948, 1964 by the author. Published by Chilton Book Company, Radnor, Pennsylvania. By permission of the publisher(134). *The Pie Book.* Copyright © 1949 by Mrs. Louis P. de Gouy. Published by Dover Publications, Inc. By permission of the publisher(103, 114).

De Lune, Pierre, *Le Nouveau Cuisinier.* Paris, 1656(136).

d'Ermo, Dominique, *The Chef's Dessert Cookbook.* © 1976 by Dominique d'Ermo. By permission of the publisher(112).

Diat, Louis, *French Cooking for Americans.* Copyright 1941, 1946 by Louis Diat. © Copyright renewed 1969, by Mrs. Louis D. Diat. Published by J. B. Lippincott Company. By permission of Harper and Row Publishers, Inc.(150).

Dodd, Marguerite, *America's Cookbook.* Copyright ©

1963 by Marguerite Dodd. Published by Charles Scribner's Sons. By permission of the publisher(93).

du Chesne, Joseph, *Le Pourtraict de la Santé.* Published in Paris, 1606(139).

The Eastern Shore Cookbook. © 1919 by the Epworth League of Still Pond Methodist Episcopal Church(108).

Elisabeth, Madame, *599 Nouvelles Recettes de Cuisine de Madame Elisabeth.* Published by Éditions Baudinière, Paris(94).

Escudier, Jean Noel and Peta J. Fuller, *The Wonderful Food of Provence.* Copyright © 1968 by Robert Rebstock and Peta J. Fuller. Published by Houghton-Mifflin Company. By permission of the publisher(137).

Famularo, Joe and Louise Imperiale, *The Festive Famularo Kitchen.* © Copyright 1977 by Joe Famularo and Louise Imperiale. Published by Atheneum Publishers. By permission of the publisher(127).

Farmer, Fannie Merritt, *The Original Boston Cooking-School Cook Book.* © Copyright MDCCXCVI by Fannie Merritt Farmer(106).

Favorite Recipes of America: Desserts. © 1966 by Favorite Recipes Press. Published by Favorite Recipes Press. By permission of the publisher(119—Mrs. Okey Patterson).

Favorite Recipes of the Great Plains. © 1966 by Favorite Recipes Press. Published by Favorite Recipes Press. By permission of the publisher(132—Mrs. Betty Hamilton).

Fitzgibbon, Theodora, *A Taste of Paris.* Copyright © 1974 by Theodora Fitzgibbon. Published by J. M. Dent & Sons Ltd. and Houghton-Mifflin Company, Inc. By permission of the publisher(126).

Flexner, Marion, *Out of Kentucky Kitchens.* © Copyright 1949 by Marion Flexner. Published by Bramhall House. By permission of the publisher(108, 128).

Foods of the World, *The Cooking of the British Isles; Latin American Cooking; Russian Cooking.* Copyright © 1969 Time Inc.; Copyright © 1968 Time Inc.; Copyright © 1969 Time-Life Books Inc.(160; 159; 157).

Giaguinto, Adolfo, *I Dolci in Famiglia.* Copyright Edizioni Mediterranee s.r.l. Rome. Published by Edizioni Mediterranee s.r.l. Translated by permission of the publisher(123).

Gilbert, Philéas, *La Cuisine de Tous les Mois.* Published by Abel Goubaud, Editeur, Paris, 1893(145).

Greenberg, Florence, *Jewish Cookery.* © Copyright Florence Greenberg, 1963. Published by Penguin Books Ltd., 1967. First published by Jewish Chronicle Publications, 1947. By permission of The Jewish Chronicle Ltd.(106).

Greene, Bert, *Bert Greene's Kitchen Bouquets.* © 1979 by Bert Greene. Published by Contemporary Books, Inc. By permission of the publisher(117, 119, 130).

Grigson, Jane, *English Food.* © Copyright Jane Grigson 1974. First published by Macmillan, 1974. Published by Penguin Books Ltd., London, 1977. By permission of Macmillan, London and Basingstoke(139).

Guérard, Michel, *Michel Guérard's Cuisine Gourmande.* © Macmillan London Ltd., 1977, 1978. Originally published in French as "La Cuisine Gourmande." © Éditions Robert Laffont S.A., Paris, 1978. Published by Macmillan London Ltd. By permission of Macmillan, London and Basingstoke(141).

Hanneman, L. John, *Patisserie.* © L. J. Hanneman 1971. Published by William Heinemann Ltd., London. By permission of the publisher(141).

Hartley, Dorothy, *Food in England.* © Copyright 1954 by Dorothy Hartley. Published by Macdonald and Jane's, London, 1954. By permission of Macdonald and Jane's Publishers Limited(103).

Hazelton, Nika, *American Home Cooking.* © Copyright 1980 by Nika Hazelton. Published by The Viking Press. By permission of the publisher(90, 93, 96, 115).

Hewitt, Jean, *The New York Times Large Type Cookbook.* © Copyright 1968 by The New York Times Company. Published by Golden Press. By permission of The New York Times Book Company, Inc.(98, 120, 130).

Hutchinson, Peggy, *Old English Cookery.*

© W. Foulsham & Co. Ltd. Published by W. Foulsham & Co. Ltd., London. By permission of the publisher (125, 134).
Irish Recipes Traditional and Modern. Published by Mount Salus Press Limited, Dublin. By permission of the publisher(144).
Junior League of Gainesville, Florida, *Gator Country Cooks.* © Copyright 1975. Published by S. C. Toof & Co. By permission of the Junior League of Gainesville(97—Mrs. T. B. Skiff; 137—Mrs. John G. Kitchens).
Kamman, Madeleine, *The Making of a Cook.* Copyright © 1971 by Madeleine Kamman. Published by Atheneum Publishers. By permission of the publisher(100). *When French Women Cook.* Copyright © 1976 by Madeleine Kamman. Published by Atheneum Publishers. By permission of the publisher(142).
Kaufman, William I. and Sister Mary Ursula Cooper, *The Art of Creole Cookery.* © 1962 by William I. Kaufman and Emelda Maria Cooper. Published by Doubleday & Co. By permission of the authors(118).
Keller, Jean, *Les Pâtisseries et les Bonbons.* © Culture, Art, Loisirs 1979. Published by Culture, Art, Loisirs, Paris. Translated by permission of the publisher(160).
Kiehnel, Hermine and Maria Hädecke, *Das Neue Kiehnle-Kochbuch.* © Walter Hädecke Verlag, (vorm. Süddeutsches Verlagshaus) Weil der Stadt, 1960. Published by Walter Hädecke Verlag, Weil der Stadt. Translated by permission of the publisher(105).
Kinsey, Mrs. W. E., *The "Next Meal" Cookery Book.* Published by Kelly & Walsh Limited, Hong Kong, 1927. By permission of the publisher(135).
Kluger, Marilyn, *The Wild Flavor.* Copyright © 1970, 1971, 1973 by Marilyn Kluger. Published by Toward-McCann & Geoghegan, Inc. By permission of John Schaffner, Literary Agency(92, 100, 128).
Kraus, Barbara (Editor), *The Cookbook of the United Nations.* Copyright © 1970 by United Nations Association of the United States of America. Published by the United Nations Association of the United States of America. By permission of the publisher(126).
Kürtz, Jutta, *Das Kochbuch aus Schleswig-Holstein.* © Copyright, 1976 by Verlagsteam Wolfgang Hölker. Published by Verlag Wolfgang Hölker, Münster. Translated by permission of the publisher(101).
Lang, George, *The Cuisine of Hungary.* © Copyright 1971 by George Lang. Published by Atheneum Publishers. By permission of the publisher(91, 118, 151, 152).
Lenotre, Gaston, *Lenotre's Desserts and Pastries.* © 1977 Barron's Educational Series. Published by Barron's Educational Series. By permission of the publisher(140, 144).
Lepore, Alfred, *Ferrara's Little Italian Cookbook.* Copyright © 1968 by Ferrara Confectionary Company. Published by Berkley Publishing Company. By permission of Walker & Company(158).
L'Escole Parfaite des Officiers de Bouche. Published by Jean Ribou, Paris, 1662(116, 132, 133).
Les Desserts de Nos Provinces. © Librairie Hachette, 1974. Published by Librairie Hachette, Paris. Translated by permission of the publisher(99, 102, 126-127).
Leslie, Miss, *Miss Leslie's Seventy-Five Receipts.* Copyright 1827. Published by C. S. Francis and Company(145).
Lucas, Dione and Marion Gorman, *The Dione Lucas Book of French Cooking.* Copyright 1947 by Dione Lucas. © Copyright 1973 by Mark Lucas and Marion F. Gorman. Published by Little, Brown and Company. By permission of the publisher(104).
McCullough, Glenn, *Georgia Receipts.* © 1971 by The Georgia Press Association. Published by The Georgia Press Association. By permission of the publisher(96, 110).
MacNiven, Ruth, *Montserrat Cooking.* Copyright © 1969 by The Montserrat Old Peoples Welfare Association, Montserrat. Published by The Montserrat Old Peoples Welfare Association. By permission of the publisher(129).
Mapie, the Countess de Toulouse-Lautrec, *La Cuisine de France.* Copyright © 1964 by The Orion Press. Translated by Charlotte Turgeon. Published by The Orion Press. By permission of The Viking Press Inc.(89, 92, 94).
Mason, Anne, *Swiss Cooking.* Copyright © 1964 by Anne Mason. Published by André Deutsch Limited, London. By permission of the publisher(115).
Mengo, António de Macedo, *Copa e Cozinha.* © Celir/Apesar de Tudo. Published by Celir/Apesar de Tudo, Porto, 1977. Translated by permission of the publisher(102).
Menon, *Les Soupers de la Cour,* Volume 3. 1755(142).
Morphy, Countess, (Editor), *Recipes of All Nations.* First published by Herbert Joseph Limited, London, 1935. By permission of the publisher(156).
Morphy, Countess, *Sweets and Puddings.* The Kitchen Library, Volume 6. First published by Herbert Joseph Limited, London, 1936. By permission of the publisher(90).
Nignon, Edouard, *Les Plaisirs de la Table.* Published by the author © 1920. Reprinted by Éditions Daniel Morcrette, B. P. 26,95270 Luzarches, France, 1979. Translated by permission of the publisher(91, 101).
O'Connor, Hyla, *The Early American Cookbook.* © 1974 by Alan Landsburg Productions, Inc. Published by Prentice-Hall, Inc. By permission of the publisher(108).
Oliver, Raymond, *Raymond Oliver's La Cuisine Secrets of Modern French Cooking.* Copyright © 1969 by Leon Amiel Publisher. Published by Leon Amiel Publisher. By permission of Tudor Publishing Co., Inc.(98, 112, 145).
Olney, Judith, *Summer Food.* © Copyright 1978 by Judith Olney. Published by Atheneum Publishers, 1978. By permission of the publisher(149).
Olney, Richard, *Simple French Food.* © Copyright 1974 Richard Olney. Published by Jill Norman Books Ltd., London, 1980. By permission of Jill Norman(88, 100).
Peck, Paula, *The Art of Fine Baking.* © Copyright 1961 by Paula Peck. Published by Simon and Schuster, a Division of Gulf & Western Corporation. By permission of John Schaffner Agency, Literary Agent(143).
Pellaprat, Henri Paul, *The Great Book of French Cuisine.* Copyright © 1966, 1971 by René Kramer, Publisher Castagnola/Lugano, Switzerland. By permission of Harper & Row, Publishers, Inc.(161). Le Nouveau Guide Culinaire. © Copyright by René Kramer, Éditeur, Castagnola-Lugano, 1973. Published by René Kramer, Editeur, CH 6976 Lugano-Castagnola. Translated by permission of the publisher(147, 148).
Pépin, Jacques, *La Méthode.* Copyright © 1980 by Jacques Pépin. Published by Times Books, a division of Quadrangle/The New York Times Book Co., Inc. By permission of the publisher(145, 146).
Petits Propos Culinaires (Volume 2, August 1979). © Prospect Books 1979. Published by Prospect Books, London and Washington D.C. By permission of the publisher(136, 138).
Phillips, Bert, *The Pastry Chef.* © 1965. Published by A. S. Barnes. By permission of the author(151).
Plucinska, I., *Ksiazka Kucharska.* 1st Edition 1926. Published by Wydawnictwo Poznanskie, Poland, 1945. Translated by permission of the publisher(107).
Poulson, Joan, *Old Thames Valley Recipes.* Text © Joan Poulson 1977. Published by Hendon Publishing Co. Ltd., Nelson. By permission of the publisher(133).
Reboul, J. B., *La Cuisinière Provençale.* Published by Tacussel, Éditeur, Marseilles. Translated by permission of the publisher(89, 146).
Reese, Ralph, *The Flavor of Pittsburgh.* © 1976 by the Pittsburgh Diners Guild, Inc. Published by Superior Printing Co. By permission of the Pittsburgh Diners Guild, Inc. (105—Chef Richard Doehler; 131—Dorothy S. Fontana).
Reich, Lilly Joss, *The Viennese Pastry Cookbook.* Copyright © 1970 by Lilly Joss Reich. Published by Macmillan Publishing Co., Inc. By permission of the publisher(105, 125).
Reynière, La, *200 Recettes des Meilleures Cuisinieres de France.* © Albin Michel, 1978. Published by Éditions Albin Michel, Paris. Translated by permission of the publisher(142).
Rombauer, Irma and J. Marion Rombauer Becker, *Joy of Cooking.* © 1931, 1936, 1941, 1942, 1943, 1946, 1951, 1952, 1953, 1962, 1963, 1964, 1974 by The Bobbs-Merrill Company, Inc. Published by The Bobbs-Merrill Company, Inc. By permission of the publisher(109).
St. Paul's Church Recipe Club, *The Regional Cooking of Greece.* Copyright © 1981 by the St. Paul's Greek Orthodox Church of Hempstead, Long Island. Published by Doubleday & Company, Inc. By permission of the publisher(153).
Sass, Lorna, *To the Queen's Taste.* Copyright © 1976 by Lorna J. Sass. Published by John Murray (Publishers) Ltd., London. By permission of the Metropolitan Museum of Art, New York(99).
Seidel, Elinor, (Editor), *Chefs, Scholars & Movable Feasts.* Published by the University of Maryland University College. By permission of the publisher(120—Marge Drazek; 155—Felicia Drazek).
Seranne, Ann, *The Complete Book of Desserts.* © 1952, 1963 by Ann Seranne. Originally published 1964 by Faber and Faber Limited, London. Also published 1967 by Faber and Faber Limited for The Cookery Book Club, London. By permission of Faber and Faber Limited(155). *The Complete Book of Home Baking.* Copyright 1950 by Doubleday & Company, Inc. Published by Doubleday & Company, Inc. By permission of the publisher(102, 160).
Southern Railways Ladies Club Cookbook. Published by the Southern Company for the Southern Railway Ladies Clubs. By permission of the publisher(108—Lavernia Ayers; 129—Lillian Hudson).
Sugden, Claire, *The Romantic and Practical Side of Cookery.* © 1931 by Louis S. Siegfried, New York(94, 128, 133).
Szathmáry, Louis, *The Chef's Secret Cook Book.* Copyright © 1971 by Louis Szathmáry. Published by Times Books, a division of Quadrangle/The New York Times Book Co., Inc. By permission of the publisher(147, 148).
Taber, Gladys, *Stillmeadow Kitchen.* Copyright 1947 by Gladys Taber. Published by Macrae Smith Company. By permission of Constance Taber Colby(92).
Tartan, Beth, *The Good Old Days Cookbook.* © 1971 by Westover Publishing Co. By permission of Crown Publishers Inc.(111, 118).
Theoharous, Anne, *Cooking the Greek Way.* © Copyright 1977 by Anne Theoharous. Published in Great Britain 1979 by Methuen Paperbacks Ltd., London. First published as *Cooking and Baking the Greek Way* by Holt, Rinehart and Winston, Inc. By permission of Methuen Paperbacks Ltd., and Holt, Rinehart and Winston, Inc.(154).
Tobias, Doris and Mary Merris, *The Golden Lemon.* © Copyright 1978 by Doris Tobias and Mary Merris. Published by Atheneum Publishers, 1978. By permission of the publisher(112).
Toklas, Alice B., *The Alice B. Toklas Cook Book.* Copyright, 1954, by Alice B. Toklas. Published by Harper and Row Publishers, Inc. By permission of the publisher(132).
Townsend, Mrs. Grace, *Imperial Cook Book.* Copyright 1890 by Mrs. Grace Townsend. Published by L. P. Miller & Company(95, 137).
Tracy, Marion, *Favorite American Regional Recipes.* © 1952 by Indiana University Press. Published by Dover Publication, Inc. By permission of the publisher(97—Winnefred Cannon Jardine; 99—Sarah Ellen Merritt; 101—Dorothy Robertson).
Troisgros, Jean and Pierre, *The Nouvelle Cuisine of Jean & Pierre Troisgros.* Copyright © 1978 in the English translation by William Morrow and Company, Inc. Published by William Morrow and Company, Inc. Originally published under the title *Cuisiniers à Roanne.* Copyright © 1977 by Éditions Robert Laffont, S.A. By permission of William Morrow and Company, Inc. (95, 140).
Vence, Céline and Robert Courtine, *The Grand Masters of French Cuisine.* © Copyright 1978 by G. P. Putnam's Sons. Originally published in France as *Les Grands Maîtres de la Cuisine Francaise.* © Copyright 1972 Éditions Bordas. Published by G. P. Putnam's Sons. By permission of G. P. Putnam's Sons(114).
Verge, Roger, *Cuisine of the South of France.* English translation © 1980 by William Morrow and Company, Inc. Originally published under the title *Ma Cuisine du Soleil.* Copyright © 1979 by Éditions Robert Laffont, S.A. Published by William Morrow and Company, Inc. 1980. By permission of William Morrow and Company, Inc. (113).
Vielfaure, Nicole and Christine Beauviala, *Fêtes, Coutumes et Gâteaux.* © Christine Bonneton Editeur. Published by Christine Bonneton Éditeur, 4300 Le Puy, France.

Translated by permission of the publisher(149).
Viron, Charles, *Charles Viron's French Country Cook-book.* Copyright © 1972 by Hawthorne Books, Inc. Published by Hawthorne Books, Inc. By permission of Elsevier/Nelson Books(120).
Volpicelli, Luigi and Secondino Freda, *L'Antiartusi: 1,000 Ricette.* © 1978 Pan Editrice, Milan. Published by Pan Editrice, Milan. Translated by permission of the publisher(106).
Voltz, Jeanne A., *The Flavor of The South.* Copyright © 1977 by Jeanne A. Voltz. Published by Doubleday & Company, Inc. By permission of the publisher(110).
von Welanetz, Diana and Paul, *The Pleasure of Your Company.* Copyright © 1976 by Diana and Paul von

Welanetz. Published by Atheneum Publishers. By permission of the publisher(116).
Waldo, Myra, *Myra Waldo's Dessert Cookbook.* Copyright © 1973 by Myra Waldo. Published by Macmillan Publishing Co., Inc. By permission of the publisher(111).
White, Florence, (Editor), *Good Things in England.* Published by arrangement with Jonathan Cape Ltd., 1968 by The Cookery Book Club, London. By permission of Jonathan Cape Ltd., London(95, 106).
Witwicka, H. and S. Soskine, *La Cuisine Russe Classique.* © Éditions Albin Michel, 1968 and 1978. Published by Editions Albin Michel, Paris. Translated by permission of the publisher(93).
Wolfert, Paula, *Mediterranean Cooking.* Copyright ©

1977 by Paula Wolfert. Published by Times Books, a division of Quadrangle/The New York Times Book Co., Inc. By permission of the publisher(153, 154).
Woodlawn Plantation Cookbook. Copyright © 1979 by The Woodlawn Plantation/Pope Leighey House Council. Published by The Woodlawn Plantation/Pope Leighey House Council. By permission of the publisher(131).
The World Atlas of Food. © Copyright Mitchell Beazley Publishers Limited 1974. Published by Mitchell Beazley Limited, London. By permission of the publisher(121).
Zawistowska, Z., *Z. Naszej Kuchni.* Copyright by the author. Originally published by RSW Prasa-Ksiazka-Ruch, Warsaw. Translated by permission of Agencja Autorska, Warsaw, for the author(91).

Acknowledgments

The indexes for this book were prepared by Louise W. Hedberg. The editors are particularly indebted to Maura Bean, U.S. Department of Agriculture, Berkeley, California; Donald K. Dubois and Robert Rodriguez, American Institute of Baking, Manhattan, Kansas; Gail Duff, Kent, England; Susan Foresman, Arlington, Virginia; Albert Kumin, Rhinebeck, New York; Ann O'Sullivan, Majorca,

Spain; Jean Reynolds, London; and Stacy Zacharias, Alexandria, Virginia.

The editors also wish to thank: Dr. Ruth Baldwin and Dr. Owen Cotterill, University of Missouri, Columbia; Katherine Boulukos, St. Paul's Greek Orthodox Church, Hempstead, New York; Dr. M. Burge and Wendy Godfrey, Tate & Lyle, London; Marisa Centis, London; Neyla Freeman, London; Maggi Heinz, London; Hudson Brothers Greengrocers, Washington, D.C.; Dr. John Hal Johnson, Brigham Young University, Provo, Utah; Maria

Johnson, Hertfordshire, England; Jo Oxley, Surrey, England; Nizam Ozghur, Nizam's Restaurant, Vienna, Virginia; Lou Seibert Pappas, *Times Tribune*, Palo Alto, California; Margot Kopsidas Phillips, Chicago, Illinois; Nancy Purves Pollard, La Cuisine, Alexandria, Virginia; Marina Polvay, Miami Shores, Florida; Michael Schwab, London; Cathy Sharpe, Annandale, Virginia; Dr. R. H. Smith, Aberdeen, Scotland; Louis Szathmary, Chicago, Illinois; Anne Theoharous, Sherman, Connecticut; Paula Wolfert, New York, New York; Dr. Charles Wood, Virginia Polytechnic Institute, Blacksburg.

Picture Credits

The sources for the pictures in this book are listed below. Credits for each of the photographers and illustrators are listed by page number in sequence with successive pages indicated by hyphens; where necessary, the locations of pictures within pages are also indicated — separated from page numbers by dashes.

Photographs by Aldo Tutino: cover, 8-9—bottom, 11—top, 12-14, 20-21, 23—bottom right, 24-31, 34-39, 42-43, 45—bottom, 46, 49—bottom right, 52-62, 71, 76-77—bottom, 78-86.

Other photographs (alphabetically): Tom Belshaw, 10, 11—bottom left, 17—bottom, 22—top left and bottom, 23—top and bottom left, 51—top right and bottom right. Alan Duns, 4, 11—bottom center and bottom right, 16—top, 40-41, 44—bottom, 45—top right, 68, 69—top and bottom left. John Elliott, 8—top right, 9—top left, 16—bottom, 17—top, 45—top center, 48, 49—top, bottom left and bottom center, 64—top left and bottom. Louis Klein, 2. Bob Komar, 8—top left, 9—top right, 18-19, 22—top right, 32-33, 44—top, 45—top left, 50, 51—top left, top center, bottom left, bottom center, 64—top right and bottom center, 64—top left and bottom center, 65-67, 69—bottom right, 70, 72, 74-75, 76-77—top. Illustrations: From the Mary Evans Picture Library and pri-

vate sources and *Food & Drink: A Pictorial Archive from Nineteenth Century Sources* by Jim Harter, published by Dover Publications, Inc., 1979, 6-7, 88-167.

Library of Congress Cataloguing in Publication Data
Time-Life Books.
   Pies & pastries.
   (The Good cook, techniques and recipes)
   Includes index.
   1. Pastry. I. Title. II. Series: Good cook, techniques and recipes.
TX773.T55   1981   641.8'65   80-20378
ISBN 0-8094-2897-0
ISBN 0-8094-2895-4 (retail ed.)
ISBN 0-8094-2896-2 (lib. bdg.)

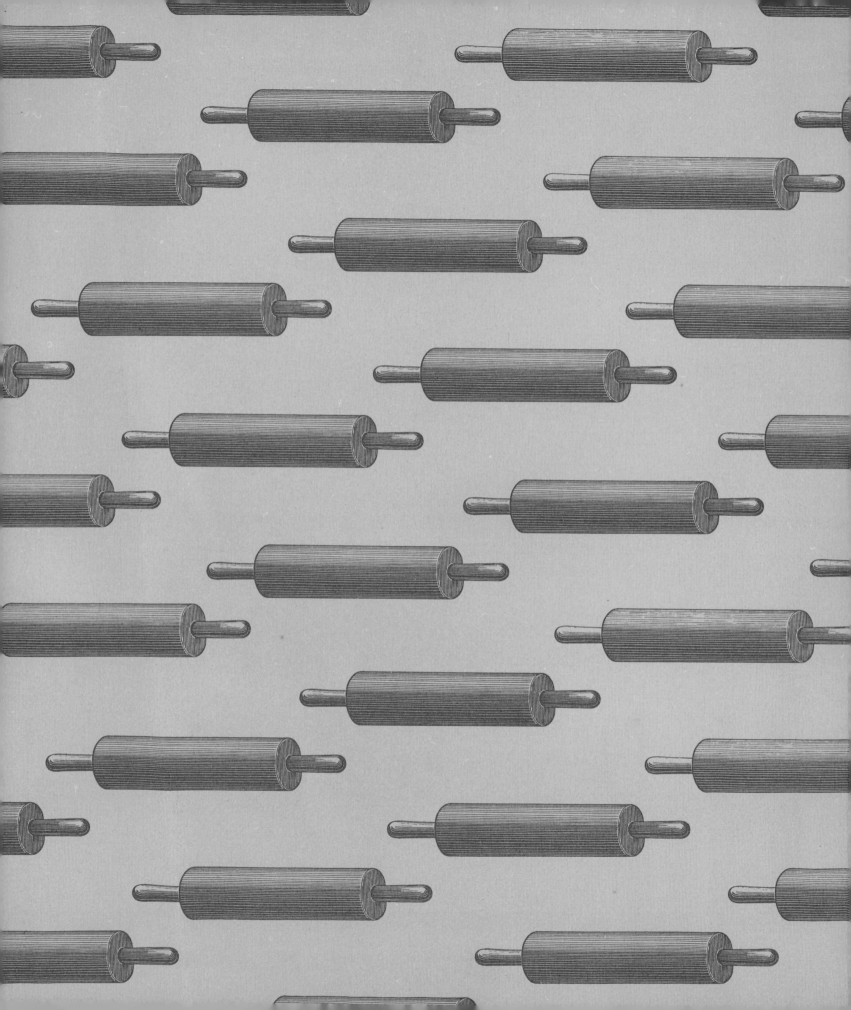